More Advance Praise for

TOMBOY

"*Tomboy* is a revelation, an impassioned and emphatic considera-
tion of how gender is manufactured and sold, and how it can both
oppress and empower. This is way more than a book for parents
navigating how to raise individuals in a world of stubborn binaries; it's for all of us who want to understand that world, and how
we might become our true selves within it."

—Lauren Sandler, author of *One and
Only* and *This is All I Got*

"Lisa Selin Davis uses *Tomboy* as a launch pad for a thought-
provoking and enlightening exploration of the troubled pink and
blue waters of gender categories—and the words that can be life
rafts to help us float above them or stones pulling us in deeper."

—Deborah Tannen, professor of linguistics
at Georgetown University and author
of *You Just Don't Understand, You're
Wearing THAT?*, and *You're the
Only One I Can Tell*

"This book will surprise, delight, and challenge everything you
think you know about gender. Davis's writing is lively and lucid; a
sage and compassionate guide on this rocky terrain. Every parent
needs to read this book."

—Jennifer Block, author of *Everything Below the Waist*

TOMBOY

TOMBOY

THE SURPRISING HISTORY
AND FUTURE OF GIRLS
WHO DARE TO BE DIFFERENT

Lisa Selin Davis

hachette
BOOKS

NEW YORK

Hachette Go, an imprint of Hachette Books
Hachette Book Group
1290 Avenue of the Americas
New York, NY 10104
HachetteGo.com
Facebook.com/HachetteGo
Instagram.com/HachetteGo

First Edition: May 2020

Hachette Books is a division of Hachette Book Group, Inc.
The Hachette Books and Hachette Go name and logos are trademarks of Hachette Book Group, Inc.

The publisher is not responsible for websites (or their content) that are not owned by the publisher.

The Hachette Speakers Bureau provides a wide range of authors for speaking events. To find out more, go to www.hachettespeakersbureau.com or call (866) 376-6591.

Print book interior design by Six Red Marbles, Inc.

Library of Congress Cataloging-in-Publication Data has been applied for.

ISBNs: 9780316458313 (hardcover); 9780316458290 (ebook); 9780306874710 (library ebook); 9781549152986 (audio downloadable)

Library of Congress Control Number: 2020930612

Printed in the United States of America

LSC-C

10 9 8 7 6 5 4 3 2 1

To Alex, Enna, and Athena

"The most normal girl is the 'tom-boy'—whose numbers increase among us in these wiser days—a healthy young creature, who is human through and through."

—*Charlotte Perkins Gilman,*
Women and Economics, *1898*

CONTENTS

Contents

III
Tomboys, All Grown Up

Introduction

A TOMBOY EMERGES

It started with a tie and a button-down shirt.

When my daughter was three, she asked for that ensemble for Christmas. We had no idea where she'd gotten the idea, since my husband and I both went to work in T-shirts and jeans, but my mother found her a white shirt and a clip-on navy tie with silver horses from Target. Not long after, she saw my husband slip on a blazer—we can't remember if he was going to a funeral or a bar mitzvah—and her jaw dropped as if she'd spied a double rainbow stretching across the sky.

"What is *that*?" she asked. "I want one of those."

My stepmother still had the red polyester blazer with brass buttons that my little brother had worn as a kid, and my mom added to the mix a fedora she'd picked up at Buy Buy Baby. Voila: The coolest looking three-year-old any of us had ever seen emerged. She was a pint-sized Annie Hall or Patti Smith.

With the clothing shifts emerged a style of play that was a bit different from that of the other preschool girls. She was delighted to play princess—as long as she could be a police officer or the royal dog. She played with boys and girls—but maybe a little more with the boys. She was sporty and strong by age four, when she requested a short haircut, "like Ellis's," she said, naming her male preschool pal.

So many of the little girls around us seemed to look and play alike: long hair and dresses, taking on female roles in make-believe games. They pined for pink and sparkles, preferring to be Cinderella over Spider-Man for Halloween. As a proper lefty feminist, I had largely avoided the Barbies and pink paraphernalia that have come to define modern girlhood, and I was relieved to find her skipping the princess phase that I'd heard so many girls go through. It seemed to emphasize appearance over adventure, magic over action, self-consciousness over self-confidence.

Still, I knew that most girls gravitated toward those things regardless of parental disapproval, and I wondered at—if I'm honest, worried about—her lack of interest in them, envisioning everything from social rejection to gender dysphoria. But I let her dress and look and play as she pleased, even as I mourned the loss of her caramel-colored curls. Soon enough, it seemed her differences were actually advantages. She had twice as many friend options as most kids, and parents praised the cuteness of the girl in the tie and fireman's hat.

As her younger sister, with whom I was far more lenient/exhausted, embraced the traditional trappings of femininity and all the pink sparkly dresses and Barbies I allowed her to get her hands on, my older daughter entered elementary school fully clad in boys' clothes, with short hair, a pack of little boy pals, and an air of self-possession. In the beginning, there were bathroom incidents (there still are), with kids insisting she was in the wrong one, and some children struggled to accept that she was a girl. A few had to be educated with what became our stock refrain: "Girls can look and act all kinds of ways." But it didn't take long for them to understand and accept her. They got it.

One day in first grade she came home and announced that she was a tomboy. "That's a girl who has short hair and likes sports," she informed me, smiling widely, passing on the definition that someone in her class—I still don't know who—had provided.

A tomboy? That word, the idea, had never occurred to me.

But at its mention, I thought back to the 1970s, to the many tomboys in the various schools I attended, and on the playgrounds I frequented, in Upstate New York, Georgia, and western Massachusetts, the three main places I spent my childhood. Even I, a non-tomboy who craved the Barbies my feminist mom wouldn't let me have and coveted the frilly, fancy clothes of wealthier girls, had short hair and wore striped turtlenecks and corduroys most of the time. So did the other little girls. So did the little boys.

Tomboys were in my favorite TV shows and movies as a kid, from Laura Ingalls on *Little House on the Prairie* to Jo Polniaczek on *The Facts of Life*, who sported a leather jacket, talked tough, and fixed her own motorcycle—otherwise known as the coolest girl ever and the one even straight girls had crushes on. They were the heroines of America's most beloved works of literature, from Jo March in *Little Women* to Scout Finch in *To Kill a Mockingbird*.

These tomboys, admired by both boys and girls, were precocious, outspoken, and unbeholden to the silent or explicit rules of gender around them. They often adopted male nicknames, like both Jos, or Frankie from Carson McCullers's *The Member of the Wedding*. They rejected feminine fashion, or anything that could be labeled fashion at all. They were athletic and played primarily or at least partially with boys. And they played *like* boys—that is, they were interested in pursuits that American society had labeled as masculine, from baseball to tree climbing. They behaved differently than many of the other girls, which made them compelling and complex; it's what made them heroines.

In fact, tomboys were once so beloved that many adult women who probably weren't particularly tomboyish claimed to have been tomboys. An early 1970s study found that *78 percent* of college women said they were tomboys growing up.[1] More recent studies show that between a third and half of adult women say they were childhood tomboys—a huge decline, but still a strong showing.[2] The word "tomboy" is found in or borrowed by over forty non-English languages, and more than forty others have their own version of it: *garçon manqué* (failed, lost, or missing boy) in French; *Wildfang* (little rascal or domesticated wild animal) in German.[3] Kim Jong-un's little sister, Kim Yo-jong, has been described as "sweet but with a tomboy streak."[4]

Legions of famous and important women have heralded their tomboy pasts: Janet Jackson, Keira Knightley, Ava Gardner, Martina Navratilova, Reese Witherspoon, Joan Collins, Robin Roberts, Hillary Rodham Clinton, and Jean Jennings, one of the first women in computer coding, all said they were tomboys growing up. "Vanessa and I were both what we call tomboys; that is, we played cricket, scrambled over rocks, climbed trees, were said not to care for clothes and so on," Virginia Woolf said.[5]

Cher credited her miraculously enduring physique to her tomboy past. "You have to work out. But, thank God, I always was a tomboy, so I don't mind doing it," she told *People* in 2018. Dolly

Parton, arguably the most feminine human on the face of the earth—a tomboy. Belinda Carlisle! Julia Child! Lupita Nyong'o!

It seemed like they were everywhere when I was a kid in the seventies, these feisty pigtailed or shorthaired girls in dungarees and T-shirts, playing ball, scraping knees, and getting their hands dirty; a kid like mine might have gone unremarked among them. But tomboys were so uncommon among my daughter's crowd in 2015 that I hadn't even conjured the term from my memory.

When the word did reenter my life, I didn't bother to critique it—why, I would ask later, use a word with "boy" to describe a sporty, independent-minded girl?—and part of me wondered why a child who identified as a girl, but who preferred short hair and track pants, needed a separate label. But it did help me understand my daughter's inclinations and differences. The act of naming something brings relief, the psychological exhalation gifted by taxonomy. *Oh, she's just a tomboy*, I thought.

But in writing this book, I have come to see that there's no such thing as "just a tomboy." I've come to see the values and judgments embedded in that phrase—the sexism, homophobia, and transphobia, the idea that tomboyism is normal only if it's a phase resulting in a feminine, heterosexual, and cisgender woman—one whose assigned sex and gender identity align. I've come to see that childhood tomboys grow up to claim many different sexualities and gender identities. And I've come to see that only cisgender girls have had this privilege of blurring boundaries and crossing lines. There is no positive term for a boy version of a tomboy, not sissy (derived from sister) or Nancy boy, no historically positive word for a girl who continues such masculinity after puberty. It is because we both tend to approve of masculinity and have considered tomboys harmless because they are girls that this allowance has been made. Rarely does anyone think a boy's "sissy" phase is cool. Rarely do they even see boys' feminine behavior as a phase while tomboyism is often imagined that way.

But it took me a long time to see this. My understanding began to change when my daughter was in third grade, and a teacher at the after-school program she'd been attending for six months stopped me at pickup. "I just wanted to check," she said. "Your child wants to be called a boy, right? Or is she a boy that wants to be called a girl? Which is it again?"

"She's a girl," I reminded her. The teacher seemed hesitant. *Girls can look and act all kinds of ways* was apparently harder for adults to understand than kids. This was becoming a recurring situation: adults' questioning of my daughter's gender identity and skepticism at her response (admittedly something many trans kids have to face daily—and they can't use their anatomy as "proof" that they are who they say they are). It happened regularly in doctor's offices, classrooms, and on baseball diamonds, with adults who had known her for some time, whose goal was to be sensitive and inclusive. Our lovely pediatric nurse practitioner almost always asked if she wanted a new pronoun. The very kind teachers and administrators at school asked if she wanted to change in the boys' locker room.

In many ways, this was a wonderful thing, a crucial cultural shift. Caitlin Jenner had been out for two years and *Time* had pronounced a transgender tipping point. Transgender high school student Gavin Grimm was suing his Virginia school board for its discriminatory bathroom policies. Trans adults and kids were an

6

occupying topic of the public mind. Asking a child his or her or their preferred pronouns was progress, reflecting our increasing awareness of trans rights and the human right to have one's gender identity affirmed, which I support unequivocally.

But adults' questioning and skepticism of my daughter's gender identity seemed like zealousness to put kids in boxes—new boxes, but boxes all the same—and they seemed to be based on binaries and gender stereotypes, the idea that short hair and track pants and sports fundamentally *were* boy things, even in 2017. I can't blame those well-meaning adults for thinking so. There were so few short-haired girls in sweatpants playing with boys, even in our dark blue dot in a royal-blue city, with one of the most active LGBTQ+ communities in the world. While many have finally come to see gender as a spectrum, often young children hew to the pole ends.

When I relayed the conversation with the after-school teacher to my daughter, she looked at me calmly and said, "More girls should look like this so it's more popular so grown-ups won't be so confused." I hugged her and marveled at her wisdom, but it also set into motion what proved to be an unstoppable inquiry: Why *did* so few girls look like her these days? According to her own declaration, she was a tomboy, a type with which the world had been familiar for nearly two hundred years. They weren't entirely extinct as a species, and clearly were still in the collective consciousness enough for a six-year-old to invoke the term to describe my child two years before. But there were certainly far fewer tomboys than when I was a kid, in the media and on the playground. Why was such a person no longer understood? Where had the tomboys gone?

I pondered my daughter's experience in a hotly contested op-ed for the *New York Times* in 2017. Partially in response to the criticisms (detailed in chapter 12), I began to study gender generally and tomboys specifically. Soon, I discovered that the retreat of the classic 1970s and '80s tomboys of my youth started long before the profile of trans kids rose. That retreat stems from a Big Bang of convergent cultural shifts: unchecked capitalism, advances in reproductive technology, homophobia, anti-feminist backlash, a declining birthrate, deregulation of kids' TV, and the rise of "girl power." All of those forces and more contributed to today's era of the "hyper-gendered childhood," the labeling of every single item, activity, piece of clothing, toy, color, and personality trait as either masculine or feminine. I believe those categories have been artificially, stiflingly narrowed, especially when it comes to children, and that there's nothing static about what those words convey. As I researched, I found that those overly restrictive categories have had tremendous social and psychological implications for children.

That narrowing is now giving way to a much-needed explosion. Today, with the rise of non-binary and genderfluid identities, with Xs on birth certificates instead of Fs and Ms, and increasing consumer pressure on marketers to strip the boy and girl markers from toys and clothes, a gender revolution is taking place. Meanwhile, there are somewhere between 1 in 100 and 1 in 2,000 intersex babies born each year (depending on sources of statistics and definitions), whose biological or chromosomal makeup or anatomy don't fit neatly into a single sex category.[6] Their parents are now less frequently pressured into surgeries that would make their children's bodies look conventionally male or female; in some states, such surgeries are illegal. Thus, our ideas of assigned or biological sex are likely to expand along with our ideas about gender—all the cultural associations and expectations associated with sex, along with a person's self-representation, or how that person is treated based on gender presentation.

Yet this is also the era of gender-reveal parties, and everything from candy to pens, toys to clothes, every item associated with childhood stuffed into separate pink or blue packaging. In many ways, early childhood is as binary as it ever was, and in some cases, more so.

In the midst of this upheaval, I wanted to find out what tomboys could teach us about gender as our culture grapples with what it means to be a boy or a girl, man or woman, masculine or feminine, or none or all of those things. I spoke to sociologists, biologists, anthropologists, neuroscientists, psychologists, historians, Shakespearean scholars, clothing designers, gender therapists, people of many sexualities and gender identities, and tomboys from eight to eighty, asking three main questions, the sections of this book:

- Where did the pink/blue divide come from, and where do tomboys fit within it?
- What motivates childhood tomboys to straddle or cross that divide?
- Who do those tomboys grow up to be?

Amid the studies and stories, I discovered common narratives of tomboys who were physically active, proud of their muscles, self-confident, and open to both traditionally feminine and masculine playmates and toys. They were, as one researcher put it, egalitarians.[7] When puberty hit, those similar tomboy stories diverged into

9

tremendously diverse adulthoods. My hope is that reexamining what we already thought we knew about tomboys will create *more* understanding of and appreciation for gender diversity.

Many people feel that "boy" and "girl" are only gender or social identities, and don't refer to hormones, chromosomes, or anatomy as the words "male" and "female" do. That is, those words don't refer to sex—biology—but the social meaning of sex: gender. But in this book, unless otherwise noted, I use "boy" and "girl" the way that most of the research I consulted and most of the researchers I spoke with used them: as shorthand for those who are assigned male or female at birth. The broader truth is that some people who identify as tomboys may not have been assigned female at birth, and some people who claim the mantle of tomboys may not identify as girls.

Gender is one of the hardest subjects to talk about. It may be a spectrum (and some people even object to that idea because it's a line between the poles of man and woman, instead of a more inclusive sphere), but it is made up of individual dots, and each of us sees gender from the perspective of our own dot. Many experts I spoke to—academics, doctors, specialists—had differing opinions and plenty of research to back them up. So did laypeople, who had equally strong opinions because of their lived experience, which gave them their own expertise. They had competing gender belief systems, and complete faith in what they believed. Over decades and generations, experts found new and opposing truths, each time declaring that they knew all there was to know about gender, sex, and sexuality, but most of what early experts knew is in dispute. The single unequivocal truth about gender I could locate was this: It's complicated.

Our shifting understandings of gender over the last two centuries have had profound effects on how we raise children and divide the stuff of their childhoods into pink and blue columns. My goal is to get parents, especially, to question where their ideas of normalcy for boys and girls come from—and even where they got the idea that those are the only two kinds of kids—and understand how we as a society perpetuate those ideas.

Sometimes tomboys are cute little girls in fireman—fire*fighter*—hats. Sometimes they are radical gender warriors, "gender heroes," as the writer Karleen Pendleton Jiménez called them, who manage to rebel against restrictive norms, at times against tremendous backlash, at others with relative impunity. And sometimes they are just following their instincts, doing what they like, oblivious to how adults categorize them. What if there were room for every boy, girl, intersex, trans, non-binary, and every other kind of kid to explore and express their gender? What if we could all feel the freedom that tomboys historically have, and enjoy that same declaration of gender independence?

Long before the debates about bathrooms and binaries, tomboys showed us that there are all kinds of ways to *do gender*, as the theorists say. They offer us a perch from which to view the beauty, mystery, and complexity of gender.

I

The Creation of the Pink/ Blue Divide

Chapter 1

WHAT THE HECK IS A TOMBOY, ANYWAY?

"She is gentle! She is wild! She's a riddle! She's a child!"
— *Richard Rodgers, "Maria," from* The Sound of Music

One of the first things I did when I embarked on this project was set up a Google alert for the word "tomboy." When my daughter came home in first grade with her new descriptor, I didn't think much about the word itself. I thought of what it evoked: a sporty young girl in ripped overalls or shorts, with skinned knees and messy hair, playing ball with the boys, running with her shirt off down the street or across the field. Maybe a kid with swagger and confidence, a tough talker, who either doesn't give a hoot about gender norms that tell her she's supposed to be demure and passive, stuck in a dress and on the sidelines, or doesn't think those rules apply to her and makes up her own. I thought of all the kids that young Kristy McNichol and Jodie Foster played.

But almost no references to young girls graced my inbox. Day after day, I was provided with a roundup of season three of the Russian reality makeover show *From Tomboy to Lady*, or lots of hot animated tomboy avatars from gamers chatting on Reddit or 4chan. There were more than 2.8 million #tomboy images on Instagram, most of them showing androgynous-looking models and actresses, or long-haired women kissing each other, or just pictures of Kristen Stewart walking the red carpet in sneakers and leather pants.

There were references to the pan-gender underwear company TomboyX, which describes a tomboy as "an energetic, sometimes boisterous girl" who "dresses and sometimes behaves the way boys are expected to" and "who is not afraid to stand up, stand out, be heard and be seen." Based on my experience, it's hard to find gender-neutral kids' boxer briefs, but sadly TomboyX doesn't market its wares to the young girls who inspired its name.

On Facebook, there were dozens of tomboy groups, almost all of them dedicated to a kind of butch lesbian sexuality, and sometimes transgender identity, in Asian countries from Thailand to China to the Philippines. *THAT'S MY TOMBOY PHILIPPINES*, *Femmes and Tomboys*, and *TOMBOYS LOVE GIRLS* each had tens of thousands of members. *Tom suay* is Thai for "beautiful butch."

Yet there were but five members of the group *Tomboys just being Tomboys*, which had no posts and just one photo, of a tawny-skinned girl sticking out her tongue. That was pretty much it for childhood tomboys on social media.

When I did find current, contemporary references to young girls in my inbox, they were almost always in articles and blog posts from mothers insisting that their daughters not be called tomboys—even though I found scant evidence that girls today are commonly referred to that way. These writers denounced the word as outdated and offensive, noting that making a separate category for sporty, assertive girls implies that the normal state of girlhood is inactive and quiet. Why should we use a term with *boy* in it to describe these Jos and Punkys and Scouts, indicating that they are both a lesser form of boy and a better form of girl?

Meanwhile, the word "tomboy" has sometimes been foisted upon trans people, to tell them that their core gender identities aren't valid. Saying someone is "just a tomboy" can also be code for: "I don't believe that you are trans."

So, yes, the word in all its deployments is full of flaws, misuses, even abuses. In fact, it always was.

A Brief History of the Word "Tomboy"

The "tom" part of tomboy likely comes from the twelfth-century Middle English *thom*, meaning "boy type"—like tomcat, tom turkey. And the "boy" is, well, boy. The term, when it was coined in 1556, meant an extra-boisterous boy, a dose of prepubescent toxic masculinity.

Not long after, the meaning shifted to describe a lascivious woman whose sexual appetites rivaled men's. By 1656, it had begun to describe a girl who acted more like a rambunctious boy, a definition that stuck, even if for the first two hundred years or so it was an insult. But in mid-1800s antebellum America, "tomboy" began shifting from a slur to a term of pride.

In many ways, the mass media and publishing industries, which ballooned after the Civil War, created and popularized the

Credit: From *Freaks and Frolics of Little Girls and Boys* by Josephine Pollard (New York: McLoughlin Bros, 1888)

modern concept of the tomboy. They supplied books to the growing demographic of middle-class children who went to school instead of worked, who were partaking of this new time and space called childhood. These books told girls and boys how, and how not, to behave. The emerging products of women's magazines and children's literature trafficked in gendered cultural normalcy.

Amid the tales of naughty boys who were more interested in

spinning tops than reading books, and girls who were too vain, were tales of girls who, when told that they should be sweet and sedentary and deferential and demure, said *no way*.[1] Those girls became known in American media and culture as tomboys. Adult women in the Victorian era, predominantly middle-class white women, were largely constrained by the gender roles of what was known as the "cult of true womanhood," sometimes called the "cult of domesticity." This ideology promoted the ideal of women sticking to the private sphere, tending to children and cultivating piety, purity, domesticity, and submissiveness (though some were also cultivating their own industries and romances). But some of their daughters were doing wildly "masculine" things like playing sports with boys, even if they were expected to desist once they became mothers themselves.

Early on, "tomboy" was a divisive word. The media debated tomboyism's merits and deficits during this first nineteenth-century tomboy heyday; there are more than twenty-two thousand tomboy mentions in the Newspapers.com archive alone.[2] Sometimes tomboys were called vulgar or dangerous, with experts declaring that girls should not be raised with the malignant idea that they deserved equality with boys, or be educated with them. The biggest peril? Studying would siphon blood away from the womb.

The greatest possibility? It's nicely put in this 1891 article from San Francisco's the *Morning Call*: "The American Tomboy: She Often Becomes a Woman Men Admire and Worship." If some people believed tomboys would lose what was thought to be women's most important power—procreation—others believed tomboyism would strengthen that power; tomboys would grow up to be the healthiest and most attractive women, the most suited to reproduce.

Some encouragement of tomboyism was downright feminist. An author named L.V.F. wrote a widely reprinted 1858 editorial called "Our Daughters—Tomboys." She suggested what mothers should remember: "...if restricted (physical) education, enfeebled health, delicate nervous system, and above all a purposeless, aimless life, are not calculated to bring out the genius and build up the reputation of their sons; neither are they to be depended on to do this for their daughters."[3] That is, some people began to believe that daughters should be treated, in many ways, like sons.

Jo Changes Everybody's Mind

What really upped the cultural approval of tomboys was the rise of tomboy literature, starting with what may have been the country's first bestseller, E. D. E. N. Southworth's 1859 *The Hidden Hand*. It starred the mischievous tomboy orphan Capitola Black and electrified the kid-lit industry. Books about feisty, fending-for-themselves, often motherless girls followed (their lack of maternal influence was used to explain their tomboyism). They were misfits, and pals with fellow-misfit sissies, but also heroines. Soon there were Western books for boys that included horse-wrangling tomboy characters.

Once Louisa May Alcott's *Little Women* hit the scene in 1868, Jo March captured the hearts and imaginations of girls around the country. One of the first books written specifically for girls— by a woman who claimed not to know many girls besides her sisters, or to like the ones she did know—Alcott's novel, based on her own gender-rebellious life, starred a heroine who was not just mischievous; she was the smartest, most resourceful person around. Even if she was occasionally chastised within the book for her gender noncompliance, just about every reader loves Jo the best of all four of the March girls.

Usually in these books, tomboys were feminized by the end, married off to men, which literary critics call "tomboy taming." Even Jo married the much older Mr. Bhaer (to Alcott's own chagrin; she caved to pressure from readers and her publisher to marry her off). That is, tomboyism wasn't usually portrayed in literature as permanently deviant behavior.

In fact, it's quite likely that the tomboyism being debated was not particularly unusual. Historian Renée Sentilles, author of *American Tomboys, 1850–1915*, reviewed diaries of girls in the nineteenth century and found that many were hunting, jumping fences, and climbing trees. "Girls' fathers, brothers, and uncles readily took them into the woods for hunting and fishing, and included them in games," she wrote.[4]

Laura Ingalls Wilder wrote in her autobiography, *Pioneer Girl*, "Being, as sister Mary said, a tomboy, I led the girls into the boys' games. We played Anti-over, Pullaway, Prisoners Base and hand ball. When the boys saw how well we could play, in an hour of triumph they took us into their baseball game and we played that the rest of the summer."[5]

Laura was an exception in that she became a publishing star, but she was also an average American tomboy, doing what some girls, and boys, did.

Though throughout the century, some still objected to the idea of girls having a version of boyhood, to others, tomboyism was thought of as normal, partly because of how the Western world understood gender, sex, and sexuality in much of the nineteenth century. They were considered one thing. A boy was expected to grow up to be a heterosexual, cisgender man, and a girl a heterosexual, cisgender woman. So childhood tomboyism was, to some people's thinking, no threat for the natural, maternal instincts that would kick in at puberty. It wouldn't, couldn't, interrupt a girl's natural, charted trajectory: to become a proper wife and mother. (This would soon change, as the concept of homosexuality—sexuality as separate from sex—became more common. More on that later.)

But that didn't turn out to be true; being a tomboy probably *did* shift the trajectory for some women. As a generation of tomboys who had been raised with some notion of freedom grew up, many became "New Women," early women's rights advocates with independent spirits. Some of these early tomboys bushwhacked, paving the way for the feminists who followed. Just as some critics feared, when given an inch, tomboys took a mile.

They went on to become some of the country's first female doctors, like Elizabeth and Emily Blackwell and Sara Josephine Baker; great actresses like Charlotte Cushman, who played both male and female roles; and early feminists, leaders, and suffragists, like temperance movement leader Frances Willard and Clara Barton, founder of the American Red Cross. Each recalled their tomboy days proudly and fondly, as proof that their exceptionalism had been there from the start. Sentilles scoured tomes of late-nineteenth- and early-twentieth-century biographies of these great women, and found that *every single woman profiled* claimed a tomboy childhood. For some of them, that exceptionalism had transitioned from a liability to an advantage, and they from outsider to groundbreaker.

However debatable the word was when applied to children, grown women loved to apply it to themselves retroactively.

Eugenics, Girly-Girls, and Tomboys

Tomboys in the press were sometimes seen not only as future wonderful wives, mothers, and women, but as the heroic antidote to their opposite: feminine, vain, and indulgent girly-girls.[6] Often, they were pitted against each other in literature, the fair-skinned and fair-haired ladylike girly-girl and the raven-haired unladylike tomboy with sun-darkened skin.

In fact, race was an important factor in these early portrayals of tomboys, who were almost exclusively white but were usually dark-haired and tanned. Tomboys took on some stereotypes affixed to people of color, including African-Americans and Native Americans—a kind of cultural appropriation. As Sentilles wrote, tomboys could "play Indian without becoming Indian." Some books even claimed that the name Pocahontas translated into the word "tomboy" (some recent translations posit that it meant "mischievous one").[7] As an example, Capitola Black becomes Capitola Greyson when she's tamed and married at the end of *The Hidden Hand*. She is not just feminized, but lightened, showing how whiteness and traditional femininity, and Blackness and masculinity, were intertwined in the minds of the ruling and creative classes. Nineteenth-century tomboyism was, in fact, connected to one of the white middle class's great projects of the time: breeding the white race.

The birthrate was declining among American-born whites, and proper middle-class white women, in their twenty-five pounds of restrictive bustles, corsets, and crinolines, were aiming for the ultimate femininity of frailty. But that wasn't much good for procreation. An 1873 article stated that parents should "allow a girl to be as 'tomboyish' as her inclinations lead her to be....Let her ride, drive, row, swim, run, climb fences, and even trees, if she has a mind to. She is only laying the foundation for future good health."[8]

Good health is a code, meaning: tomboy now, successful breeder of white children later. Michelle Abate, author of *Tomboys: A Literary and Cultural History*, called tomboyism "a code of conduct" that "stressed proper hygiene, daily exercise, comfortable clothing, and wholesome nutrition...designed to boost the health of middle and upper-class white women."[9]

Tomboyism was stitched to whiteness, a form of white privilege, in the nineteenth century, which redefined and broadened acceptable behavior for a subset of American girls. Much of the documented history of American tomboys is white tomboy history; the term was rarely used in African-American newspapers in the nineteenth and early twentieth centuries, and not much applied to people of color in white newspapers until the 1950s, as sports became desegregated and the profiles of African-American female professional athletes like Althea Gibson rose.[10] Most of the psychologists, sociologists, and biologists who study tomboys are white women, and the great bulk of subjects in tomboy studies are white, which complicates—or oversimplifies—the research.

What is gender-typical depends on race and class and geography, among other factors. Tomboyism for a wealthy, urban white girl in the nineteenth century, running outdoors and having an active physical life, was a privilege, whereas being conscripted to hard physical labor outdoors was not a choice for poor or enslaved rural girls. Those girls engaging in "masculine" behaviors likely wouldn't have been called, or called themselves, tomboys; those aspects of traditional masculinity were forced upon them.

All-American Tomboys

But for those who had a choice, tomboyism became an increasingly normalized option. As the century closed, it was so common for some girls to be doing "boy" stuff that those same magazines, newspapers, and books that had cautioned against, and then celebrated, tomboys declared the word "tomboy" dead. An 1898 article from *Harper's Bazaar*, serialized in papers across the country, was titled "Passing of the Tomboy"; it called tomboy "an antiquarian's word."

"The passing of the tomboy is complete," it remarked. "The girl of to-day at her American best is a hearty, healthy, happy, graceful child."[11] Some swaths of American society had shifted from portraying tomboys as misfits to portraying them as so everyday that there was no need to categorize them separately. Young girls, born into a world in which they could climb trees and play baseball and have some version of equality with boys, should not be called tomboys, the media suggested. Instead, they should be called "all-American girls."[12]

Even back then, critics expressed what would become a recurring conundrum with the word. If there were so many girls acting "like boys" that we needed to create a new category for them, did those behaviors and activities and personality traits really belong to boys? Where did we get the idea that tree-climbing, baseball-playing, fence-hopping, independence, and assertiveness were, in some biological and not just a cultural sense, *masculine*? After all, temperance leader Frances Willard had been more keen on running, sledding, and skating than playing with dolls as a tomboy girl.[13] But G. Stanley Hall, founder of developmental psychology, estimated that up to 82 percent of boys under six, and 76 percent of boys six to twelve, liked playing with dolls at the turn of the century.[14]

The meaning of tomboy is completely dependent on a binary of opposites, with separate criteria of what's normal for boys and girls. It's a name for girls who cross the divide, who act or play or dress like a boy, who gravitate toward boy-typical things: clothes, people, toys, activities. But what's typical for boys and girls has constantly been in flux. Once whistling and bike-riding were considered things only boys could and should do, and a century ago American boys wore dresses or decorative, lacy Little Lord Fauntleroy suits and, later, plenty of pink. Now any girl can whistle and very few American boys wear pink, and even fewer wear lace and dresses. What's on either side of the divide is not static, so neither can definitions of "tomboy" be.

So What *Is* a Tomboy?

When I asked third grade identical twins Dylan and Elie, who identify as tomboys, what that word meant, they struggled to define it.

"Somebody who isn't, like, a girly-girl I guess, who doesn't play with dolls, doesn't wear, like, pink dresses [and] wears more boy clothes, I guess. Kind of like, does sports. Like, isn't the kind of normal girl," said Elie.

"Someone who's a girl but dresses and acts like, not acts but, likes sports and stuff like that," said Dylan. She knew not to say "like a boy." She knew her exception proved the fuzziness of the rule.

But what was the rule?

Are tomboys girls who play with boys? Most literary tomboys, from Jo March to Scout Finch, run with the boys in sexual tension–free friendships. Sissies and tomboys are portrayed as outsiders communing, like Jo and her best friend Laurie.

But in real life, many (but not all) tomboys have not tended to be loners or solely play with boys or do boy stuff, but instead mix male and female friends and play. Rather than shadowy figures on the outskirts of boy and girl spheres, they are included in both, the overlap in the Venn diagram, with a pass to surf between both worlds; some, though, hew far more to the boy side.

Are tomboys girls who play sports? Short answer, yes, but that can't be the sole criterion because how acceptable it is for a girl to play sports has changed. If baseball was a relatively common pastime for some nineteenth-century girls,[15] it became less so in the twentieth century. Girls were kept out of Little League until 1974, two years after Title IX of the Education Amendments of 1972 was passed, prohibiting discrimination on the basis of sex in federally funded education programs, including sports—the league "yielded to the 'social climate,'" per the *New York Times*.[16] Before that, one in twenty-seven girls played sports. Today it's two in five. But even now, few of them play baseball.

Are tomboys short-haired girls in boys' clothes? Well, in the 1800s, most little boys *and* girls—even the tomboys—had long hair and wore dresses, until they went to school around age six. Jo March wore women's clothes; there was no other option. So there was little about the way an older tomboy *looked* that distinguished her from other girls in the nineteenth century. The only difference would have been that her dresses and skirts were torn and stained from hopping fences and engaging in—note the word—tomfoolery. There are many paintings of nineteenth-century tomboys doing just that.

Credit: *The Tomboy,* by John George Brown, 1873

In the 1970s, boys and girls often dressed alike, in boyish clothes (I will soon explain why) and short hair was common for both boys and girls. Yet these days, short hair for young girls is so rare that it ruffles feathers. In 2017, a soccer team with short-haired girls was ridiculed by adults and children who refused to accept that they were girls.[17] A similar "misunderstanding" took place that same year with a short-haired girl on a Nebraska team—perhaps because they didn't have access to the word "tomboy" to normalize or contextualize the existence of such girls.[18]

Are tomboys girls who embrace traditional masculinity, or do they reject traditional femininity? One of the biggest questions asked by researchers is whether tomboys reject girl stuff or just add boy stuff. In 1973, psychiatrists Tasmiya Saghir and Eli Robins defined tomboyism as a "preference for the company of boys and for boys' activities," as well as "persistent aversion to girls' activities and girls as playmates." But when researchers included in studies *every* kid who called herself a tomboy, the definition got much wider. In 1984, psychologists Pat Plumb and Gloria Cowan surveyed girls who identified as tomboys and noted: "*Self-defined* tomboys do not reject traditionally female activities. Instead, they expand their repertoire of activities to include both gender-traditional and nontraditional activities." (Emphasis mine.)

Sometimes researchers break tomboys into groups. Are they "always" or "masculine" tomboys, who never relent, even after puberty, when so many tomboys tuck their masculinity away? Or "sometimes" or "feminine" tomboys, who can drift from a dress back to boys' clothes, from tree-climbing to proper feminine presentation, with relative ease?

While some tomboys are certainly more masculine than

others, I don't believe that there are just two types of tomboys, but rather many. Participants in a 2012 study had answers to "Are you a tomboy?" like "[I'm a] subtle tomboy," or "Yes, but barely. I'm more like my dog: a mutt."[19]

My husband and I often noted what we saw as the difference between our daughter, who looked for about six years entirely like a boy, and played with more boys than girls—an "always" tomboy, so we thought—and her friend, Madeleine, who in first grade was sporty and assertive and equally friends with boys and girls. She had a no-frills bob and wore the occasional dress: a "sometimes" tomboy, in our minds.

But my daughter has pink-streaked longer hair now, and many female friends. And on the cusp of fifth grade, Madeleine cut her hair super short and mostly plays with boys. Often kids—who have the privilege, support, and freedom to do so—toggle their masculinity and femininity throughout childhood. Many adults do the same throughout their lives, too.

Is tomboyism connected to race? As mentioned previously, the definition of tomboy also shifts based on race and class and geography. An example: To Lisa, an African-American tomboy who grew up in a Brooklyn housing project in the 1970s, tomboy meant protection. "I didn't like dresses or anything that would make me look like a girl," she said. There was poverty, and violence and hardship, the structural racism built into the bricks of her under-maintained building. Lisa had to be hard, tough, rough. "Everyone was a tomboy," she said. "It was like, who can bark the loudest? Who can have the most alpha aggression, because that's the only way you can survive in Brownsville." Tomboy was how she showed other girls and boys not to mess with her, how she showed her strength. "For us," she said, "tomboy is survival."

For Susan, a white tomboy in the 1950s growing up in a Chicago suburb, tomboy meant popularity. She was catching frogs in the creek with her tomboy pals, wearing jeans—which was still a no-no—and playing as many sports as she could. She despised dolls but loved dollhouses. In third grade, she wrestled her best friend—a boy—to the ground. "This was a crowning moment for me," she said. It didn't dissuade the boy from being her friend. In fact, it made her more of a social success.

These are just two examples, not meant to encapsulate the entire racialized experience of tomboyism. Besides, tomboyism is a cross-cultural phenomenon in many ways. As Abate writes, "In the same way that tomboyish young women can be found in every early period, genre, and phase of U.S. literature and culture, so, too, can they be located in nearly all of the nation's racial and ethnic groups."[20] Women of color from Princess Nokia to actress Priyanka Chopra proudly proclaimed themselves tomboys, too.

Whatever a tomboy is and however one defines it, like it or not, for almost two hundred years tomboy was an incredibly important word and idea. Whenever we divide things—behaviors, personalities, clothes, activities, toys, colors—into boys' and girls', there will always be people whose preferences don't fall neatly on one side of the line. And there will always be people who want to hop from one side to the other. Tomboy was a meaningful category that excused, and normalized, certain kinds of behavior and gave girls access to a whole wing of childhood that would otherwise have been closed off. It gave a name to the many girls who straddled, and sometimes hopped, the line—or at least visited the other side. Many tomboys are both liberal—accepting of others who straddle or ignore or hop the line—and liberated: free from gender's constraints. They tend to be gender egalitarians, open to what's on both sides of the pink/blue divide.

What I want to know is: Who gets to draw those lines, to forge boy and girl, masculine and feminine, as opposites? And how has it changed over time?

For if the word and idea of "tomboy" are problematic, they are symptoms of a much larger problem: the problem of hyper-gendering childhood.

ELIZABETH

I was nine when it happened, the misery that befalls almost every tomboy, the turning point when we realize we don't actually have full equality with boys. My mom said, "You have to wear a shirt."

I was still years away from getting breasts, but the other moms in our Kansas neighborhood were starting to talk. My parents were open-minded and feminist—my dad had even bought me a Tonka truck when I was little, which I loved both as a toy and a statement—but they gave in to the pressures of that particular corner of conformity.

I was furious. Before that, I'd been riding around the neighborhood shirtless on my bike with a pack of boys and some girls. I couldn't play Little League—girls weren't allowed to back then—and I could feel the oppressive weight of childhood's impending end. My options were being limited. Boys had all this freedom and girls didn't. It really frustrated me.

Sometimes I looked like a boy, in short hair and jeans, but not always. From early on my tomboyism was in my actions and attitudes. I liked to do physical things and speak up and I made of a lot of noise, the same way the boys did. I demanded attention. My hero was Leather Tuscadero, the tough-talking rock singer from *Happy Days*. I saw myself as a rebel, even if my behavior, my way of looking and being, was accepted as within the normal range. People called me a tomboy, and I didn't feel judged—I felt proud. My self-possession and confidence, my tree-climbing and ball-playing earned me the moniker.

But even then, I could sniff out the double standard. I went to school with a very femme boy and he got so much shit. He was constantly being bullied. I think that the social policing when I was a kid meant that tomboys were accepted, but boys like him never were.

Chapter 2

TOMBOYS? OKAY! SISSIES? NO WAY!

"The generally accepted rule is pink for the boys, and blue for the girls. The reason is that pink, being a more decided and stronger color, is more suitable for the boy, while blue, which is more delicate and dainty, is prettier for the girl."

—Earnshaw's Infants' Department, *1918 (via Smithsonianmag.com)*[1]

"**W**hy are there so many tomboys in this movie?" my daughter asked me. We were watching the original 1976 *Freaky Friday* starring Jodie Foster, who, along with her friends, was sporting tube socks, athletic shorts, and a T-shirt.

"Those aren't necessarily tomboys," I replied. "That's just how lots of girls dressed in the 1970s and early '80s." Sure, there were plenty of highly feminine girls' fashions—the Gunne Sax dresses and lacy Lanz nightgowns of my childhood heart's desire—but many of us wore outfits like those of the *Freaky Friday* girls.

Lots of boys had bowl haircuts; girls had Dorothy Hamill haircuts. Turns out, they were the same haircut! In the 1980 movie

Credit: My pals and I rocking 1970s unisex looks (plus a bonnet and Dr. Scholl's)

Little Darlings, tomboy icon Kristy McNichol and her love interest Matt Dillon wear the same T-shirts and jeans and even have the same feathered, shoulder-length hair. Many people I talked to who were tomboys in the 1970s and early '80s said they were not the only girls like them around, riding bikes and running wild, having what some researchers have called a "boyhood for girls." Tomboys were common, in life and in the media.

One of the most famous tomboy images is a 1981 ad for LEGO. It features a girl in dungarees and a striped shirt, her long red hair in braids, holding up the colorful design she made herself. The

Credit: Used with permission. ©2019 The LEGO Group
[Disclaimer: All information in this publication is collected and interpreted by its authors and does not represent the opinion of the LEGO Group.]

tagline—"What it is is beautiful"—and the copy made no mention of gender, and the plastic bricks had no gender color-coding.

It might seem that we went from the tomboy heyday of the 1800s, where the baseball-playing, tree-climbing, dress-wearing tomboy was lauded as "an eager, earnest, impulsive, bright-eyed, glad-hearted, kind-souled, living and real specimen of the genus feminine," as she was described in 1858,[2] straight to the tomboy heyday in which I was raised, 120 years later.

But in fact, our continually evolving understanding of sex,

gender, and sexuality changed the way kids dressed and played for most of the twentieth century. Between the Victorian tomboy movement and the revival in the 1970s was a long period in which we created the first round of the pink-and-blue divide, and began to gender children's earliest years.

Every Boy Likes to Tinker, Every Girl Likes to Play House

Credit: *The Land of Sunshine: A Southern California Magazine*, 1901

Until the 1920s, most American children under age six were having some version of a gender-neutral early childhood. According to historian Jo B. Paoletti, author of *Pink and Blue: Telling the Boys from the Girls in America*, most American babies of both sexes wore white dresses—they were practical in an era when people mostly made their own clothes, and easy to clean. Many little girls *and* boys donned dresses of other colors—with bows and ruffles and lace—and didn't cut their hair until they went to school. Fashion writers advised that boys aged two or three could graduate to kilts and blouses but shouldn't wear trousers until they turned five. Little girls could wear overalls if they wore them over dresses. When they got older, boys wore pants and girls wore dresses.

Credit: Boys in Little Lord Fauntleroy suits, 1914, via Zazzle (Creative Commons usage)

A similar trend was found in kids' playthings. Toy ads in the very first part of the twentieth century had "no reference to the gender of the target child, and very few gender cues," Dr. Elizabeth Sweet, a sociologist who studies the history of gendering toys, told me. There wasn't a pink Big Wheel to be found.

Why? Remember that sex, gender, and sexuality were all thought of as one thing—the word "homosexual," coined in the mid-1800s in Germany, wasn't in widespread use, and gender identity, as separate from sex assigned at birth, wasn't yet a common Western concept. Because assigned sex and sexuality were connected in people's minds, adults didn't want to think of little kids as future men or women, as later sexual beings, so they downplayed gender differences. Thus, children were dressed according to age, not assigned sex.

But change was coming. The late nineteenth and early twentieth centuries saw the rise of sexology—the study of human sexuality—and of popular psychology, along with the continued growth of publishing and the mass media that spread their gospel. The first medical textbook in English on homosexuality, Havelock Ellis's *Sexual Inversion*, was published in 1897. Sigmund Freud was getting more well known, asserting that kids went through "psychosexual" stages on their way to adulthood, and that early experiences and families shaped our personalities and proclivities. Sexuality came to be seen as distinct from sex: that is, one could be a man and be attracted to other men. Of course, homosexual *behavior* had existed before; but now, according to the men who studied it, such behavior had a name, a distinct classification: homosexual as social category.

Key to this "discovery" of sexuality were thoughts on its origin: Homosexuality was seen as the result of nurture, not nature. So letting boys access too much of the feminine could make them gay—an outcome considered unacceptable, even horrifying, to mainstream American society (though a few early sexologists, Karl Heinrich Ulrichs, saw homosexuality as natural human behavior).[3] G. Stanley Hall, a leading child expert of the day, considered distinct gender roles for boys and girls paramount, and insisted that boys learn early to be straight men.

How to make that happen? Have little boys look and play like little men, so they'd know how to become them. The sharper and earlier the distinctions, the better boys would learn their masculine roles and eschew "abnormal" effeminacy, and thus homosexuality. The clothing details that had been gender neutral—lace, ruffles, bows, and flowers—got stripped off boys' clothes, replaced by images of sports and transportation and male figures and the more "manly" animals, like bears and dogs. Dresses and skirts and frills for boys were no longer allowed after the first quarter of the twentieth century. Girls were left to inhabit the land of lacy flowered things—anything delicate, beautiful, complex, associated with handiwork became entwined with femininity—where boys dared never tread again. Children were groomed to inhabit adult gender roles.

Toys, too, began to prepare kids for their future adult performances of gender. "Every boy likes to tinker around and try to build things," read an ad Sweet found from 1925. "With an Erector Set he can satisfy this inclination and gain mental development without apparent effort.... He will learn the fundamentals of engineering." Meanwhile, read another: "Mothers! Here is a real practical toy for little girls. Every little girl likes to play house, to sweep, and to do mother's work for her."[4]

Some people did fear that tomboyism would lead to lesbianism. But because tomboyism had at times been connected to good health, promoted in the media, and seen as an ideal precursor to childrearing in the century before, many early childhood psychologists thought tomboyism was normal, even preferable. Tomboy play clothes were still acceptable and available, and *Good Housekeeping* heralded the tomboy in 1912 as "a new type of American girl, new not only physically but mentally and morally."[5] Girl Scouts was created that same year, a natural counterpart to the Boy Scouts, albeit with more of a focus on proper table-setting than tying knots.

Tomboys were A-Okay, but anything that could contribute to a boy becoming a sissy? No way!

When Pink Was a Boys' Color

Initially, colors weren't an integral part of the project of gendering childhood and keeping boys from becoming too feminine or gay. All colors were still available to kids, but that started shifting in the late 1920s, too. Advances in dye technology meant many kinds of consumer goods and clothes and toys could be sold in a rainbow of colors, including pink, which had been a hard color to produce before.[6]

Color became part of identity and self-expression. Simply put, having an identity that is expressed through stuff requires enough stuff, and enough money to buy the stuff. In the roaring twenties, with more women in the workforce after World War I, and more cash to spend in American pockets, those pockets became increasingly gendered by color. But what colors went with which genders was still up for grabs.

A chart printed in *Time* magazine in 1927 revealed that department stores promoted differing ideas about which colors were appropriate for boys versus girls. Filene's declared pink a boys' color, as did Best's and Marshall Field's. Macy's, Wanamaker's, and Bullock's said pink was for girls. Catholics associated light blue with girls, à la images of the Virgin Mary.[7] The French associated pink pastels with women, and Americans with children's rosy cheeks. There was no consensus.

For the most part, pink and blue were interchangeable as baby colors for the first half of the twentieth century. Boys were still wearing pink dress shirts and could have pink icing on their cupcakes without people assuming future homosexuality, and girls had access to a full rainbow of colors besides pink. In the 1950s, when pink fanatic Mamie Eisenhower, wife of President Dwight D., came along, with her pink ball gowns and pink decor and "Mamie pink" mid-century bathrooms, pink became even more associated with women. With the growth of the teenage demographic, the *pink* = *girl* thing grew like kudzu. Pink began to communicate to members of an entire sex that they belonged—and to boys that they didn't. That's why, many years later, the University of Iowa football team would paint the visitors' locker room pink.[8]

Stuff = Sex

The baby boomers became the first American generation in which almost every child was raised wearing gender-specific dress, which had profound implications for what they, and eventually we, thought was normal for boys and girls to look like and wear.

Most children learn to categorize themselves by sex by age two, and fully affix gendered expectations and stereotypes to those categories, learned from the culture, their parents, and their peers, by age three. By the middle of the twentieth century, even three-year-olds could identify their own sex, and the sex of another child, by clothes. The more they could distinguish between categories, and the more those categories were positioned as in opposition to each other rather than peacefully coexisting, the more they could police their peers' behavior. And with each generation, especially when there were increases in the middle class and consumer spending, the associations got stronger and more important—not just to the grown-ups but to kids, especially boys, as any parent of a bullied, pink-loving boy knows.

By the 1920s, many psychologists conceived of sex and sexuality separately. That is, being male or female didn't determine sexual attraction. Then the understanding got deeper. In the mid-1950s, psychologists who were studying intersex people— those whose reproductive and/or sexual anatomies don't align with typical definitions of female or male—observed that they had gendered behaviors, expressions, and identities even when their biological sex was unclear. That separated gender—the cultural expectations and norms, the performance—from sex, the

44

biological stuff. Separate from both was sexuality. Researchers coined the term "gender role," which came to mean what society expects of us or considers appropriate based on the sex we're assigned. But just because gender roles were increasingly understood as culturally influenced didn't mean that people weren't punished for deviating from them.

Tomboys were still a big part of popular culture in the 1950s and '60s, with beloved characters like Anybodys in *West Side Story* or Scout Finch in *To Kill a Mockingbird* in books and on stage and screen. With the headline "'TOMBOY' PHASE CALLED NATURAL," the *New York Times* assured parents in a 1950 article that a rowdy period for girls from ages seven to ten was normal, and that "little girls can be at times just about as noisy, dirty and sassy as little boys."[9] Note that it was supposed to evaporate at age ten—crossing the line into masculinity after puberty was not part of this normal, natural phase. Tomboys' embrace was dependent on their desisting and not traveling too far, from straddling to crossing a line. "Always" tomboys—those who were too masculine, who didn't properly retreat from tomboyism at the appropriate times and abide by their adolescent and adult gender roles—could be criticized, even pathologized, portrayed as "aberrant" butch lesbians. But mostly the concern from the mass media was still about young boys and grown women.

The era's increasingly gendered colors and clothes and toys contained other important functions and messages. Just as they had during the Civil War and World War I, women moved into men's work roles during World War II, sampling a taste of freedom in the Rosie the Riveter era. Women had gotten a dose of feminism. Afterward, they needed to be told, shown how, to return to their power-diminished state.

Historian Paoletti found articles from *Parents* magazine in the fifties that explicitly told moms—some of whom had been Rosie the Riveter types—how to raise girls to be wives and mothers, how to emphasize sex roles so they wouldn't be "seriously handicapped adults." No wonder women's clothes got so curvy and feminine in the 1950s, after masculinizing during the flapper era. The message was that women should return to and stay in their lanes.

And tomboys? They were still tolerated, with Gidgets and Scouts in books and on screens, but not as often celebrated as the best way to be girls. Then, tomboys' fate changed once more, when second-wave feminism resurrected them.

Feminism and Nonsexist Parenting

In the 1960s and '70s, tomboys rose to prominence again with the sexual revolution, the rise of the counterculture, feminism, and the questioning and rejection of gender roles. For adult women, claiming to have been a tomboy meant renouncing those restrictive expectations retroactively. One reason up to 78 percent of women in the 1970s said they'd been tomboys growing up was that it expressed their feminism. It was a way of saying they were above the low bar society held them to, and always had been.

If baby boomers were the first generation raised with the gendering of young kids' clothes, the first real taste of the pink/blue divide, now some became members of the procreating counterculture, poised to reject the gender stratification that had been imposed on them. Some partook of "nonsexist parenting," the idea—albeit one that had been kicked around in the mid-1800s, when Jo March made her debut—that girls deserved parity with boys and access to their worlds. Raising daughters to reject gender roles meant deliberately rearing a generation of tomboys. As Paoletti wrote, "In the mid-1970s, the objective of feminist parents was to empower girls by stripping their clothing of every last vestige of traditional femininity and replacing the ideal little lady of their childhood with the tomboy."[10]

Credit: Lisa Selin Davis

That ideology permeated the consumer marketplace. According to Paoletti, 1970s Sears catalogs (aka "the Amazon.com of the twentieth century," per Sweet) marketed many styles of clothes to both boys and girls, offering almost no pink toddler clothing.

There were boys'-to-girls' size conversion charts: How much clearer could the message be that little girls could reach over the line into the land of boys?

Toys followed the same pattern. Less than 2 percent of the toys in those catalogs were marketed to a specific gender in the seventies, per Sweet's research. There were lots of toy ads showing girls as doctors and pilots (though not with boys as ballet dancers and nurses). Science- and domestic-themed toys were sold in many colors, with images of boys and girls in ads working and playing together.

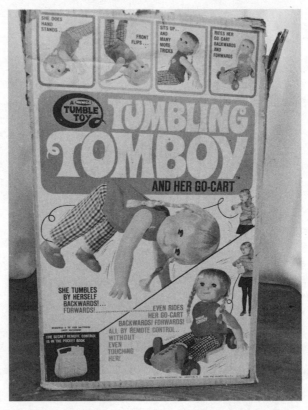

Credit: Lisa Selin Davis

There were still lots of dolls, but among the Barbies appeared a crop of tomboys. Mattel's Hug'n Talk dolls from the seventies featured a tomboy with short red hair, green overalls, and an orange-and-red striped shirt. The Topper Go-Go doll line showcased a tomboy baseball player with freckles, a dirty face, messy clothes, and a baseball hat. Remco's Tumbling Tomboy had a blond, pig-tailed girl in plaid pants as well as an African-American version in the late 1960s, a rarity in the world of tomboy media and toys, which was so interwoven with whiteness. Then again, Mattel's 1970s line the Honey Hill Bunch was a racially diverse group of girl cloth dolls, most of whom were wearing pants and had accessories ranging from guitars to purses.

And of course there were the famous LEGO tomboy ads, which were the brainchild of one of advertising's rare female creative directors, Judy Lotas. "I had two young daughters at the time," Lotas told me. Whenever she'd go up to Connecticut to meet with the LEGO folks at headquarters, she'd come back with armloads of LEGO bricks and her daughters would not just build things out of them, but they'd present the finished products to her proudly. Lotas convinced LEGO that this should be the campaign: kids crafting their own constructions and displaying them with pride.

But she had to fight to feature girls prominently in the ads. "It's not just boys," she told LEGO executives. "Girls do it, too." She knew this because she'd seen it in her own home; her daughters were just as into LEGO bricks as the boys were.

Lotas was adamant that boys and girls be equally represented in the ads, but she told the child models to show up in their own clothes. So that little girl, the icon of the 1970s and '80s tomboy look? That's just what she was wearing because so many little girls dressed that way. While one girl wears lavender overalls and a pink turtleneck in the other print ads in the campaign, most of the kids' clothes are interchangeable, as are their creations.

One reason so many kids looked like Jodie Foster or Kristy McNichol in my childhood, even me, is that wearing "boys'" clothes was a readily available and uncontroversial option. Tomboys were encouraged, and easily clothed. And toys and media that tried to represent the vast experience of girlhood had a tomboy, or several, among them. One look at skimpy-outfitted, high-heeled Bratz dolls and you can see how much that later changed.

When I looked back to see how these gendered waves had crested and receded, it seemed that war and the economy had played a leading role. During and after the Civil War in the mid-1800s, when women assumed greater power in the economy, the first major movement of tomboyism began. After World War I, the flapper movement took hold, offering more masculine, corset-free clothes for liberated women. World War II promoted Rosie the Riveters. During each war, economic times were tight, and women filled men's roles while they went off to fight: War begat feminism. And often the children of feminists were raised as tomboys.

But as money flowed into the economy and the middle classes surged later in the twentieth century, more items were gendered. This served two purposes: to sell twice as much stuff, and to push women back into their places. When each tomboy heyday ended, childhood became gendered as never before. The 1990s produced the most hyper-gendered childhoods yet.

KATHARINE

She called herself Jimmy.

As a tomboy in the 1910s, Katharine Hepburn shaved her head, wore her brother's clothes, and wished she was a boy because "I thought boys had all the fun."[1] "Jimmy" could access the privileges that belonged, in her day, only to little boys.

Katharine—Kate—wore pants long before it was common or even legal for women to do so, when cross-dressing, or "appearing in public in a dress not belonging to his or her sex," or "masquerading as a man" was a criminal act, and women (and men who did the opposite) could be and sometimes were arrested for donning trousers. (Ohio's 1848 law forbidding someone wearing "dress not belonging to his or her sex" in public wasn't overturned until 1974.)[2]

Even after she became famous, Kate had the gall to wear jeans to the set, and when they were taken from her dressing room in an attempt to coax her to wear skirts, she refused to work until they were returned. In 1951, when the management at Claridge's Hotel in London told her that women couldn't wear slacks in the lobby, she took the staff entrance instead.

Kate was known for the tough and independent characters she played: a professional golfer in *Pat and Mike* and an aviator in *Christopher Strong*. Her directors often gave her notes on being softer, more feminine. Her idea of a love scene with a man, director George Stevens once said, "involved standing up straight and talking to him strong, eye to eye."[3]

It was as if she never fully surrendered Jimmy, or her tomboyishness, maintaining that prepubescent spunkiness that made people see her as alluring and distant, aloof, unfeminine, graceful, awkward, seductive, off-putting, dashing, and all-out unusual, both icon and iconoclast. She was "the patron saint of the independent American female."[4]

Like many childhood tomboys, she didn't feel beholden to the gender roles that trap so many people and often needle tomboys into conforming once they hit puberty. "I have not lived as a woman. I have lived as a man," she told Barbara Walters in 1981. "I've just done what I damn well wanted to."[5]

Chapter 3

SPORTY SPICE DROPKICKS
THE TOMBOY

She's a power girl in a nineties world,
She's a downtown swinging dude.

—*Spice Girls, "The Lady Is a Vamp"*

Some people think little girls should be seen and not heard
But I think, "Oh bondage, up yours!"

—*X-Ray Spex, "Oh Bondage! Up Yours!"*

Seduced by the $49 sale price and succumbing to the pressure to keep up with the neighborhood Joneses who had given their children iPads in preschool, I bought two Kindle Fires for my then five- and seven-year-old daughters. The devices were, as advertised, very easy to set up: I signed in, entered my children's birthdays and then...their genders.

As anyone raising a gender-independent kid, or trying to, knows, "What is your child's gender?" can be a difficult, unpleasant, or annoying question to answer. I always wish *Why do you want to know?* was an option in the drop-down menu.

In the case of Amazon's tablet, they wanted to know because they would filter every single app, video, and book that loaded onto it by the way I replied. Answer "boy" and the items they suggested were filled with sports themes and bold colors. Answer "girl" and it was as if a bottle of calamine lotion had dripped down the screen, coloring every app pink and bestowing upon it a magical fairy-tale theme. A tomboy option would have resulted in a nice magenta hue, a pleasant mix of action and magic.

I lodged a complaint with Amazon and tried, in vain, to get them to let me go filter-less. I'm no longer interested in walling off my kids from all things pink and princessy. I like pink (or I think I do—I have no idea how much my cultural conditioning has affected my ability to have independent preferences). What I want is to stop limiting and gendering choices, to let all children have basketballs *and* pink sparkles.

Why has that gotten so hard?

The Forces Converge

Gender roles are elastic, springing back generationally, with more force each time we push on them. If the baby boomers were the first generation with fully gendered kids' clothes and toys, some of whom grew up to reject the gendered experience of their childhoods, their kids went on to raise the most hyper-gendered generation in American history.

So many cultural and economic shifts collided to form this explosion of hyper-gendering. There was anti-feminist backlash and the conservative Reagan era, which pushed nonsexist parenting and feminism out of the way, making room for girl power. This coincided with the end of 1970s recession, which transformed into the "Greed Is Good" 1980s. At the same time, a class of stores known as "nobrow," like Wal-Mart and Target, majorly expanded. These retail outlets brought better design to middle- and working-class people, urban and rural. If once one needed money to express high femininity in clothing—hence my unfulfilled childhood desires for Gunne Sax dresses—now the girliest of goods could be sold to kids of all classes, making feminine fashion cheap and available to all. This redrew the boundaries of the girly-girl/tomboy trope. Girly-girls had been rich and fair, pitted against their poorer, darker tomboy counterparts, like *Little House*'s highly feminine and wealthy Nellie Oleson versus poorer tomboy Laura Ingalls. Now any girl could be girly.

The rise of video games and the deregulation of kids' TV led to program-length ads for toys or video games masquerading as shows—hello, *He-Man*, *Care Bears*, and *My Little Pony*—putting pressure on toy makers to snatch back segments of the blossoming kid demographic being lost to screens.

All this happened as birthrates declined again. It became imperative for marketers to come up with new ways to sell clothes and toys, to prevent hand-me-downs from happening. The pink/blue divide was perfect for disrupting that circuit. To wit: In 1987, the first mass-market book for parenting boys, *The Little Boy Book*, was published, showing the media and publishing industries how much easier it was to sell *any* products if they were marketed toward one sex; *The Little Girl Book* followed not long after. The explosively popular *Men Are from Mars, Women Are from Venus*, published in 1992, provided new fodder to old ideas about gender roles: that males and females were *from different planets*. A kind of commercial gender essentialism came to dominate the market. Maybe we were equal, both good planets, but we were fundamentally different, and thus we needed to buy different things.

Amid these shifts was the increasing commonness of prenatal testing, allowing parents to know the sex of their babies in utero. Suddenly, parents could pave a hyper-gendered path, painting their future kids' rooms pink or blue, assembling a collection of gender-specific toys and clothes and color palettes, a hyper-gendered world that kids could be socialized into from *before* birth. It became common, imperative, that people announce the assigned sex of their babies, that everybody know it immediately and get it right.

Historian Jo B. Paoletti found that the rate of newborn girls' ear-piercing rose in the late 1980s, as did baby headbands and barrettes, and in 1985 Luvs introduced pink diapers for girl babies and blue for boys, with the padding in slightly different spots. Hyper-gendering became part of our parenting mindset, the opposite of how it had been one hundred years before. It was ubiquitous and endless, and just really good for selling stuff.

If the project of the 1920s was to create toys and clothes that ensured little boys would be cisgender, heterosexual men, and the project of the 1970s was to create tomboys, now the project required that everything girls did and bought be marked as girly and that boys didn't go near them. Down the assembly line came pink bikes and pink keyboards and pink pens and pink *everything*, clearly and cleverly marketed to and for girls and girls *only*. We went from "no pink allowed" to the full-on pinkification of girlhood—a land of "no boys allowed." Sociologist Elizabeth Sweet found that gendered toys accounted for around half of the Sears catalog's offerings in the mid-nineties, as they had between the wars.

Grrrl Power Versus Girl Power

The pinkification of girlhood was personified, exemplified, and intensified by the Spice Girls, a British pop girl group—composed of Melanie Brown ("Scary Spice"), Melanie Chisholm ("Sporty Spice"), Emma Bunton ("Baby Spice"), Geri Halliwell ("Ginger Spice"), and Victoria Beckham ("Posh Spice")—that made its debut in 1994. They were an unmatched set—different personalities, races (well, one of them), skill sets—but all the same level of smoking hot.

The most successful British band since the Beatles sold more than 31 million copies of their debut album, *Spice*. They popularized the slogan "Girl Power," which was also the name of their first book and often slathered across their merchandise and outfits—though it had originally come out of the feminist punk scene, conceived as "Grrrl Power," to reject the importance of prettiness and proper feminine behavior.[1] Oh well!

Many felt that the Spice Girls, with their message of unbreakable bonds (*"If you wanna be my lover, you gotta get with my friends"*) empowered young women: Spice Girls as gateway liberation. "You could be sporty and a woman, or very girly and equally a woman," a writer named Irina Gonzalez, who grew up as an avid Spice Girls fan but not as a tomboy, told me. The Spice Girls taught her to "feel good about yourself because you're a woman." Sporty Spice pulled from the tomboy tradition, showing girls how they could retain some tomboyish elements and still be a sex object; this was the dawn of the pretty, feminine tomboy.

But Spice Girls' brand of girly-girl power was inextricable

from highly feminine beauty, so sexualized, so commercial. They weren't just selling merch but an aspirational brand of ultra-feminine empowerment that wouldn't dare make use of the other F-word, feminism—Gonzalez's Spice Girl–loving pals never used that dirty word. Girl Power became code for strong, attractive, confident, heavily made-up girly-girls, and the massive amounts of Girl Power–branded merchandise they would buy. It was female empowerment packaged, literally and figuratively, for the girly.

In post–Title IX America, when girls had legal access in public education to everything boys did, a kind of separate-but-equal commercial philosophy permeated the culture, featuring girl versions of boy stuff, including power. Many experienced it as progress—no longer did girls have to look or act masculine to access the boys' sphere. Girls could now be strong or independent or sporty or smart without sacrificing their femininity. But it was also backlash: Girly-girl power was tomboyism stripped of its gender-bends, telling powerful girls to stay in their feminine lanes, and that their greatest power was prettiness. As literature professor Michelle Abate puts it, the new model was epitomized by "a young girl who plays softball instead of baseball and whose hair is pulled back in a long ponytail rather than cropped in a short crew cut."[2]

Added to the all-pink power package was the Disney princess line of toys and clothes, as chronicled in Peggy Orenstein's *Cinderella Ate My Daughter*. The line started in 2000 and almost instantly racked up $300 million in sales, a cue to retailers everywhere that this pinkification business is a limitless gold mine. It reached the $3 billion mark by 2006,[3] and is now many times that. Today, just about every item conceivable is gender color-coded, from computer tablets to toothpaste. Somehow, this gendering is both omnipresent and invisible—something I hadn't thought about until I compared the unisex Big Wheel of my childhood to the princess-pink version today.

Even as women continued to butt their heads against the glass ceiling, as we decried the leaky pipeline (women dropping out of science and tech careers), the lingering epidemics of girls' low self-esteem and eating disorders and now Snapchat filter–inspired plastic surgery, marketers created—and parents bought—items that contained an insidious message to be girly, and that edged out masculine or tomboyish girls. Fewer such girls appeared in the media, and fewer toys that featured tomboys or might appeal to them as a demographic were sold.

Girly-girl power really did inspire a lot of girls, including the many who loved Sporty Spice. But it left a lot of kids out in the cold.

LEGO in the Pink

Gender-coding can and has been wielded in the name of equity, luring girls into activities that have been pitched as "for boys," telling them, via a pink-and-purple signal, "Hey, you can be interested in pursuits that will lead you to a job at Google some-day, too." (Except that women still only comprise 24 percent of leadership roles there.[4])

Thirty years after being known as the pinnacle of gender-equitable toy advertising, LEGO participated in this shift, too, adding pink and purple bricks in the early nineties. Then in 2012 they introduced their Friends line; according to Elizabeth Sweet, they were convinced that girls had their own special play needs and interests.[5]

The Friends are a racially diverse crew of big-headed, tiny-bodied girls—Shrinky-Dinked Spice Girls—who live in pink-clad bedrooms and have horse stables and heart-shaped boxes. "They love music, science, sports, nature, and art," we're told, but you wouldn't know it from the toys themselves. The copy for the (discontinued) Heartlake News Van suggested that girls "break the big story of the world's best cake" and prepare it for broadcast. After which they should "get Emma ready at the makeup table so she looks her best for the camera."

By contrast, "boy" LEGO sets have police "command centers," Master Falls building kits, water striders, superheroes, helicopters, and no makeup tables. LEGO Friends are more like dolls and dollhouses than they are like construction toys. They don't build the same skills. What they build is big revenue for LEGO. Sales surpassed company expectations, and Friends was among its best-selling products in 2018, steadily increasing its market share of girls since its introduction.[6] So, yeah, more girls play with LEGO products, but essentially a less enriching kind. Unfortunately, LEGO declined my request for an interview because I would have liked to hear their thoughts on this inequity, and the potential fallout from it (and if they will be putting boys on the Friends packaging anytime soon).

Because there *is* fallout. Toys, and how kids play, really do make a huge difference in the skills they develop and who they become. A 2005 study rated 126 toys and found that the boys' were "violent, competitive, exciting, and somewhat dangerous," whereas the girls' were "associated with physical attractiveness, nurturance, and domestic skill."[7] Boys' toys tend to promote exploration and problem-solving and independence. LEGO bricks in particular are known to promote spatial and fine motor skills, while LEGO Friends? Not as much. Girls' toys and games tend to restrict those things, though they tend to foster the valuable skills of communication and nurturing.

How interesting, considering there is research, and folklore, showing how boys have better spatial-temporal skills than girls, and that there are male and female brains with different innate abilities baked in (more on this later). Girls socialized to play with boys, and to play as boys sometimes do—tomboys, usually— might be more prepared for the work world, more positioned to develop those qualities we mistakenly think of as masculine, like being independent or brave, than typical girls.

And boys, well, there's a whole emotional world they can't access because the hyper-gendering of kids' material worlds makes it feel unsafe for them to try. Segregating toys restricts the development of different kinds of intelligence, from spatial to emotional, that *all* kids would do well to learn. Assigned sex need not limit or dictate skill sets. But it often does. As effective as it is to sell toys to kids based on gender stereotypes, it's not actually good for kids.

Writer Lori Day tracked down the child in the original 1981 tomboy LEGO ad, Rachel Giordano, now a naturopathic doctor in the Northwest, and the two lamented over the shift between classic LEGO sets and the Friends line. Giordano told Day, "In 1981, LEGOs were simple and gender-neutral, and the creativity of the child produced the message. In 2014, it's the reverse: the toy delivers a message to the child, and this message is weirdly about gender."[8] Giordano credited toys like LEGO, and the lack of gender segregation in her childhood, with helping shape her creativity and her science-mindedness, leading to her medical career.

In her TEDx Talk, *Parenting a Gender Non-Conforming Child*, Michele Yulo displays an image of the covers of 2016 issues of *Boys' Life* and *Girls' Life* magazines, side by side. *Girls' Life* has a picture of a pretty blond girl, likely because of the stereotype that "girls like people." The articles cover fashion, waking up pretty,

Credit: Screenshot from Michele Yulo's TEDxUtica Talk, *Parenting a Gender Non-Conforming Child*

first kisses, dream hair, and how to get straight A's. *Boys' Life* has a mosaic of objects—because "boys like things," the stereotype goes. "Explore Your Future" reads the title. "Astronaut? Artist? Firefighter? Chef? Here's how to be what you want to be."

Is it any wonder that girls suffer more from low self-esteem and eating disorders, and that more boys become astronauts and firefighters?

What Is Innate?

There's little evidence of consumer demand driving these sweeping changes in the gendering of children's toys in the twentieth century, but there is certainly plenty of evidence, in the form of revenue, that children and their parents have heartily supported them. Marketers and parents clearly believe that they are giving kids what they want, and from there they argue backwards: It's successful so it must be what they want, and it must be biological. Amazon PR rep Robin Handaly wrote to me, when I inquired about the gender filtering in the Kindle Fire, that "the reasoning behind [the filtering] is to make it easy for kids to find the content they love, right out of the box."

Amazon doesn't actually tag its twenty thousand content offerings, from books to apps to videos, as "boy" or "girl," according to Handaly. "The New & Popular category row provides content suggestions based on what other boys and girls of that age range have previously chosen within FreeTime Unlimited—it is not curated by the FreeTime team."

That is, what gets pushed to the forefront of the girl filter gets there because girls have already chosen it. "And, as kids use the FreeTime Unlimited service, the content they see will become more personalized to their preferences," Handaly wrote. The more girls chose the pink stuff and boys the blue, the more they got sorted that way by the algorithm. The algorithm may be designed with marketing in mind, but it is reinforced by consumer choices, more of a self-fulfilling prophecy with each click. The stronger the association between gender and color, the more intense the preferences.

But it's a myth that only girls like dolls, for instance. GI Joe was created for boys who played with Ken dolls—secretly, because they'd learned that they shouldn't.[9] *Every* boy does not want to tinker and build and *every* girl does not like to play house. In fact, most tomboys have historically wanted to do both. What if it isn't that tomboys like "boy" toys and clothes? What if tomboys just like toys that we mistakenly, or insidiously, market as "for boys"? And what if the way we market those things reinforces gender differences that we have come to believe are innate, and positions them as opposites when they don't belong on opposite sides?

Despite the fact that the connection between pink and dresses and femininity is quite recent, people truly believe that pink is a more delicate color, and blue more robust, that girls' love of pink is innate and that their sons were born to love LEGO bricks, somehow an artifact of their chromosomes or reproductive organs. The messages those material goods convey are those we impose upon them and then collectively accept, believing the mirage of color-coded gender, conflating what's common or popular with what's natural or biological.

The trajectory of tomboyism shows us how much of what is thought of as normal and natural for boys and girls is culturally created, and how that can shift. The more commonly we see behaviors in society, the more we think they are natural, but that's not necessarily the most sensible order. Sometimes the more common it is, the more normal it becomes, the more natural it seems.

From Uniformity to Diversity

Until quite recently, it's been hard to find things for kids that *aren't* divided by gender; I couldn't search for kids' bedding on a housewares website without selecting a gender. Girls' Goldfish crackers, man candles, girl socks, and boy bubble bath abound.

There are hopeful and helpful changes afoot, as consumers battle back and insist that retailers offer toys and clothes with fewer gender markers. But even as we celebrate or negotiate or debate diversity at this moment, I often see a striking uniformity within groups of young boys and within groups of young girls, and very little between them. Maybe it's helped along by fast fashion, luring even wealthy parents to the $5 sale prices at Old Navy, making so many kids look the same. Young girls often have long hair and wear skintight, pocket-less thin leggings with dresses. If they have sneakers, they are usually pink or purple, adorned with sparkles and hearts. Many young boys have short hair and wear athletic clothes in muted tones. This trend was confirmed around the country, save for in—big surprise!—Los Angeles, Portland, the Bay Area, and Seattle, the country's most liberal spots, where there is more appreciation of gender diversity, and a more concerted effort to promote it. (Surprisingly, many people I talked to confirmed my experience that New York City is a step behind in this department; a cisgender, dress-wearing, pink-loving boy left his Brooklyn school due to what his parents described as a hostile environment; they later sued the NYC Department of Education.[10])

Of course there are exceptions everywhere, but today, when a little girl is wearing boys' clothes, or has short hair, or plays with boys or with the toys marketed to them, it is often remarkable. I know because of the number of remarks my kid and those I interviewed receive. During my research, I heard myriad stories of boys who love pink and princesses and girls who love baseball and action figures—aka dolls—and I am the mother of two daughters who enjoy both Barbies (at least destroying them) and wrestling. Why not open up the possibilities of all toys and activities to all kids?

Many kids are affected by this cultural inflexibility. "I just feel like when people think of girls they always think of long hair and pink," said eight-year-old tomboy Elie. "I have short hair. I don't wear pink at all. People always think I'm a boy, but I think that's kind of rude. I would think that girls can have short hair and wear, like, boy clothes."

I asked her how it felt when that happened. "It's kind of annoying when people are always like, *Oh my god, she's a girl?* They act like it's such a big deal."

Her twin tomboy sister, Dylan, had a different reaction. "I'm usually fine with it," she said. "It's just a little annoying because people always just, like, assume, oh, you have long hair so you have to be a girl and you have short hair so you have to be a boy. They never just ask first. And it's always, on the girls' bathroom sign, the girl in the dress and the boy in the pants. And at my school bathroom the boys' walls are blue and in the girls' the walls are pink."

Though being egalitarian, feeling free to access both sides of the gender divide, can happen easily for some tomboys, we can make it happen for other kids. A 2018 study looked at effects of showing four- to seven-year-old kids images of their peers playing with either gender-stereotypic or counter-stereotypic toys.[11] In one set of images, a girl played with, and professed her love for, a car. A boy did the same for My Little Pony. In the other set, the opposite happened. When the kids were later asked if certain toys were for boys or girls, like tool kits or dolls, the kids who had seen the pictures fighting stereotypes were less likely to stereotype the toys. These kids were then more likely to want to play with kids of the opposite sex. If you put boys *and* girls on the packaging, if you remove the gendered messaging, it changes, and broadens, the way kids play.

Luckily, Amazon—arguably the biggest consumer-shaping force in the world—is working on gender equity. "We strongly promote self-discovery of content for every child regardless of gender," their PR rep wrote to me in 2019. "We are already working toward removing gender as a required input in the FreeTime child profile set-up process."

CASPAR

My uniform was hoodies and baggie jeans, castoffs from my older brother. For the most part, my parents didn't care—I was allowed to express as I wanted, and they didn't force me into one toy aisle or another. Every once in a while, for a wedding, a special family event, I was expected to wear a dress, and that's when I clashed with my parents. But generally they accepted me because they had an explanation for the way I looked and played: I was a tomboy.

For a little while, that made sense to me, too. Except that there were other girls around me claiming that same term, and girls in literature and film called tomboys, and they seemed so unlike me. There seemed to be two kinds of tomboys—those like me, who were achingly, unbearably uncomfortable, who could not emotionally withstand the costume and performance of femininity, and the tomboy who was generally comfortable with being female. They, too, were bucking trends and rejecting stereotypes, but there was something fundamentally different about the way they moved through the world: an ease, a freedom, that the word "tomboy" bestowed upon them, but not upon me.

I was trying, without having the proper vocabulary, to articulate the difference that I had sensed between me and other people who were in this category. There was something deeply rooted inside me that told me that designation—girl—was wrong, and it had nothing to do with gender stereotypes. It had to do with the very core of my being. But people around me would insist, "Well, you're just a tomboy. That's all there is to it because that's all there is. You can't be anything else. This has to be the label that explains you because there's no other label."

It was the early 2000s, and the concept, the reality, of trans kids had not entered my corner of the UK. "You're just a tomboy," people would tell me. "Just a tomboy," they'd insist. That's where the word became used as a weapon against me.

As puberty approached, I was starting to tell strangers that I had a boy name, to go into boys' bathrooms, to not correct people who thought I was a boy, to cross lines into territories where other tomboys dared not tread. Those other tomboys were conforming, feminizing, and the grown-ups around me were still insisting that I was just a tomboy, that it was a phase, that it would end.

It would be years before I would grow up and learn about trans people, learn that, in fact, I was trans and "not just a tomboy"—a phrase so important to me that it became the title of my memoir in 2018.

Chapter 4

ODE TO JO

Jo: Blair, can I borrow your black liner?
Blair: Well okay, but I think a soft brown would make you look not as cheap.
Jo: It's for my bike, I scuffed it. Lucky for me your makeup covers everything.

—*From* The Facts of Life, *1984*[1]

Everybody's favorite character was Jo. With her dark hair and her irreverence, her rejection of high society and lack of need for approval, she was a tomboy heroine to little girls everywhere.

I could easily be talking about Jo March from *Little Women*, a book that helped define, popularize, and normalize the concept of the tomboy in post–Civil War America. *Little Women* has never been out of print and has been made into at least four movies, including a 2019 version, an opera, a Broadway play, and a Japanese anime series. Jo March inspired a generation of early feminists, and women writers, to think for themselves and forge their own paths.

But the Jo I speak of is Jo Polniaczek from the 1980s sitcom *The*

Facts of Life. Jo P. was a scholarship kid at a fancy girls' boarding school who wore her hair in two little ponytails that connected to a big one in the back, rocked a leather jacket, dressed up as Peter Fonda in *Easy Rider* for Halloween, and fixed her own motorcycle. Her nemesis was wealthy and highly feminine Blair Warner, with her mane of feathered blond hair and tight Jordache jeans; the traditional theme of the dark, poor tomboy versus the fair, rich girly-girl was in full swing on that show, and I have only met one woman in all my days who liked Blair best.

I was eight when Jo joined *The Facts of Life* for its second season in 1980, and she was among many tomboys on the big and small screen in that era, from Punky Brewster to Billie Jean (the title character of the 1985 movie, not the tennis star, though she counts, too). Such tomboys included Addie Loggins in 1973's *Paper Moon* and Amanda Whurlitzer in 1976's *The Bad News Bears*—both played by Tatum O'Neal. There was Watts in the 1987 romantic comedy *Some Kind of Wonderful*, played by Mary Stuart Masterson, who had short hair, played the drums, and wore a leather jacket and jean shorts, and the tomboy/lesbian character Idgie, whom Masterson played in 1991's *Fried Green Tomatoes*. Most tomboys in earlier media had been dark-haired, with sun-darkened skin—white girls co-opting facets of Blackness, and what white people thought of as Black women's innate masculinity. But more 1970s and '80s tomboys were pale and blond, no longer required to transgress racial lines in order to transgress gender lines, even if many such tomboys were still depicted as working class.

Though she wasn't a tomboy herself, Mary Stuart Masterson grew up in New York City in the 1970s, "with these women's libbers all around me," she told me. She'd gone to an all-girls' school but had been friends with boys and had never embraced the stereotypically feminine stuff. She could recognize the characters she played in the media, in the people around her, and in herself.

Sometimes these nontraditionally feminine girls were given flak about not doing femininity right—certainly Jo and Blair fought over which of them men would find more attractive, and Jo's tomboyism, along with her working-class background, was confused with loose morals by upscale private school boys. But if that happened, the nontraditional girls were able to hold their ground. The plot lines of these TV shows and movies weren't always about makeovers and feminine redemption. The tomboys were often accepted and even celebrated for their nonconforming ways.

But characters like Jo, Watts, and Idgie soon became less common in the mass media.

Pocahontas, Buffy, and New Heroines

Around the time that Girl Power and Sporty Spice were drop-kicking the tomboy off the screen, a new publishing trend emerged: girl crisis literature, inspired in part by the American Association of University Women's 1991 report *Shortchanging Girls, Shortchanging America*.[2] The report found that girls' self-esteem plummeted in adolescence and that boys were outperforming them all over the map, in school and at work. Mary Pipher's 1994 book *Reviving Ophelia: Saving the Selves of Adolescent Girls* joined several similarly themed books that same year, and literature about the crisis of low self-esteem, declining academic performance, and eating disorders among America's female adolescents itself became an industry. It promoted a problem that Girl Power—the sexy, commercialized version, not the Riot Grrrl version—seemed to solve in a way that the promotion of tomboyism in the 1970s hadn't. Girl Power must have reached far more girls than tomboyism did.

The crisis, it turns out, was mostly found among middle-class white girls, something the media, so populated by middle-class white people, failed to note. If white girls were becoming meek in adolescence, African-American girls were being reprimanded for not being meek enough—a continuing problem. Today, African-American girls get suspended *six times* as often as white girls, not because they misbehave more, but because they get punished more for the same behaviors.[3] When girls of color are aggressive, it's often seen as unfeminine and uncool by people in power. When middle-class white girls are aggressive, it's empowerment. For reference: John McEnroe's on-court tantrums were criticized, but generally seen as benign, and parlayed into comedy and marketing opportunities. Serena Williams has been punished for hers. Often, the double-standards of race and gender rear their heads together.

But Girl Power and girl crisis literature, however white, did change the media landscape. A new crop of shows with smart, complex female—and feminine—heroines made their debuts in the late nineties, from Nickelodeon's *Clarissa Explains It All* to *The Powerpuff Girls*. A few more assertive, nonwhite (but still problematic) characters entered the mix, as well. Mulan and Pocahontas, while critiqued for their slanted portrayal of race and historical events, appeared among the cabal of waiting-to-be-rescued white Disney princesses who came before. Feminine action heroines popped up on the small screen, from *Buffy the Vampire Slayer* to *Xena: Warrior Princess*. Far tougher than Wonder Woman, whose breasts bounced impractically while chasing down bad guys in high-heeled boots, these new heroines' outfits made sense from a physics standpoint.

But pink-powered action heroines were definitely highly feminine, and definitely not like the 1970s and '80s tomboys who had filled our screens. Who needs a tomboy like Jo Polniaczek, fixing motorcycles and talking smack in a leather jacket with an unfeminine scowl on her (admittedly very pretty) face, when you've got Buffy, somehow defanging a vampire while appearing totally unthreatening? Many of these new female characters were strong but less masculine than traditional tomboys.

Who runs the world? *Girls*, Beyoncé told us in 2011, while riding a bucking steed in high-heeled boots, surrounded by a cast of scantily clad women.

Taming the Tomboy

When I asked a group of children's media professionals for examples of post-1990s tomboys, they mentioned Rainbow Dash on *My Little Pony*, or *The Powerpuff Girls*—often cited as the first feminist show for kids. They listed Anna from *Frozen*, *Nella the Princess Knight*, *Moana*, Jessie from the *Toy Story* franchise, Edith from *Despicable Me*, Merida from *Brave*, Judy Hopps from *Zootopia*. (Post-1990s tomboys seem to be more common in animated, and not always human, form.) They mentioned the Disney show *Liv and Maddie*, in which Liv is the girliest girl on the planet and

Maddie, her identical twin sister, is the tomboy because she's competitive and likes sports. But both girls, played by Dove Cameron, are quite traditionally feminine-looking. They mentioned movies like *Miss Congeniality*, but I don't see as much of our beloved Jo in them as I'd like.

Even when tomboyish characters appeared in films like *Bend It Like Beckham* or *The Hunger Games*, the post–Girl Power characters were much more feminine, and romance was still at the heart of their stories, with tomboy taming—transforming an independent tomboy into somebody's wife or girlfriend—in full effect. This happened in nineteenth-century tomboy novels, too. Much to Louisa May Alcott's dismay, as mentioned earlier, she was forced by pressure from her publisher and her rabidly devoted readers—a Victorian-era version of Twitter—to marry Jo off.

This is not to say that there is anything wrong with being a feminine and/or heterosexual tomboy who marries, but rather that the rich variety of tomboy experiences, and their diverse gender expressions and sexualities, have not been well represented by the media, and even less so since the 1990s.

Or at least, that's what it seemed like to me. But to Columbia University English and gender studies professor Jack Halberstam, there's very little difference between any of these tomboys, Jo and Addie and Maddie and Watts. All of them were feminine tomboys who occupied "a pre-cisgender or pre-heterosexual stage, and that's why it could be indulged," he told me. "It was never considered to be a threat because it had already been given a space in the society, from *Little Women* on." That is, these characters were allowed and encouraged and beloved because they seemed straight and cisgender. They weren't crossing the line into lesbian and/or trans territory, into places once (and still, in many cases) considered deviant.

Today, in fact, there *are* more shows with gender nonconforming and trans characters, hugely important because representation matters. As communications professor George Gerbner wrote in 1976: "Representation in the fictional world signifies social existence; absence means symbolic annihilation."[4] The media shape our ideas of normalcy, and many gender-rebelling young characters on big and small screens are now presented as variations, not deviations, of gender: non-binary actor Ellie Desautels playing transgender student Michael Hallowell on NBC's *Rise*; non-binary character Syd on the rebooted *One Day at a Time*; or Mark, the boy who wears girls' clothes, on *The Conners*, along with characters on *Modern Family*, *Glee*, and *Degrassi: Next Class*. The organization GLAAD, which tracks depictions of LGBTQ+ people in the media, found that 6.4 percent of main characters on broadcast TV were LGBTQ+ in 2017–2018—the highest number ever,[5] and higher than the percentage of Americans who identify as LGBT, 4.5 percent per a 2017 Gallup poll (though that number seems far too small to me).[6]

This is huge progress, especially when the few trans and even gay adult characters in the past were often portrayed as psychotic or homicidal, the villains in movies like *Basic Instinct*, *Psycho*, *Silence of the Lambs*, and *Monster*.

Troubled Childhoods

It's truly fantastic to have gender nonconformity represented. But interestingly, in the few shows I could find that starred characters who resembled the TV tomboys of my youth, the nonconforming characters' gender was portrayed as causing conflict.

In Netflix's short-lived 2017 series *Gypsy*, the tomboyish daughter of a therapist and a lawyer, Dolly, was often in battle with her family and classmates. She was too aggressive and had the audacity to ask for short hair, confounding the other wealthy mothers who were so relieved that their own daughters were "straightforward girly-girls." On Netflix's *Good Girls*, about suburban moms-turned-bank-robbers, parents fought over their daughter Sadie's gender nonconformity—it wasn't a cool and understood mode, but a source of familial pain, at least for the father. In the second season, Sadie came out as transgender and transitioned (just as the actor who plays Sadie, Isaiah Stannard, did).

So did we boot tomboys off the screen and replace them with trans characters? After all, in 2019 British theater director Emma Rice staged Enid Blyton's beloved tale of girls' school adventures, *Malory Towers*, casting tomboy Bill—short for Wilhelmina and described as "all grins and freckles and very short hair, mad on horses, has seven brothers, says just exactly what she thinks"—as a trans boy.[7] This caused celebration by some for its inclusivity, especially because Rice cast a non-binary actor in the role. For others, the casting caused consternation, for narrowing the breadth of girls' experiences; many women use a masculine nickname without changing their identities, and many of Blyton's other characters—like George, short for Georgina—were tomboys, too.

Perhaps, suggested Halberstam, it's not that the TV tomboys of my youth, and those of the more distant past, have disappeared. If those non-cisgender identities had been available back then, some of those more masculine 1970s tomboys, and even 1870s tomboys, likely would have claimed them, and thus they are at long last being represented in the gender nonconforming and/or trans category that truly fits them. Maybe we're finally replacing the always, masculine, and threatening tomboys, like short-haired Frankie in the 1952 film *The Member of the Wedding*, once forced to identify as a girl because there was no other option, with the person she/he/they were always meant to be. Some writers and critics have suggested that characters from Jo March (and her creator Louisa May Alcott) to the tomboy Anybodys from *West Side Story* were actually trans and not tomboys—that is, cisgender girls who looked and played like boys—after all.

Maybe these current depictions are more realistic, and are rife with conflict over gender because gender culture wars are so prevalent right now. Or maybe, as a non-binary trans acquaintance of mine suggested, the media is more focused on trans characters right now because of their increasing visibility, both responding to and stoking a fascination among society as a whole. The representations may be imperfect, focusing mostly on gender dysphoria and on gender-conforming trans people, who switch from one side of the binary to the other. But they are a step toward a wider representation of normal. "It doesn't mean that the past was a golden age. It means that in the past the tomboy had a time and a place and was not threatening at all. She was just a different kind of girl," Halberstam said.

Maybe, he suggested, a cisgender, somewhat straight-ish person like me couldn't discern the difference because I didn't see myself in any tomboys at all, let alone have the capacity to distinguish between them. That is, I couldn't look at tomboys from a queer perspective.

All this is true, and these points are incredibly important. And yet I still believe that we could use a few more scowling, motorcycle-fixing, leather jacket–clad cisgender drummer girls, the Jos and Jodies and Kristys and Mary Stuarts, so that *many* kinds of kids can see their experience represented. Maybe she *is* just a different kind of girl, as Halberstam suggested, but let's add her back into the mix.

Halberstam pointed out that we still occasionally see the classic tomboy, like the hockey-playing Riley in Disney's *Inside Out* (animated, once again), or *Star Wars'* Rey. Arya Stark, the tomboyish character on *Game of Thrones*, is so popular that Arya became a common baby name in 2019.[8] Max and Eleven are tomboy*ish* characters on *Stranger Things*, but that show is set in the 1980s and thus replicates those 1980s casts—and they get more feminine by season three. With the explosion of streaming channels, I'm sure there are many more masculine girl characters than those I've counted, but from the mainstream they have surely faded.

"There are hardly any tomboy or butch role models," for kids, said Karleen Pendleton Jiménez, a professor of education at Trent University and author of, among other books, *Tomboys and Other Gender Heroes*. "Why would anyone think they could grow up to be butch or be a tomboy?" (We had this conversation before Billie Eilish won her Grammys and offered young girls a rare and much-needed tomboyish look, an exception to the oversexualized rule. Hopefully we'll have more characters on big and small screens like her.)

While we can be grateful that the spectrum has gotten wider, and that we have both many strong adult female characters and younger, non-cisgender characters, fewer young, sporty, sassy, and masculine girls are present in the American media. The dragon-fighting princesses who replaced them, who wouldn't dare use the word "tomboy," are feminine: sugar and spice and everything nice, plus karate lessons. We have shows like *The Kicks*, about a girls' soccer team, but the girls are mostly long-haired and traditionally feminine. None look like the masculine tomboys I talked to. I've heard from many young girls who have short hair and wear athletic clothes and are told, either by gender-policing children or well-meaning adults, that they must be boys, which shows me that our spectrum is not yet wide or deep or complex enough. Representation matters, even for cisgender girls whose gender expression puts them at odds with today's post–Girl Power stereotypes.

Kids of all genders and races who see themselves represented in professions, in TV shows, on toy packages, for instance, believe that wider paths are possible for them. *Kicks*, in fact, profoundly grew my younger daughter's interest in soccer. As Geena Davis's Institute on Gender and Media puts it, "If she can see it, she can be it."

The 2011 French film *Tomboy*, written and directed by Céline Sciamma, is a rare exception. It follows ten-year-old Laure, who poses as a boy, right down to packing underwear and kissing a neighborhood girl. Spoiler alert: Laure is outed by the end of the film, heartbreakingly forced into a dress, but viewers get the sense that Laure's destiny is still unknown. Will Laure come out as trans? Gay? Straight? Cis? Non-binary? Is Laure "just a tomboy" embracing masculinity, or will he or she or they transition? We don't know. We have to live with the ambiguity. But we get the sense that Laure is going to be okay, and we see a complex exploration of gender on the big screen.

Media Problems That Remain

Though the classic 1980s tomboy is largely gone from screens, big and small, I heard the refrain many times while researching this book that that was okay. The word and concept of "tomboy" are outdated, people told me, and we don't need girls like Frankie Addams or Amanda Whurlitzer or Jo P anymore because girls can do anything boys can do—play soccer, slay dragons, or whatever Rainbow Dash does—without looking like or being called a tomboy.

Yet statistics about girls' representation in the media reveal that in fact we have much more work to do. A 2018 study found that just 38 percent of main characters on kids' TV shows are female, and that girls are twice as likely to use magic to solve problems, while boys use physical power and STEM skills.[9] According to one study, the more TV four-year-olds watch, the more likely they'll believe that boys and men are better than girls and women.[10] In family films, males outnumber females three to one. More than 80 percent of working characters in such films are male, yet around 70 percent of real-life mothers work. We're not living in a golden age of female representation now, either.[11]

The Facts of Life was an early attempt at TV diversity and intersectionality. It wasn't a stellar show, and on the pilot episode, a different tomboy girl is teased for being a proto-lesbian, until housemother Mrs. Garrett assures her that her heterosexual feelings will soon kick in; there was still an underlying message that tomboys were okay only if they were straight, like Jo. But the show had some relatable characters who were important to the kids who watched them. It was grappling with what it meant to be a girl in a world in which second wave feminism was dying out and being replaced by what would become the hyper-gendered consumer culture of the 1980s and '90s.

Perhaps repackaging the domain of tomboys—the rough-and-tumble play, the interest in science, the sportiness, the toughness, the independence—in a pink sparkly sheath made many more girls feel they could access it. Girls have made tremendous gains since we transitioned from tomboys to Sporty Spice, closing the achievement gap with boys in most STEM fields, save for computer science, physics, and engineering (hey, the things that pay the most!). Maybe we continued to expand girlhood, and as we added representation of trans characters in the media, all we did was strip out a certain brand of acceptable 1980s young female masculinity. But to me it's a real loss. I believe we should see representation of trans kids, non-binary folks, *and* masculine cisgender girls in the media, and that we have the knowledge and infrastructure to make room for them all.

And what of the original Jo—Jo March? She changed the literary landscape, and the dreams of girls, forever. We can't say how many American girls were called or identified as tomboys in the nineteenth century. It's a chicken-and-egg question: Was Jo March popular because so many girls recognized themselves in her, or did her popularity, did the representation of that experience, encourage more girls to be like her? We don't really know. What we know is that, given the option to access what had hitherto been off-limits, girls resoundingly said yes.

GLENIS

I've always been serious, no-nonsense, straightforward, and unconcerned about the approval of others.

I was born in the sixties in South Carolina, to a jazz and blues piano-playing military man and a quintessential Southern Black Christian woman—both loving and tough—and I came out swinging. I had three brothers and one girly-girl sister, and I knew from a young age which side of the line I wanted to be on. I could run as fast as the boys, and I always ran with them. I was a kinesthetic wonder kid, like my brothers.

My mother sewed all our clothes, and insisted that I and all my siblings be well dressed and well behaved. I tolerated the hot-combing and braiding of my hair, and the wearing of dresses for church. I coveted my father's uniforms, so my mother made me military-inspired jumpers and smocks for school, but the minute I got home, it was dungarees and a T-shirt and my favorite green Keds. In high school, my mother made me a satin cummerbund for a school dance, which even the wealthiest girl, whose clothes came mail-ordered from overseas department stores, admired. It wasn't that I was gender-bending. I wasn't trying to make any kind of statement other than being myself.

I was always comfortable and confident, but my differences were hard on my parents, who favored my sister and disapproved of my masculine energy. I was called a tomboy, much to my mother's chagrin, who wanted me to be like my sister. I got in trouble a lot because I had these girl standards that I wasn't living up to, even though I was a cheerleader, when I wasn't running track, and once I even won a beauty contest.

In junior high school, I started reading. First there were the tomboy heroines, the Pippi Longstockings and Ramona Beasleys. They were white girls, but their behavior was so much like mine. And for the most part, those tomboys got away with it, were even congratulated for it. In their fictional worlds, it was better to be a tomboy. And then I read Alice Walker and Zora Neale Hurston, books and poetry featuring strong Black women, who may not have been tomboys but sure as heck didn't conform to some narrow definition of femininity, who weren't weak or demure or giving in easily to some man.

Through literature, through representation, I could recognize the heroine in myself. I became a teacher and a poet, and that inner tomboy never left me. I never really fell in line.

II

Why Tomboys Do
What They Do

Chapter 5

THE BEST OF BOTH WORLDS

"The general finding was that all mature, intellectually creative women were tomboys when they were young."
—*Rev. Dr. Thomas Boslooper*, New York Times, *1967*

It's common for boys and girls to play together, and exhibit similar behaviors, before age two. But around the time they hit preschool, they begin to segregate, and be segregated, by sex. This may happen less in a home or a neighborhood where there are fewer kids around, but once kids get into a bigger social environment, they increasingly divide.

Likely this has to do with cognitive development. After age two, most kids' brains mature enough to understand that in American society there are two sex categories, and to which they belong (the reality is that there are categories beyond the neat male/female binary, but not many children are taught that). By three, most know the stereotypes associated with those categories, what stuff and colors and activities go with each, and most children stick to their sex-segregated script, playing with the toys and kids marked as gender-appropriate; psychologists call this "stereotype-behavior congruence."

What these young kids don't yet understand is what's known in psychology as "gender constancy"—the idea that they can change their gender expression and gendered behaviors and still maintain membership in the group. They might not understand that a person in a pink dress can be a boy, and a person playing Batman and running shirtless can be a girl. So as boys' and girls' interests and ways of playing diverge, due to both biological and social factors, they gender police themselves and one another. They tease boys for wearing pink and playing princess, or girls for having a "boy" haircut and playing the prince. They learn what sociologists Candace West and Don H. Zimmerman call "doing gender" to themselves and others, reinforcing and reproducing stereotypes and sex-typed behaviors through interactions in gendered peer cultures that form and blossom (or fester, depending on your point of view).[1] They master the group rules, embracing them and imposing them, working hard to belong and to weed out those who don't.

Except that tomboys don't do gender the same way. They don't stick to the script. They're stereotype-behavior *in*congruent.

Some of that is because they can be. Girls who play with and like boys are usually accepted, and often praised, while boys who play with and like girls, well, we don't even have a non-mean name for them.

But some of it is because of how their stereotype-behavior incongruence teaches them about gender, and how they then craft gender stereotypes differently. They tend to pick their friends not based on their sex but on what they *do*. That is, many of us have assumed that kids are dividing based on sex, into male and female groups. But some are also dividing by *gender*, hewing to groups of kids who look and play in similar ways, regardless of bodies. Tomboys can belong to the girl group and still play with the boy group, accessing both sides of the divide. Thus, they may learn and understand gender differently than others, which could have implications for the rest of their lives. And it could be an advantage.

A Wider Idea of "My Own Kind"

Most kids will like the toys, and playmates, marked as appropriate for them. As Arizona State University child development professor Carol Martin noted in a 2012 study on tomboys and stereotype-behavior congruence, "A young girl who thinks 'dolls are for girls' is likely to approach and become interested in playing with dolls and she would likely avoid playing with trucks if she stereotypes these as being 'for boys.'"[2]

However, when some young children are drawn to toys that aren't clearly gender-marked, they extrapolate from their own preferences: They make up a new story to fit their reality. A girl who cottons to a silver balloon, say—anything with an unknown gender category—will assume it's a girls' toy simply because she likes it and she's a girl.

Martin hypothesized that this is what happens with tomboys. They develop atypical preferences and behaviors—perhaps due to biological factors, perhaps due to an egalitarian family environment (more about these ideas later) or a gender-expansive peer culture. Then they craft stereotypes around them: *I'm a girl and I like playing ball or with boys, so those things must be okay for girls.*

In Martin's 2012 study, she found that tomboys and non-tomboys liked the same number of "feminine" activities—they liked playing with dolls and other girls—but tomboys were more interested in boy stuff, like football, than non-tomboys were. Non-tomboys were more likely to exhibit stereotype-congruent behavior, preferences that linked up with their gender stereotypes, than tomboys. Non-tomboys stuck to the script. Tomboys wrote their own.

They still stereotyped, Martin observed, but because they disrupted the stereotypes themselves, they were more creative about the process, not slotting activities and items so neatly into boy and girl categories. They justified their interest in what's on the boy side of the boy/girl line, and made sense of the world in their own way from there.

The most important word that keeps popping up in these studies is "flexibility."

Tomboys "show flexibility in their stereotypes concerning what girls do and do not like," Martin wrote.

"Tomboys, rather than having rigidly gendered or masculine interests, may be more flexible," asserted a 2013 study by psychologist Sheana Ahlqvist and colleagues called *The Potential Benefits and Risks of Identifying as a Tomboy.*[3] "Girls who identified as tomboys were significantly more likely than the other groups to mention gender-based interests and activities and to define tomboyism explicitly in terms of flexibility."

One study found that even though tomboys had lots of male friends, little interest in dolls (despite the wealth of evidence that boys did and do like dolls), played the part of boys in make-believe games, and sometimes expressed a desire to be a boy, they had good relationships with girls. The authors noted, "None of the tomboys were rejected by their peers."[4]

Neither were they exclusive about the sex of their playmates. Of the more than 180 people I surveyed who once identified or currently identify as tomboys, around 40 percent said their friend groups were equally split between boys and girls, with 30 percent saying their friends were almost all boys and 25 percent almost all girls. Few had only male friends, and even fewer had only female friends. Even some tomboys who rejected dresses and makeup and dolls didn't always reject other girls, or feel rejected by them.

Not only were tomboys less likely to sanction themselves; they were less likely to impose gender sanctions on other children and more likely to be accepting of others who violated gender norms—hence the tomboy-sissy friendship trope. They show less of what social psychologists call "in-group bias": the preference for your own kind. A similar trend was found among transgender children: They were less likely to gender stereotype and more tolerant of gender nonconformity than their peers, as were their siblings.[5] In other words, their atypical preferences or expressions or identities set them on a different, and wider, path than lots of other conforming kids, a path with more acceptance for themselves and others.

This doesn't mean tomboys have it easy, or that all tomboys feel flexible and free. A tomboy's social success can depend on the degree of her traditional masculinity. A girl who is more of a short-haired, masculine, "always" tomboy can be at a deeper disadvantage than one who is closer to a ponytailed, feminine "sometimes" tomboy, and consistently read as a girl; some "excessively" mascu-line girls were subject to intensive treatment to feminize them in the 1970s (see *Becky*, following chapter 6). Often, there is a tension between girls who straddle the line of acceptability and those who cross it.

There's some research showing that sports can mitigate the teasing and bullying that "always" tomboys can be exposed to—an athletic girl can sometimes get away with more traditional mascu-linity, but one without that excuse could have a harder time.[6] But of course there are plenty of masculine girls paying a social cost to be themselves, just as there are plenty of softball players wearing makeup and twisting ribbons into their hair, asserting femininity and athleticism together.

Adding or Subtracting?

So what's the difference between kids who hew more to the always side of things than those who pool around more in the some-times section? As mentioned earlier, some researchers break these groups into those who embrace traditional masculinity versus those who embrace masculinity while also rejecting traditional femininity: the line-straddlers versus the crossers.

Seton Hall University sociology professor C. Lynn Carr, who has studied tomboys since the 1990s, found that the most com-mon reason tomboys preferred masculine activities and inter-ests was that they were "more fun." With the boys, these tomboys took apart and fixed things, got dirty, played outdoors—they embraced masculinity, adding things culturally marked as "for boys" to the mix.[7]

That was part of the motivation for a thirty-five-year-old former tomboy named Allison, who grew up with three sisters in Somerville, Massachusetts, then a working-class town. "We went to Girl Scouts for a little while and they just wanted to sell cookies and have sleepovers and stuff like that," she told me. "I coveted being in the Boy Scouts so badly because as far as I knew they made soapbox cars and went camping and I wanted to do that so badly. And then other kind of 'boy things' like comic books and turning rocks over to see what was underneath them—all that got me labeled as a tomboy." Though, as we know from stories of nineteenth-century tomboys, there have always been girls who liked to do the same.

But there were also those who rejected traditional femininity. The words Carr's tomboys used to describe girl stuff—dresses, playing with dolls—were "boredom" and "frustration." Softball was not as good as baseball. Girl Scouts not as adventurous as Boy Scouts. Girls were "silly, boring, or incomprehensible," chitchatting and not running down a field after a ball. Femininity just didn't feel available or right, and they could sense that it mattered less than masculinity in American society. They discerned that the boys' side of the line is the better place to be, and that being a tomboy got them there.

Cultural anthropologist and queer studies pioneer Esther Newton put it beautifully, if depressingly, in her memoir *My Butch Career*: "My child body was a strong and capable instrument somehow stuffed into the word 'girl,'" the former tomboy wrote about her 1940s childhood. "I was the first kid up the jungle gym, as good as any of the boys at stoop ball. All my friends were boys—girls were dumb. I had nothing in common with them. But because of my XX chromosomes, my body is female and I was stuck in the girl gender, linked worldwide to hard work, low pay, disrespect, and cheating husbands. Impossible to refuse girlhood, so I refused femininity."[8]

Masculinity can also be a haven, and being feminine—girly—can make a girl feel vulnerable. Some of Carr's tomboys were incest or sexual abuse survivors, or had witnessed violence against women; making themselves unappealing to heterosexual men, or emulating men, was "a retreat to the perceived safety of masculinity."

"If you were soft and prissy, we felt sorry for you, honey. We felt sorry for you. It wasn't happening. In our culture, women were trying to raise a tomboy so that no one could take advantage of them," Lisa, who grew up in the housing projects in Brooklyn in the 1970s, told me. "You had to be dressed down and be ready for the kill. You know, you could not be too cute."

Ten of Carr's participants said they had tried to pass as or wanted to be boys, though there was no commonly available option to identify as trans or non-binary, as there is today (discussed at length later); tomboy was all they had.

So some tomboys reject the feminine, or reject the sexualization that typically comes with their sex assigned at birth, and protect themselves or relieve their psychological pain with masculinity—whether consciously or not. Some just do what they want to do. Either way, there may be some psychological benefits for tomboys who have access to both sides of the line. These tomboys tend to be what's known as "psychologically androgynous."

Fully Effective and Healthy Human Functioning

		FEMININE	
		Lo	Hi
MASCULINE	Lo	Undifferentiated	Traditional Female
	Hi	Traditional Male	Androgynous

The term "psychological androgyny" was coined in the 1970s by psychologist Sandra Bem, who created the Bem Sex-Role Inventory (BSRI). The psychological test measured how masculine, feminine, androgynous (both), or undifferentiated (neither) people were. Psychological androgyny has nothing to do with looks; it's about combining personality traits that American culture has broken down into masculine and feminine. Per the BSRI, feminine traits were, for instance, affectionate, sympathetic, warm, soft-spoken, and tender. Masculine traits were dominant, forceful, competitive, and independent. Hence, the BSRI had many critics, including me. Once again, I ask: If there are so many independent, forceful, and dominant girls that we carved an entire category for them, why say they are masculine?

There have been attempts to replace those words, to use *instrumentality* for traits like competence and assertiveness—those thought of as masculine—and *expressiveness* for empathy and emotionality, which are thought of as feminine. But I don't see them knocking masculine and feminine out of the vernacular anytime soon.

Despite many legitimate objections, the BSRI was a useful way of mapping how many of each traits a person had. Bem's belief was that the more psychologically androgynous someone was—the more one had of both traits—the better, and that hewing to the pole ends of traditional masculinity or femininity was worse.

"Masculinity and femininity may each become negative and even destructive when they are represented in extreme and unadulterated form," Bem wrote. "For fully effective and healthy human functioning, both masculinity and femininity must each be tempered by the other, and the two must be integrated into a more balanced, a more fully human, a truly androgynous personality."[9] Bem was getting at ideas of gender now playing out in the media, both mass and social: that accessing only the masculine stuff can lead to toxic masculinity and rape culture, and access to only the feminine can lead to the plagues of eating disorders, depression, and low self-esteem.

Even if some objected to her idea that everybody should be a mishmash of these traits, there is plenty of research to back her up, much of it hinting that tomboys' hall pass to both the boy and girl sides puts them in a uniquely positive position. A study on childhood tomboyism pointed to a connection between psychological androgyny and situational flexibility,[10] and psychological androgyny is correlated to high self-esteem, marital satisfaction, parental effectiveness, and achievement motivation[11]—that is, a host of highly desirable outcomes.

The benefits extend beyond the interpersonal, to careers. A 2002 study found that "higher self-ratings on the tomboy scale correlated with confidence in career success."[12] Meanwhile, a 2006 book, *Alpha Girls*, found that more androgynous girls had higher self-esteem and lower anxiety, were less prone to substance abuse, and were less promiscuous. Even though these girls had been exposed to the high femininity of girl power, what made them so effective was their combination of feminine and masculine traits.

Psychological androgyny could connect, not just to low anxiety and high self-esteem, but to creativity. In 1963, psychologist Ellis Paul Torrance published a paper showing that creative girls were perceived as more masculine than less creative girls, just as creative boys were seen as more feminine. "Creativity, by its very nature, requires both sensitivity and independence," he wrote, noting that, in our society, sensitivity is seen as feminine and independence as masculine.[13] The world's great creatives already knew this. Former tomboy Virginia Woolf surmised that a writer should be "woman-manly or man-womanly....Some collaboration has to take place in the mind between the woman and the man before the art of creation can be accomplished. Some marriage of opposites has to be consummated."[14]

Set aside the word "androgynous" for a minute, which you may find either off-putting or distractedly alluring, and consider instead the traits that we (misguidedly) characterize as masculine, like self-reliance, dominance, leadership, and independence. And those we characterize as feminine, like compassion, kindness, and empathy. They are indeed wonderful traits to have, but it's nice to have that dominance tempered with compassion, the leadership meshed with empathy. Those things *should* go together. But none of those things belongs to a single sex.

Until we made concerted efforts in the 1990s (perhaps due to girl power and girl crisis literature) to raise the hopes and dreams and self-esteem of little girls, tomboys were more likely than non-tomboys to possess the traits deemed as masculine, or to pursue things that developed those traits. Access to both sides of the pink-and-blue divide not only gives tomboys male and female friends, boy and girl games and toys, but license to display a whole host of personality traits that many children are policed out of.

The most common characteristic I noticed in tomboys was high self-esteem, from a nine-year-old telling me, "I know who I am," to an eighty-one-year-old telling me, "I didn't need their approval then and I don't need it now." Perhaps this comes from being socialized with boys. Tomboys may absorb the benefits of male privilege via those "masculine" traits while still feeling free to access the "feminine" ones.

I'm not saying that there's a direct link between psychological androgyny and supreme mental hygiene. But the words most associated with tomboys—"freedom," "flexibility," "egalitarianism"— have much broader implications beyond toys and clothes and playmates. The more we gender the stuff of childhood—the colors and toys and outfits and personality traits—the less chance to become egalitarian, flexible, and free. As former tomboy Allison told me, "Letting the sex you were assigned at birth lead your path to personhood is a shitty idea." When we focus on how a child is *supposed* to be, based on stereotypes connected to their assigned sex or gender identity, we overemphasize gender roles. As Torrance wrote, that's a "serious block to the development of many talents."

A former tomboy named Natasha told me that her 1980s tomboy childhood directly prepared her for her career: She belongs to the only 3 percent of advertising creative directors who are female. "I was always comfortable with boys," she said. "I'm in a Fantasy Football league with nine other guys and we talk trash to each other and I very much feel like one of the guys, but I'm comfortable with my femininity. I guess I just have the best of both worlds."

SARAH

The cutoff point was junior high. Before that, everything had been fine. Great, even. I'd had a short, spiky haircut all through elementary school and I'd been super popular. Friends with the boys. Friends with the girls. Playing with dolls. Playing with balls. Running around the woods in my comfortable, practical boy clothes, and nobody cared, especially not me.

I guess I was a tomboy. I didn't care about looking like a girl. It just didn't seem important. It had nothing to do with gender. It was about comfort.

I grew up in the eighties in a Boston suburb where there was a lot of uniformity. Most of the girls dressed the same, in cuffed jeans and white Keds and a specific Champion sweatshirt. They did the same things, went to the same summer camp. But they knew me, and didn't care that I was a little different in what I did and how I looked, in my short hair and my often boyish clothes. They accepted me. More important, I accepted myself—I had no interest in conformity.

But the summer before junior high started, looks and conformity became important to everybody around me. The night before the first day of school, a friend delivered the message that my boyfriend didn't want to go out anymore. At the bus stop on the first day of school, the kids who'd been my friends for years wouldn't speak to me. Once five elementary schools dumped into one junior high, the stakes were raised, and I was suddenly declared unfriendable. Simply because I looked like a boy, I became a target. I wasn't invited to sleepovers. I was picked last in gym. Every day in Spanish class, a boy named Mark would whisper insults under his breath to me until I'd cry.

But I dug in my heels. I cut my hair shorter.

I couldn't change who I was to make other people comfortable. Why did it matter to someone else what I wore or how long my hair was? I knew who I was, and what I liked, and as painful as it was to be scorned for my proclivities, it would have been more painful to turn away from them. Maybe it was some sort of tomboy training that allowed me to be true to myself. Maybe it was old-fashioned stubbornness. I've always been pretty sure about who I am and pretty comfortable in my own skin.

Chapter 6

ARE TOMBOYS BORN OR MADE?

"One is not born, but rather one becomes, a woman."

—*Simone de Beauvoir*

"Men mistakenly expect women to think, communicate, and react the way men do; women mistakenly expect men to feel, communicate, and respond the way women do."

—*John Gray*, Men Are from Mars, Women Are from Venus: The Classic Guide to Understanding the Opposite Sex

"He's such a *boy*," my friend said as her son smashed a wooden bulldozer into a pile of LEGO bricks. Her daughter had no interest in those items—or smashing anything for that matter—but not for the mom's lack of trying to generate some. She had offered her children the same choices, but her six-year-old son played rough and rowdy with boys, and loved baseball and climbing trees, while her four-year-old daughter played sweet and sedentary with girls, pined for Barbies, and preferred pink and purple "girl" LEGO Friends. They just came out that way, my friend said. It's biological.

A lot of the tomboys I talked to used those terms to describe their inclinations: biological, innate. "It was my nature," said Ellen, who grew up in Western New York in the 1960s. She had two older brothers and there was a gang of neighborhood boys, and they were doing the things she wanted to do—for her, the word "boy" came from "tomboy," not the other way around. "What was fun was not hanging out playing with dolls. What was fun was being outside and running around and sledding and playing baseball."

The love of pink and purple is not innate, and the love of baseball and tree-climbing doesn't belong to one sex, as Victorian tomboys showed us. That said, a sturdy body of research suggests a biological basis for some gendered behaviors: Nature, along with nurture, plays a vital role in what we do and who we are.

Yes, much of gender, and what's culturally coded as masculine and feminine, is a social construct, produced and reproduced in society, performances. But some gendered behaviors start with a biological push, perhaps a hormonal seed that affects the brain.

Inquiry into these hormonal seeds has led to the radioactive debate over "male brains" and "female brains," and whether people, including scientists, can and should extrapolate from scientific research to make sweeping statements about essential gender differences.

And to the question of whether tomboys are born or made.

Testosterone and Tomboy Behaviors

All humans have a mix of both "male" and "female" hormones that inspire different kinds of bodily changes and regulate certain functions. The "male" hormones, those that trigger development of the male reproductive system and later things like facial hair growth, voice deepening, and muscle mass, are androgens, including testosterone, androstenedione, and dihydrotestosterone—but most people mistakenly just say testosterone. "Female" hormones are estrogens. There is no one chemical compound called estrogen; rather, it's an umbrella term for estrone, estradiol, estriol, and estetrol (produced only during pregnancy), which are related to things like breast growth and menstrual cycles. Each of our bodies is in hormonal flux, on a daily basis and over a lifetime, or even if we drink out of too many plastic water bottles lined with BPA—which was the first synthetic estrogen ever invented, back in 1891, though it was deemed too toxic to ever be prescribed.[1]

Since the 1960s, researchers have been studying girls who are exposed to androgens in utero, either via the mother's own levels or a disease that alters hormone production, to see how it affects their behavior.

One such experiment was conducted by two professors from the University of Cambridge, neuroscientist and psychologist Melissa Hines and professor of family research Susan Golombok. They took hormone readings from hundreds of pregnant women. Three-and-a-half years later, they followed up with a behavioral questionnaire that measured gender role behavior—that is, stereotype-behavior congruence. Did the women's daughters play with guns or jewelry, tools or dolls? Did they play with boys or girls? Did they role-play *as* boys or girls? Did they like rough-and-tumble play? Pretty things? Snakes? Did they take risks or avoid them?

Their findings, published in 2002, suggested that some moms with higher testosterone levels were more likely to have tomboyish girls, the ones who liked rough-and-tumble play and snakes and role-played as boys.[2] These kids largely identified as girls and had female genitalia, but their *preferences* were masculinized, lessening the link between the stereotypes and the behavior. Even when they controlled for a variety of human social influences that might affect gendered behavior, including the presence of older siblings, the level of maternal education, or an adult male's presence in the home, the researchers found that the background variables didn't explain away some correlation between testosterone and tomboy proclivities.

Many studies with similar results focus on a different population: girls with a disease called congenital adrenal hyperplasia (CAH). They have XX chromosomes and female internal reproductive organs, but while they're developing in utero, their bodies don't produce enough of two hormones: cortisol, a necessary hormone for managing stress and blood sugar, and aldosterone, which regulates the body's salt and water. As their adrenal glands crank up to make more, they overproduce androgens, exposing these female fetuses to a higher-than-typical dose of male hormones.

As they grow up, girls with CAH tend to be shorter than typical girls, have more hair growth and acne, and irregular periods. The disease can be quite dangerous and requires lifelong hormonal maintenance, but it is most known for the androgens' non-dangerous effects: CAH often masculinizes genitalia, making them look ambiguous or resulting in enlarged clitorises that can resemble a small penis, or labia fused to look like a scrotum.[3]

The earliest studies, done in the 1960s, interviewed girls with CAH about their proclivities and play, finding that "genetic females masculinized in utero and reared as girls have a high chance of being tomboys in their behavior."[4] By that, the researchers meant things such as favoring "vigorous activity, especially outdoors"; being self-assertive; eschewing jewelry, makeup, and hairstyles; favoring utilitarian clothes; rejecting dolls; prioritizing careers over marriage; and having a high sex drive.

Behold a recurring problem with this kind of research: In the 1960s, the criteria for tomboyism were defined not by members of the counterculture but by buttoned-up professional psychologists in the ivory tower, with old-fashioned attachments to and acceptance of gender stereotypes.[5] Thus they classified behaviors such as declining to wear a necklace, wanting a career more than a husband, or liking sex as indications of tomboy behavior, when they are well within the range of normal for anyone. A decade later, many parents would rear their daughters to be tomboys, hoping they *would* eschew jewelry and focus more on career than marriage! Measures of masculinity and femininity are often rooted in stereotypes, dependent on how personality traits, colors, behaviors, and toys are connected to anatomic sex in the minds of researchers and the public at a given time.

So researchers have gotten more granular over the years and conducted better studies. They found that more girls with CAH than girls without are interested in male-typical occupations like mechanic and engineer. They tend to play with girls more than boys, but skew toward playing with trucks more than Barbies. They're more likely to prefer not to wear dresses.[6] Some have better geographical and mechanical knowledge than typical girls, or their sisters without CAH.[7]

They are also less likely to be cisgender than typical girls; maybe 5 percent versus around 0.5 percent in the general adult population will have a non-cisgender identity, but those numbers are incredibly hard to pin down.[8] Also, they'll likely increase as more people find the language to come out as trans and feel safe doing so.

Around 30 percent of girls with CAH might not be heterosexual, higher than the general population, but those numbers are equally hard to measure, since sexuality can be about behavior or fantasy or attraction or identity. By one estimate, 3.5 percent of American adults *identify* as lesbian, gay, or bisexual, but 8.2 percent have had same-sex relations and 11 percent acknowledge same-sex attraction. Alfred Kinsey's 1948 book *Sexual Behavior in the Human Male*, and the subsequent Kinsey Scale, found that sexuality is fluid, and that there are not just two kinds of mutually exclusive people, homosexual and heterosexual.[9]

Penn State professor of psychology Sheri Berenbaum, who has been studying girls with CAH for decades, boils the research down to: "Hormones influence activity interest a lot; sexual orientation quite a bit less; and gender identity even less."

Studies of nonhuman mammals indicate similar outcomes: injecting cross-sex hormones into gestating mothers can lead the offspring to behave more like the opposite sex. Most often cited is research with rhesus monkeys that manipulated the amount of testosterone in female fetuses at different times in gestation. Depending on when the testosterone was introduced, it could later result in females engaging in the amount of rough play and mounting more typical of male monkeys. Sex hormones and sex-typed behaviors are definitely doing some kind of dance.

Most of us can concede that. Hormones direct our bodies and behaviors in all kinds of ways, as anyone with PMS or going through perimenopause can tell you. Hormones "kick in" during and after pregnancy—nurturing behavior switches on in the biological mother after she's flooded with hormones like oxytocin. Hormones surge during gestation, to differentiate fetal genitalia, and they surge at puberty, to ready us for procreation. Then, once those procreation years are over, they die down, and we get a bit more similar again.

The story could end there: Yes, hormones have some effect on behavior. Tomboys have some innate inclinations. But does that mean that tomboys have "male brains"?

That's what proponents of brain organization theory seem to suggest.

The Biology of Male and Female Brains

Here's how it goes: Between six and seven weeks after conception, a fetus with a Y chromosome, previously identical to XX fetuses, expresses a gene that leads to the development of testes and, a few weeks later, the production of testosterone and other androgens, which, assuming the fetus has the receptors to synthesize them, masculinizes the genitals and the reproductive system.[10] Without the intervention of these hormones, the body proceeds in the female direction.

Per brain organization theory, prenatal hormone exposure causes sexual differentiation of the brain as well as the body. Thus, the brain of someone with testes is organized slightly differently than the brain of someone with ovaries, and along with their penises and testes, those assigned male at birth get their math and spatial skills and those assigned female get their natural demureness and kindness.

Simon Baron-Cohen, cousin of comedian Sasha and professor of developmental psychopathology, has written of what he terms the "essential difference" of male and female brains, arguing that male brains on average are "systematizing": They naturally try to analyze systems and discern the rules that govern them (as one might say I am attempting to do here, with our culture's sex-gender system). Female brains, he says, are "empathizing." "The empathizer intuitively figures out how people are feeling, and how to treat people with care and sensitivity," he wrote in 2003.[11] (He also discusses a third, less common option, the "balanced" brain. Baron-Cohen didn't respond to my request for an interview.)

Since girls with CAH get a surge of androgens, their brains may get masculinized, too, leading to nontypical interests and skill sets. That is, perhaps young females with CAH have brains that are more "male." And since tomboys also tend to have more male-typical interests, maybe they have more androgens, and maybe they have male brains, too.

The problem with this deduction is that scientists haven't agreed on how different male and female brains are, or what the differences mean. Hundreds of studies and articles argue every possible side of this debate; TED talks with opposing viewpoints, op-eds, and books abound, but there is *no consensus* about whether or not there are fundamentally different male and female brains.

There are some average variations. Males tend to be bigger than females and thus their brains are bigger on average, too. For years, male scientists extrapolated that size difference accounted for females' inferior intelligence. But we know that, ahem, size doesn't matter because, if it did, elephants and sperm whales would be getting all the physics degrees. And there are plenty of women who are taller and bigger than men, or do just fine with smaller hearts, livers, and lungs. Also, I feel comfortable pointing out without citing a specific scientific study: Men are not smarter than women. So size difference doesn't correlate to any fundamental difference in behavior or skill sets or smarts.

There are small, statistical differences in microanatomy, too: Males tend to have larger ventricles—the holes in the brain that contain cerebral spinal fluid. Males on average have bigger hypothalamuses, which regulate many bodily processes, including hormone production, and statistically smaller corpora callosa (connecting the two hemispheres and integrating cognitive, motor, and sensory skills). Males tend to have larger amygdalae (processing emotions, the fight-or-flight part of the brain). Females tend to have a thicker cortex (processing sensory information) and more gray matter (sensory perception and muscle control). And boys' brains, on average, mature more slowly than girls'.

But within these small, average differences are tremendous variations. It's how people interpret and extrapolate from those differences that makes this topic so tricky.

The classic breakdown is that, because of prenatal hormone-inspired brain organization, women like people, men like things. Women like ideas, men like data. This paradigm is used to explain why there are "women" jobs like nursing and why boys are more likely to study advanced physics than girls. Women get 54.5 percent of graduate degrees in biology and agricultural sciences, and almost 77.9 percent of graduate degrees in health and medicine— huge leaps from just a couple of decades ago when it was thought that small, female brains couldn't handle such disciplines. But a 2017 report found that women earn only 25.2 percent of engineering, 32.1 percent of math and computer science, and 27.7 percent of physics graduate degrees.[12]

Writer and sexual neuroscientist Debra Soh suggested to me that the reason for this discrepancy is that fields like biology and medicine are socially engaging, and women on average are exposed to lower levels of testosterone in utero, so they gravitate toward more socially engaging activities and occupations. People, not things. Engineering and coding, where you are "staring at a computer screen by yourself, looking at numbers and nonsensical words," as she puts it, are still dominated by men because they are numbers jobs. Things, not people. So even though the once common assumption that women were inherently incapable of being biologists or doctors has been proven wrong by women soaring in those fields, some people still believe that certain fields are underrepresented because of physiology.

In a 2005 speech, former Harvard University president Larry Summers said the dearth of women in STEM fields could be partially attributed to "issues of intrinsic aptitude"—meaning, there are fewer women in science because they don't have male science brains. Then there was the infamous 2017 "Google Memo," in which software engineer James Damore argued that one reason Google engineers were disproportionately male was that "the distribution of preferences and abilities of men and women differ in part due to biological causes and that these differences may explain why we don't see equal representation of women in tech and leadership."[13]

Soh identifies as a woman, is beautiful and feminine-looking, but believes that she was probably exposed to higher than normal testosterone levels in utero. She didn't call herself a tomboy, but she told me, "I was always more like a boy. I was always more interested in boys' toys. I looked like a boy." As an adult, she said, "I still feel very much like a man." She's focused on her career. She's blunt. She's outspoken. She's not afraid to be disagreeable. "I thought this was probably due to some sort of socialization, maybe because my parents were so open," she told me. But then she studied sex differences in the brain. "As I've learned more about the science of it, the whole idea of socialization doesn't really make as much sense to me."

The sexually dimorphic brain is not a popular idea among the left wing—both Summers and Damore lost their jobs because of outrage over the suggestion that women are inherently less apt to master certain scientific fields. But there is some evidence that men on average have better spatial abilities, including what's known as mental rotation, or the ability to imagine an object rotating—and some evidence that it's true for girls with CAH, too. Whether those skills are the result of androgen exposure in utero or later socialization, we don't know. But Soh, while not a practicing scientist, attributes these skills to prenatal testosterone, and said that exposure to it is "associated with interest in more mechanically interesting activities and occupations."

Expanding on this idea, a myriad of articles, in both the scientific and popular presses, also claim that trans women have brain patterns similar to cisgender women's, but if that were unassailably true, there would have to be such a thing as a cis woman's brain patterns.[14] I'm not saying that's wrong. I'm simply saying that we've not yet settled that debate.

For clarity, I called Dr. Joshua Safer, executive director of the Center for Transgender Medicine and Surgery at Mount Sinai Hospital, as I'd read that he had said "there is a masculine brain and a feminine brain."[15] But when I spoke with him, he told me that he wasn't talking about density of gray matter, or gendered skill sets, or figuring out which parts of which brain are boy and which are girl—he wasn't basing that statement on contested science.

Instead, he told me, "People have gender identity independent of any of their other body parts, suggesting that there's some hardwired thing." Even people with no genitals tend to have a gender identity. Therefore, Safer said, "It seems to be something in your brain."

That is, trans people, whose gender identities and sex assigned at birth don't align in traditional ways, show us that some aspects of gender are located in the brain, regardless of the body below it. But whether that incongruence is there at birth—fully innate—or develops later, no one yet knows. Probably both.

Debunking Gendered Brains

Neuroscientists like Lise Eliot, author of *Pink Brain, Blue Brain*, Gina Rippon, author of *The Gendered Brain*, and Daphna Joel, author of *Gender Mosaic: Beyond the Myth of the Male and Female Brain*, have convincingly (to me) argued that small, statistical differences in microanatomy don't add up to fully male and female brains—or personalities or skill sets. Eliot told me that research on girls with CAH hasn't produced neuroimaging evidence of masculinization in brain structure or function, and the girls' cognitive abilities and verbal skills seem unaffected by prenatal androgens, even if their spatial abilities tend to be greater than those of unaffected girls. And the truth is, the behavior of CAH girls in Berenbaum's studies was somewhere between a control group of unaffected girls and a control group of tomboys—that is, the tomboys who didn't have CAH had *more* boy-typical behavior.

The androgens clearly did *something* to their brains because, as Berenbaum put it, "behavior is subserved by the brain," but what, and how much, is the result of biology versus all the other forces of gender—the cognition, the socialization? We don't know.

In her book *Brain Storm: The Flaws in the Science of Sex Differences*, Rebecca M. Jordan-Young systematically went through hundreds of studies that have been used to claim the innateness of behavior and skill sets based on hormones, sex, and brain organization theory. She found *no consistency* between them, no overarching claim that could be made. Many of the studies cited one another, even if their findings were contradictory. Some studies showed that the brains of gay men and straight women were the same. Sometimes they showed that all gay people had the same brains. And how does one determine what's biologically masculine or feminine when what's culturally masculine and feminine is in flux? Their inputs and outputs were so different that they couldn't be compared.

"If you throw out all the citations that are debunked, nothing comes out," said Robert Ostertag, author of *Sex Science Self: A Social History of Estrogen, Testosterone, and Identity*. "It's just a house of cards."

Even the studies on how female monkeys act more like males if you dose them with androgens in utero fail to account for monkey socialization; those female monkeys may have had male-looking genitalia, and the monkey moms may have treated them differently as such. Extrapolating from other animals like rats and monkeys to humans is problematic. Those creatures don't have tech companies and retailers dividing their tablets into girls' and boys', promoting the pink-and-blue divide. Animals don't face forces like marketing shaping their ideas of what's normal, natural, and right.

Thus, we don't know for sure if these average differences between males and females are there at birth, the result of exposure to prenatal androgens, or of socialization, developing later in life. We're not scanning the brains of newborns and giving them visual-spatial skill tests to find out. Structural differences in the brain can be the result of environment and/or behavior, and increasingly, the scientific community focuses on and acknowledges neuroplasticity—the idea that the brain changes in response to experience, and doesn't just settle in place due to in utero or postnatal hormone exposure.

Meanwhile, hormones are as complicated as everything else about gender: Ostertag reports that testosterone can cause breast growth in men, and stallion urine has more estrogens than androgens.[16] Hormones are just one star in the constellation of gender, one factor in many that make a girl into a tomboy, and they aren't circulating in some corporeal vacuum. They're affected by the external environment, both cultural and physical, in a hormone-behavior-cognition-socialization feedback loop.

In other words, tomboys aren't the result of just nature *or* nurture. It is a mix, which shapes gender awareness, and funnels children's behavior and their adult skills and proclivities. It's prenatal hormonal exposure *and* postnatal socialization. It's genes *and* the environment, and the way those interact over a childhood, a lifetime. We can't draw straight lines between hormones, parts of the brain, and tomboyism. We can observe correlations. And gender is not one thing, in one place in the body. "We're looking for some place to measure it," Ostertag said. "It's all over the place. It's all over our bodies. It's all over our life experience."

When we say something is hardwired, we take for granted a relationship, a sequence of events: in this case, that the brain is ordered a certain way because of assigned sex and its organizing effects in utero, and that behavior follows. But there are many other statistics that break down along identity lines that show us how faulty such equations can be.

Allow me to digress: In the nineteenth century, white people used the "science" of craniometry—measuring the main part of the human skull—to insinuate that African-Americans were fundamentally less intelligent than whites. But we know not to be essentialists when it comes to race. If there are differences in health, finances, death rates, achievement, they're not biological. They're from the societally created disadvantages African-Americans face. African-Americans make around 75 percent of what white Americans do,[17] and are more likely to be incarcerated,[18] and to die in childbirth,[19] and their death rate is higher in just about everything from heart disease to homicide.[20] It's not race causing those differences; it's ra*cism*.

Women earn less than men, are more likely to be in poverty, and to have poor health. But we know that's not because of biology. That's not sex but se*xism*: the way women are treated, stereotyped, oppressed, and discriminated against because of their assigned sex.

Obviously, there are differences between males and females, those who line up neatly on either side of the binary. There is no human procreation without sexual differentiation—at least not yet. Males are more likely than females to have heart disease, Parkinson's, autism, kidney stones, and pancreatitis. More females than males have strokes, osteoporosis, migraines, Alzheimer's, and MS.[21] Some of those differences are due to sex—biology—and some due to gender—societal and cultural experiences.

A problem with trying to map what skills and traits belong, biologically, on the male or female side, is that what's on each side shifts, mostly as women push themselves into professions or places where once only men had access, and when men abandon those places once a quorum of women fills in. In the nineteenth century, boys were better at languages, but girls *outperformed* boys at science, including physics; a common phrase was "Science for Ladies, Classics for Gentlemen."[22] One study showed that girls retain scientific knowledge better when their textbooks have pictures of female scientists, and guess what?[23] At least one nineteenth-century textbook featured an image on the cover of a young woman teaching a girl how to use a microscope.[24]

We once thought whistling, wearing pants, climbing trees, playing baseball, and riding bikes were things boys were inherently better at or more suited to, and tomboys were the only girls partaking of them, but now they're fine for all girls. Nursing used to be considered a man's job because it was part of medicine, until Florence Nightingale popularized it as a feminine profession. The same with bank telling, which was a man's job because it had to do with numbers, until it diminished in status and so many women took it on that it passed the tipping point, beginning in

World War II.[25] We think of Evelyn or Ashley or Beverly or Carol or Hillary or Lynn or Whitney as girls' names, but they used to be considered boys' names, until too many parents bestowed them upon girls.

Oh, and the field of computer programming? It was largely inhabited by women, six of whom programmed the first large-scale, electronic-speed computer, ENIAC, in the 1940s. Building the hardware was considered a man's job, and the more clerical work of programming was considered a feminine endeavor. That view held until the 1960s, when men figured out that programming was difficult and pushed women out of the field.[26]

Meanwhile, the percentage of women in computer science has declined since the 1990s. Did women's brains get even *more* female in the last twenty-five years? Soh suggested that the shift was due to an increase in the variety of occupational choices available to women, like law and medicine. But it's safe to assume that tech bro culture plays a major role. If there are fewer females in physics and computer science than males, can we really chalk that up to the brain, when females used to be *better* represented in those fields? It's funny—or not—how many people are essentialists only when it comes to gender, behavior, and the brain.

And let's not forget that "boy" toys like LEGO bricks promote those spatial skills, that we direct kids toward specific activities that enhance and reinforce skills or traits or interests based on their sex, whether there is a biological impetus for them or not. Maybe men—and tomboys, and girls with CAH—have better visual-spatial skills because they get more boy LEGO sets, fewer LEGO Friends.

I'm oversimplifying, but if you multiply the boy-versus-girl toy issue into how we talk to kids, what activities we sign them up for, how we segregate them, it is impossible to ignore the imprint of socialization. Tomboys, and girls with CAH, who play with boys and boy stuff, may have innate proclivities, but they are also generally part of boys' peer culture in a way that typical girls usually aren't.

I noticed this with my own children. My older daughter was mostly playing with boys from kindergarten through third grade. Many parents of those boys signed their sons up for sports teams, and asked my kid if she wanted to play, so she has done soccer and baseball since she was five. She was drafted into a sporty culture. No kids, or parents, asked my younger, non-tomboy daughter to join their sports teams, despite the fact that she's lightning quick on her feet. They assumed, by way of her dresses and rainbows and hearts and sparkles, that she would not want to play. She was drafted into a different culture, and we've had to work hard to open up her world to include sports, to encourage the flexibility that comes naturally to those who straddle the pink/blue divide.

Think back to what Carol Martin said about girls who develop atypical gender preferences, which sets them on a path of being more open-minded, more likely to straddle that line. It's not necessarily that androgens induced permanent brain changes in utero for these girls; it could be that hormones widened the road that tomboys, and girls with CAH, later walked down, which led them to be drafted into multiple cultures.

Both androgens and the male-typed activity interests of girls with CAH play a role in their development of spatial abilities.[27] Androgens may affect later gender-related behaviors, from playmate to toy preferences, in part by changing how these girls are socialized. We start out with small differences, but we get sorted into separate branches, which exacerbate them.

Melissa Hines, who studied the pregnant women with high testosterone and their tomboy kids, wrote that, "Prenatal androgen exposure may influence subsequent gender-related behaviours, including object (toy) choices, in part by changing processes involved in the self-socialization of gendered behaviour, rather than only by inducing permanent changes in the brain during early development."[28]

Clearer to me than the line between male and female brains, between testosterone and other forces that dictate behavior, is the line between how we've marketed the stuff of childhood as masculine or feminine, and how we've come to believe that gendered preferences are innate. And also how that can change.

BECKY

She only wanted to wear boys' pants, mostly with her favorite cowboy boots. By age seven, she refused to wear dresses, had no time for jewels, and used makeup only to draw a mustache or a beard on her face. Sometimes she lowered her voice when she talked, pretended to be a boy when she role-played. She didn't want to play with girls. She related better to boys. Sometimes she said she wanted to be one. She definitely didn't want to have a baby when she grew up.

It was the 1970s, the major time of tomboys, but Becky's single mom thought she acted too much like a boy. She was even rubbing her body up against girls in a way that seemed to her mother like something an older boy would do. So Becky's mother took her to see some psychologists at UCLA. They were going to teach her to stop being a tomboy, to behave like a girl.

Months and months of sessions—102 in the lab, 96 at home—followed, Pavlovian-style experiments in which she was praised for choosing girl toys, punished for choosing boy toys.[1] She became attached to her female therapist. Longed to please her. Learned to say that she didn't want to be a boy because boys can't have babies. Learned to stop saying "I'm getting this stuff off of me, and I ain't kidding, I better not smell like a girl," about makeup, and to say, instead, "Where's the makeup? You should have gotten the makeup. Doesn't a lady wear makeup?"[2]

After seven months, Becky was pronounced cured because she "spontaneously began wearing jewelry and perfume at home," as the report said, and because she developed a crush on an adult male examiner, old enough to be her father. She wanted him to have her phone number so he'd call her every night and every day.

It was Dr. George Rekers who oversaw the treatment, whose goal was "normalizing her gender identity and gender role behaviors." With thousands of dollars of public funding, he studied boys and girls who acted in ways he and his colleagues felt they shouldn't. He treated "sissy" boys, too, teaching them how to act like men, "curing" them of their feminine behaviors, mostly by way of shaming.

Chapter 7

BEWARE THE END OF THE PRINCESS PHASE

"The emotional, sexual, and psychological stereotyping of females begins when the doctor says: 'It's a girl.'"

—Shirley Chisholm[1]

"I don't like princesses," my daughter's seven-year-old friend proclaimed proudly. "Or pink."

"Me either," chimed in another little girl, one of six we were having over for my younger daughter's seventh birthday, along with one boy. These first-grade girls were actually both wearing quite a bit of pink, wearing dresses with "feminine" markings: rainbows, hearts, and sparkles. We had just finished doing some painting, in which they had used a lot of pink and purple but declared that they didn't like them, and were in search of a movie to watch, which, they wanted to make sure everyone knew, shouldn't be about a princess. "I hate *Frozen*," one said, and the others quickly concurred.

Like her friends, my younger daughter had once gone whole-hog into girly-girl culture. By age three they were fully into what psychologists call "PFD," or Pink Frilly Dresses. "We have noticed that a large proportion of girls pass through a stage when they virtually refuse to go out of the house unless they are wearing a dress, often pink and frilly," psychologist Diane Ruble and her colleagues wrote in a 2011 paper.[2] Some mothers in their study recalled that their daughters began to express a desire for PFD as soon as they could speak, and insisted on wearing pink to all occasions, from hiking to horseback riding. As many as 74 percent of three- to four-year-old American girls demand PFD.[3]

But why? The psychologists knew the phenomenon couldn't just be attributed to cultural norms, since many American parents spend considerable energy attempting in vain to shield their daughters from princess culture, refusing to let their kids dress as Anna and Elsa, trying hard not to pinkify their toys. They fight with all their might *against* cultural norms. Besides, as noted earlier, those norms were so recently created. Little boys stopped wearing dresses only a hundred years ago, and pink has been considered a girls' color for less time than that. But PFD is ingrained in us as if it has been around for centuries, the desire for it so pervasive and aggressive that some researchers have come to believe that it is biologically determined.

A 2003 paper by psychologist Gerianne Alexander, "An Evolutionary Perspective of Sex-Typed Toy Preferences: Pink, Blue, and the Brain," hypothesized that "a preference for red or pink appears to have an advantage for successful female reproduction." Perhaps nonhuman primates preferred "reddish-pink" over yellow or green because "infant faces compared to adult faces are reddish-pink, and red or pink may signal approach behaviors that enhance infant survival." There is an evolutionary purpose to a woman or girl liking pink, Alexander surmises, because it helps keep babies alive.[4] I take this supposition with a large grain of very white salt for the simple reason that not all babies are reddish-pink, though Alexander told me by email that even babies of color are relatively pinkish compared to adults.

Meanwhile, pink is an ungendered color in some other cultures and countries. When I mentioned that I wanted to dedicate a day to boys wearing pink, raising awareness about gender stereotypes and the history of homophobia that has kept boys out of that color in the US, an Indian-American friend observed that boys wearing pink is just an average day in much of South Asia; she called it "#MondayinIndia."

Eventually, psychologists realized that neither nature nor nurture alone could account for the intensity of PFD in the US, but the interplay of the two could, along with the development of cognitive and classification skills. That is, gender is learned biologically, socially, and cognitively: There's what your body does, what your culture teaches you, and how you learn to navigate the messages from your body and your culture. A big part of what happens is "self-socialization." Kids get this information about what gender is and how it works from the media, from their parents, and—perhaps most important—from one another, and construct a gender reality.

Ruble and her colleague Carol Martin dubbed children "gender detectives," who aggressively try to divide the world into "what boys do" and "what girls do." As mentioned earlier, at two years old, most kids understand the two assigned sex groups, and by age three, they understand the stereotypes associated with them.

They work hard to understand and perfect them, to claim their place in a group, exercising the ultimate human instinct to belong. What they don't yet understand is that gender stereotypes and assigned sex are not the same thing, so they believe that because pink and dresses are for girls, putting on a pink dress or makeup makes them girls. Playing with trucks and short hair makes them boys.

The desire for PFD is basically human tribalism. The first tribe that kids learn about is gender, and nothing communicates "girl" more than PFD, so when a girl is asserting her place in her tribe, insisting and demonstrating that she belongs, the most obvious way to do that is by embracing PFD.[5]

Professor of child psychology at California State University May Ling Halim and her colleagues studied PFD all over the world. Soon they noticed something else about it: Around age six, some American girls "go through a curious metamorphosis, in which their earlier embrace of all-things-feminine appears to transform into an identity as a tomboy," Halim wrote. This they called the "PFD-to-tomboy phenomenon."

Halim found that elementary school girls begin showing an increased preference for male-typed behaviors and activities, including playing sports, wearing pants, playing with boys and "boy" toys, refusing to wear dresses or skirts, and casting off all associations with pink. Only 30 to 40 percent of girls they surveyed had stereotypically feminine interests as they grew older. "Instead, in an apparent 180° turnabout, 'tomboyism' becomes quite common, with some girls eschewing the PFD they embraced just a few years earlier." The love of PFD is, for most girls, just a phase, erupting around age three and evaporating a few years later.

This might be the result of understanding gender constancy, as discussed in chapter 5: A man putting on makeup or a dress can still be a man. A girl playing with trucks can still be a girl. Once kids compute that gender stereotypes and assigned sex aren't the same thing, they can be flexible without surrendering their membership in their girl tribe, and they feel more comfortable reaching across the aisle to boy-typed activities or clothes. They learn that there is variation *within* gender groups, not just *between* them.

But there was a problem with this explanation: Boys didn't go through such a change. They don't turn six and suddenly decide that they want a Barbie Dream House and can finally wear that tiara-and-tutu combo they've been eyeing. In fact, they may become *more* rigid in their preferences and play, more reinforcing of stereotypes. Which prompts the question: Why do girls feel comfortable entering boys' territory around age six, but not the opposite?

Frowning on Femininity

Starting at around age four, children begin to understand that not everyone sees the world as they do, and that there are multiple viewpoints; this is known as "theory of mind"—the realization that each of us has our own beliefs, preferences, ideas, separate from other people's. As they grow older, children begin to absorb the hierarchies and statuses of different gender groups, and they intuit that generally in American society boys and boy stuff have more status than girls and girl stuff. Girls understand that the world sees them in a certain way based on their girl category, and that their category has a lower status.

Halim found that children from ages six to twelve see masculine jobs as "more important, lucrative, difficult, and higher in status compared with feminine jobs," and those differences were even starker in the minds of older kids. Children from seven to fifteen saw men as having "more power, influence, status, and respect than did women in business and politics."[6]

Young girls may not know that jobs once considered masculine, from bank teller to nurse, get devalued once they become considered feminine, when more women than men do them, and that girls may now outperform boys in school and earn more college degrees but still earn 80 cents for every man's dollar.[7] But they can intuit that they have a lower social status than boys. Kids learn early that what matters about boys is what they do and what matters about girls is appearance. When asked, "What are girls like?," preschoolers' answers are usually all about dresses, jewelry, and makeup.

In a British TV documentary, *No More Boys or Girls*, host Javid Abdelmoneim asked primary school kids in the UK what they thought were the differences between the sexes. "Men are better because they're stronger, and they've got more jobs," said one little boy. "I would describe a girl as pretty, lipstick, dresses, love hearts," said a little girl. "Boys can only do football," said a little boy. "Because they're fitter and stronger," said a girl.

This is a program from 2018, not 1958! But the message that boys have more freedom, more power, and more pizzazz is timeless. Thus, just as girls embrace PFD to gain entry to the girl group, many subsequently reject it, asserting a tomboyish side as a way to push themselves higher on the status ladder. The Austrian psychiatrist Alfred Adler called this "masculine protest": rejecting traditional gender roles to gain power, to reject inferior status. These girls disavow what is feminine as a way of disassociating themselves from the lower rank of female. So many parents are excited when the princess phase ends, but it turns out that a six-year-old girl declaring her hatred of pink and dispensing of PFD has basically internalized sexism.

When Girls Don't Heart Hearts

As girls denounce princess movies and pink, they are likely rejecting traditional femininity, and the lowered status that goes with it. Of course, my daughter and her pals were being reared in hyper-lefty New York City, where many parents would congratulate a young boy for his interest in makeup and fret over a girl's (guilty!), or think a tomboy was terrific but fear that an extra sporty boy might be headed for toxic masculinity. Even in an era when there are important and popular books like *Strong Is the New Pretty*, those of us who think we're well aware of gender stereotypes may be reinforcing them. Even those of us who think we're feminists may be devaluing femininity if we reject things because of their association with girliness, or girls. Even we may be shaming our children for conformity, despite the fact that conformity is what our culture demands.

"I've heard from parents who say, 'I have a little girl and I encourage her to play with trucks. We only got her boys' toys,'" writer and sexual neuroscientist Debra Soh told me. "But then she goes off to school and she loves dolls. She wants dolls and she only plays with dolls and they're really horrified by that. And that makes me sad because I think, well, what's wrong with that? That's what she likes. It doesn't mean that she's oppressed. It doesn't mean that she's not going to have a happy or fulfilling or successful life. And maybe she will still be a CEO one day." But Soh thinks that parents believe their girls have to be more like boys if they want to be successful, making both girls and their parents feel bad if they're not more masculine, promulgating the femininity = bad calculation.

I talked to a first-grade mom whose daughter, like my then fourth-grader, was fully decked out in boys' clothes. The mom had never let the kid wear rainbows or pink or hearts or unicorns or sparkles, and now the child didn't want to play with other girls, the mom said, because they were only into rainbows or pink or hearts or unicorns or sparkles, and that wasn't her kid's thing. There was a tinge of superiority in the mom's voice, but she was also looking to me for confirmation, as if certain that my girl in boys' clothes also looked down on those things.

I don't want to judge, but I'd learned from my research that first grade was prime time for girls realizing that their sparkle-unicorn-heart-rainbow desires were considered uncool, subservient to the balls and trucks that dominate boy-land. And I'd learned how recently we had separated boys from lace and floral patterns and the full rainbow to make sure they knew to be manly and straight. So I thought it kind of a bummer that to make girls cool, or make them think they're cool, we encourage them to reject what is mistakenly labeled as girl stuff, and thus also reject girls. If rainbows and hearts were gender-neutral, or were beloved by the majority of boys, or slotted into the masculine file, would the first-grader's mom still keep her daughter away from them? I mean, hearts and rainbows and sparkles and unicorns—are those *bad* things? Actually, they're the stuff of joy. It's that they're associated with girly-girls that makes them bad, and that's a sad equation. Rather than raising a daughter to reject what's associated with girls, how about raising sons to embrace it?

In my family, we've tried very hard to ungender colors, toys, clothes, and personality traits. Everyone in our nuclear family knows that hearts and rainbows and sparkles and unicorns are not for one sex. Nothing is off limits, nor is anything disparaged because other people associate it with girls. As she got older, my younger daughter realized she could love blue without having to reject pink, and my older daughter grew to love pink without rejecting blue.

Of course, not all girls who discard PFD are doing it because they realize that, as Simone de Beauvoir said, "to be feminine is to show oneself as weak, futile, passive, and docile."[8] Sometimes they have just developed enough cognitively to know that they can do "boy things" and not surrender their place in the girl club, that their membership is not dependent on them wearing, or liking, pink frills. They understand that one can still be a girl without being girly. They become more flexible and feel more free to do what they want to do, including play soccer or wear pants— freedoms boys who want to do ballet and wear skirts generally don't feel. Historically, tomboys, who tend to emerge in their boy-typical preferences, including the sweatpants and T-shirts talked about in the next chapter, about the same time that typical girls are enveloping themselves in PFD, are the ones who've had the most flexibility and freedom.

It is truly difficult to determine what we objectively like versus what we have been told is appropriate—remember what Carol Martin said about a girl liking dolls if she's learned that she's supposed to. Psychologist Robert B. Zajonc conducted experiments in the 1960s that revealed a "mere exposure effect." That is, the more familiar we become with things, the more apt we are to like them—mere exposure increases acceptance and embrace.[9] Often we think of conformity as socially created, a cultural construction, but nonconformity as biological or innate: a girl's femininity as artificial and her masculinity as authentic. We may see PFD as a gender constraint imposed upon children but see the rejection of it, in favor of tomboyism, as something that comes from within. But we don't know if tomboys are doing their own thing or conforming to the stereotypical expectations of a different sex.

These contradictions are hard to sort out, but I'd rather see us remove the socially created gender roadblocks than try to solve the contradiction. Discovering our identities, including our preferences, is the process of trying things out. I'd like kids to have more freedom to try.

At my daughter's party, I put on *Brave*, a Disney princess movie with a highly feminine-looking protagonist, but one who refuses to submit to her proscribed path as a future bride, and whose proper mom learns, by way of being turned into a bear, that traditional femininity isn't that important after all.

There were a few complaints at first that I broke the no-princess rule. But after a couple of minutes, the children sat there enrapt, watching this story about a young girl carving out her own path in life: a pretty tomboy, rejecting her gender role in a princess dress.

COCO

Back when she was Gabrielle, she was a *garçon manqué*, the French word for tomboy. She preferred her brother Alphonse over her other siblings, for with Alphonse she could climb trees. She could be the tomboy she thought of herself as.[1]

Her father, a good-for-nothing, neglectful, and unfaithful husband, shipped her off to an orphanage in 1895, after her mother died when she was twelve. She lived her impoverished childhood in the worlds of novels, the tragic romances of *Jane Eyre* and *Wuthering Heights*, but she was determined not to have a life that depended on being rescued by a man. She learned early how to navigate a man's world, and that to do so a woman must be dressed more like a man.

She went on to become Coco Chanel.

With her electrifying, revolutionary designs, she capitalized on the Dress Reform movement of the late nineteenth and early twentieth centuries. Though women started competing in the Olympics in 1900, working during World War I, and won the right to vote in America in 1919, Coco knew that women would not be emotionally or physically free until their clothes facilitated free movement. And the more masculine the clothes were, the more they communicated that freedom.

Coco cast off the twenty-five pounds of corsets, bustles, petticoats, and hoop skirts that many women had worn in the nineteenth century and offered the world her iconic Chanel suit: a masculine-styled jacket, sometimes with a tie, over a long skirt. She made her sporty clothes out of a flexible jersey material, which had, until then, been used for men's underwear. Even if subtler forms of controlling women's bodies—especially dieting—emerged in the 1920s, at least women's clothes now allowed them to work, to move, and to breathe. She gave women the right to comfort, the literal freedom to move, and the first fashion that could be called tomboy style.

___

Chapter 8

WHY DO TOMBOYS WEAR BOYS' CLOTHES?

"Aunt Alexandra was fanatical on the subject of my attire. I could not possibly hope to be a lady if I wore breeches; when I said I could do nothing in a dress, she said I wasn't supposed to be doing things that required pants."

—*Harper Lee,* To Kill a Mockingbird

"**P**ut me in a dress it would feel like my skin is on fire." That's how Laurel described the sensation she was experiencing by the time she was in kindergarten. Laurel grew up in the nineties and early two thousands in Durham, North Carolina, in a middle-class white family with fairly liberal parents. When her mother was pregnant, her friends would ask if she wanted a boy or a girl. She'd answer, "I'll take a healthy cross-dresser"—which is, Laurel said, pretty much what her mother got.

For the most part, Laurel's mom dressed her in "androgynous L.L.Bean sweatpants," but on those rare occasions when a dress was expected, it was torture. Then: *Space Jam* hit the big screen.

Laurel had always been sporty, but once she saw the Michael Jordan/Bugs Bunny basketball film in 1996, she became a basketball fanatic and had an excuse to dress head to toe in athletic gear, which she pretty much did from ages five to eighteen.

That was her way, she said, of opting out of what was expected of her as a girl, the space that identifying as a tomboy allowed. Wearing girls' clothes "goes against part of who I am," Laurel said. But: "If you're an athlete and that's the gear for this sport, people will understand it."

The Many Meanings of Clothes

Often the first sign of tomboyism, or at least what parents may notice first, is what a girl wears, or maybe what she doesn't. In most of the stories I heard, the desire for boys' clothes started around three, the same time other girls go all in for PFD. This is when most kids start conforming. But, as happens with toys or modes of play, some tomboys develop atypical clothing preferences. They go for the boys' duds.

For tomboys who have gender-related tension with their parents, clothing is often the biggest source of it. The dynamic depends partly—mostly—on the parents' gender beliefs and the cultural norms of the time. Some parents don't give a hoot about dresses or a girl wanting to wear boys' clothes; in the 1970s, they may have encouraged their daughters to do just that. To others, dresses, and looking the part of girl, are extremely important.

I heard dozens of similar stories to Laurel's from young tomboys who refused or preferred not to wear dresses and opted for everything from athletic clothes to three-piece suits. Sometimes their resistance was quite dramatic: Sometimes they denounced dresses, threw tantrums about them, declared their hatred for them, felt as Scout Finch did when she described her aunt's feminine clothing as "the starched walls of a pink cotton penitentiary closing in on me." Sometimes they were fine being dressed in frills for special occasions, but politely requested pants and T-shirts the rest of the time. Of the 180 current or former tomboys I surveyed, around 48 percent wore boys' clothes usually; 14 percent wore them always; and 27 percent wore them sometimes; only 11 percent never wore boys' clothes.

Of course, there were tomboys long before wearing boys' clothes was an option, but even they might have been recognizable by their clothes. As mentioned before, in the nineteenth century, when all school-aged girls wore dresses (as boys did before school age), tomboys' outfits would still be soiled or ripped from climbing trees and playing baseball and other rough outdoor play, especially in popular tomboy literature. Jo March burns her dress and stains her gloves, which, happily, gets her out of having to deal with the proper ladylike behaviors associated with dances and balls.

Ever since the middle class has been large enough to make purchases that communicate a sense of style or an aesthetic, and since we have so heavily gendered children's clothing, clothes have become symbolic representations of ourselves. They are literal and figurative uniforms that assist in the creation of our social identities and communicate what tribes we're in: hippie tie-dye, Goth black, proper princess-pink. Expression is for those who have access to options. Clothing is a language for those allowed and able to speak it.

When gender-conforming kids who are trans, those assigned

male at birth who identify as girls, or vice versa, don the clothing marketed to another sex, they may be communicating their gender identity. But what about all the other kids whose gender expression is nonconforming without it being a reflection of their gender identity? Just what are those types of tomboys communicating?

Two Kinds of Comfort

There are loads of historical and modern examples of girls seeking refuge in masculine attire, from Joan of Arc to the *bacha posh* of Afghanistan: girls raised as boys, either to save the family from the shame of not having any sons, or to bring good luck so the mother births a son next. (According to Jenny Nordberg's wonderful book *The Underground Girls of Kabul*, most Afghans believe that the mother's body determines the sex of the baby rather than the father's sperm.[1])

Some of those girls refuse to assume the feminine gender role as they are supposed to once puberty hits, refuse to relinquish the freedom, control, and status they experienced as boys in order to take on the subservience of adult women; Afghanistan is often ranked the worst or second worst place to be a woman in the world.[2] These girls dress and live as boys and run free, which they would otherwise not be allowed to do.

But in those cases, the reason for the transgression likely didn't have to do with gender identity but power: to access male spaces and privilege, to be able to live as boys and do what they do, whether that's fight in a war or bring honor to an "unfortunate" family that had only daughters.

For most American tomboys I talked to, their clothing preferences were less about identity and more about functionality. For instance: When Penny gave birth to baby Nikki in Pennsylvania in 1990, kids' clothes were already hyper-gendered. Penny had heaps of very feminine hand-me-downs from Nikki's two older girl cousins. She pierced Nikki's ears at four months, imagining the feminine child she'd grow to be. "I had a lot of really old-fashioned ideas," Penny said.

But Nikki had ideas of her own about what to wear by the time she turned three. "She started to have a really strong identity about how she presented herself and how she dressed," said Penny. Nikki asked to have her hair cut short and wanted to wear baseball caps all the time. She insisted on wearing her brother's hand-me-downs, and because everyone in the entire family is a basketball fanatic, particularly for the Phoenix Suns, Nikki religiously wore a Phoenix Suns jersey. Sports were incredibly important to her from an early age, and so her clothes needed to reflect and facilitate that.

It was "kind of a product of functionality and comfort, that I was running around and I wanted to be wearing clothes that were comfortable for me," Nikki said. "Even today it's baggy gym shorts and a comfortable T-shirt."

Nikki was okay with wearing a dress to her aunt's wedding, though she insisted on wearing sneakers, and she would comply with the requests to wear dresses to synagogue, but increasingly, as she got older, she opted for pants. "I was fine with that," Penny said. "For her bat mitzvah she wore a blue pin-striped suit and she looked like a boss—a shark. She looked great and she was comfortable, and that's always been our motto and our theme: that if Nikki is comfortable, then that's the most important thing."

Comfort, as any of us who have tried to squeeze into clothes that look great but feel bad know, can be two-pronged: There's emotional comfort, from wearing what flatters, or soothes or communicates, and physical comfort, from wearing something of the muumuu or sweatpants variety. For many adult women, in outfits that include high heels and skintight jeans, those two kinds of comfort might be in opposition, with the emotional comfort trumping the physical. For tomboys, physical and emotional comfort seem intertwined.

For Nikki, the way she looked was a boon. Penny said that at preschool graduation, many of the little boys in her class said they wanted to grow up to marry Nikki. She'd somehow gotten status from her "masculine" dress and behavior, becoming a mini version of that American tomboy so lauded in 1891 as a future "Woman That Men Admire and Worship."[3]

A Prescription to Be Passive

Nikki's mom didn't model this masculine mode of dressing, but according to one study, mothers of tomboys reported dressing in more masculine ways than mothers of non-tomboys.[4] Girls who had role models of nonstereotypically feminine attire were more likely to prefer such clothes themselves. But Nikki didn't get it from Penny. Her inclination was to model herself after the basketball fanatics in her family—and those were mostly boys.

Nikki was born in the Girl Power era, the first time that every single aspect of a child's life was completely gendered in America, from before day one. Young kids' clothes had been gendered for a good seventy years by then, but it reached a new level of pink stratification in the nineties. These hyper-gendered kids' clothes communicated not just a kid's sex but their gender role, carrying both literal and figurative messages. I noticed that as soon as my daughter started to crawl: Her knees would snag on the cute little hand-me-down dresses I put her in. The tread-less Mary Janes made being active difficult.

A UK data analyst named Mitra Abrahams slotted one thousand items of boys' and girls' clothes into categories and found two-thirds of girls' clothing had flowers, rainbows, hearts, and pictures of girls on it, while only 3.9 percent of boys' clothes carried such images. On boys' clothes, 63.9 percent of imagery was of vehicles, animals, and pictures of boys. Girls' clothes were mostly white and pink, boys' mostly blue and gray. Girls' clothes said "Professional Princess" and "Be a Kind Human," while boys' said "Roarrrr" and "I am invincible."[5]

As writer Sara Clemence pointed out in a piece for the *New York Times* in 2018 about dressing her daughter from the boys' section, "I found girls' sections filled with lightweight leggings, scoop-neck tops, and embellished shoes. I scoured the internet for girls' pants with capacious pockets and reinforced knees, and found maddeningly few options." Boys' clothes, she found, "are largely designed to be practical, while girls' are designed to be pretty."[6] That is, the clothes carry a prescription to be passive—and then we say that girls are less active than boys. We call someone a tomboy if she chooses roaring over kindness, but that was never a fair choice.

Eight-year-old tomboy twins Dylan and Elie told me of their frustration at how girls' and boys' clothes are divided. "They always put pink clothes in girls' and, like, blue and black clothes in the boys' aisle," Elie said.

Dylan remarked that girls' clothes have "flowers and glitter and rainbows" and "boys' stuff always has, like, *Star Wars* and, I don't know, like, basketballs on it or something. I guess girls can't be, like, strong or, like, rough. I guess the boys have to act more cool and girls have to always wear pink." She offered a critique of this paradigm, and exceptions to it. "Some of the girls in my class wear some pink, and they also play sports," she said.

"Do you guys play sports?" I asked them.

"Yeah," Dylan said. "And we don't wear pink at all."

Would they wear "girls'" clothes if the pink shirts had basketballs and said "Roarrr"? Would they wear "boys'" clothes if they had glitter and messages of kindness? We've manufactured these differences, not only in clothes, but in the minds of the kids who wear them.

Boys' Underwear, Boys' Shoes

As much as these clothing differences are capitalistic constructions, sometimes there *is* a relationship between donning boys' clothes and having a male gender identity. Randi Ettner, an Illinois-based psychologist who works with transgender clients, conducted a study in 2018 of forty-five lesbians, sixty-six heterosexual women, and fifty trans men, looking for correlations between their childhood habits and adult sexuality or gender identity: whether they were labeled as tomboys; how long they liked their hair; and whether they "cross-dressed," which for their purposes was defined as wearing boys' underwear and shoes. (As mentioned earlier, cross-dressing once referred to a woman in pants, and could be filed under the crime of male impersonation.)

All participants were assigned female at birth. Almost all of the trans group, who were much younger than the others and likely had access to language, role models, and information that the older cohort didn't, had socially transitioned, and most had had hormones and/or surgeries. What the psychologists didn't account for was that this much younger group was more likely to have been raised in the era of hyper-gendered childhood. The older lesbians and cisgender, heterosexual women might have been raised in a tomboy heyday, but had access to a much narrower gender vocabulary and less expansive ideas about gender identity. We don't know enough about how the cultural zeitgeist around gender affects people's senses of themselves.

That said, there were stark differences between groups. Thirty percent of the heterosexual reference group said they were known as tomboys growing up, as opposed to 73 percent of the lesbians and 90 percent of the trans men. Though perhaps a more useful survey would have compared a control group entirely of heterosexual tomboys—if you look for people born in the 1970s, you'll find lots.

None of the heterosexual women and 9 percent of the lesbians wanted to wear boys' underwear in childhood, but 78 percent of the trans men did. Half of the lesbians wanted to wear boys' shoes, while 90 percent of the trans men did, and only about a third of the lesbians and a quarter of the trans men wanted long hair. Those assigned female at birth who insisted when they were kids that they *were* boys were more likely to transition than those who only wished they were—no surprise there.

Ettner summarized it to me this way: "Those children that would ultimately transition as adults had a desire to wear boys' underwear as a child, and to wear boys' shoes, and the women who grew up as lesbians did not." She also emphasized that her work is in no way intended to show a direct line between these preferences and future identity, but rather to observe correlations. "It is reductionistic to conclude that specific childhood behaviors or preferences, in and of themselves, can predict future outcomes," she wrote in the study.

Another way to read these data is that a quarter of future trans men *weren't* interested in boys' underwear, and wanted long hair, while a third of lesbians wanted long hair and almost 10 percent wanted boys' shoes. Laurel, for whom dresses were torture, grew up to be a butch lesbian. So did a former tomboy named Ellen, who rejected dresses, too. Two trans men I spoke to, Clark and Caspar, also couldn't abide girls' clothes for a minute. Nikki, who could withstand a dress but definitely wasn't psyched about it—and was almost never forced to wear one—is straight and cisgender. Maybe Laurel, Ellen, Clark, and Caspar are "rejecting femininity," "always" tomboys who continue their childhood looks today, regardless of gender identity. And maybe Nikki is a "sometimes" tomboy, embracing masculinity without the need to cut every pink-sparkle-heart from her life. Perhaps there is a relationship between the degree to which a childhood tomboy refuses girl clothes and later sexual orientation or gender identity.

But it seems to me that maps are hard to draw. A 1950s tomboy named Miriam truly despised wearing dresses as a kid, and still does, and is straight and cis. Gabby Kirschberg, the queer founder of the style blog *Dapper Tomboy*, told me that she wore pink and dresses as a kid, but she loved to wear boys' underwear. So cross-dressing as a kid can be an indication of gender identity or sexual orientation, but not always.

The Rise of #tomboystyle

We might look to the world of adult fashion for lessons on how to be comfortable with these murky boundaries between clothes and identity. While young boys' and girls' clothes may be more glaringly gendered than at any other time in American history, and tomboy play clothes a thing of the past, the word "tomboy" persists plenty in the fashion industry. But it is divorced from its history, instead birthing a gender-bending look that shows us what happens when boys' clothes are all grown up, and no longer just for boys: #tomboystyle.

Many posts on Instagram tagged #tomboystyle feature masculine-looking women with chiseled physiques and short hair, or genderqueer people or trans men wearing feminized versions of menswear, or non-binary or androgynous models and actors like Ruby Rose and Erika Linder. In this iteration, tomboy has almost nothing to do with kids or behaviors or the gender roles and rules the word "tomboy" once helped kids navigate.

For instance, when Kirschberg founded Dapper Tomboy in 2013, she didn't know of the word's history in the English language and American popular culture. "Tomboy" was how people described her look in high school—not her behavior or identity—when she started wearing men's formal wear, especially blazers and bow ties, the kind of looks featured on her site. "I didn't have to worry about women's style or men's style, even if I wore women's clothes in a masculine way or men's clothing in a feminine way. 'Tomboy' just means expressing the way you want," she told me. "It just means this openness of fluid style." To her, "tomboy" means a look. A really cool look that defies the traditional gender boundaries of fashion, and has no connection to sexuality or gender identity or even assigned sex.

That said, while some #tomboystyle images are empowering, magazines and blogs also feature #tomboystyle fashion spreads showing women in skimpy, tight outfits with a masculine touch—a blazer over a lacy bra with a pouty, heavily made-up woman staring at the camera. There are skintight leathery outfits and cleavage-revealing dresses, occasionally interrupted by looser-fitting leisurewear. You can find T-shirts printed with the text "pretty tomboy"—*huh?*

What does pretty have to do with being a tomboy? Jamie Skerski, a communications professor at the University of Colorado, authored an article called "Tomboy Chic: Re-Fashioning Gender Rebellion." The former tomboy suggested that making tomboy a fashion statement rather than gender rebellion is another form of "tomboy taming," pressuring tomboys to surrender their ways at puberty so they can land a man. Tomboy fashion is both liberating and constricting, like the word "tomboy" itself.

The Long-Lasting Effects of Dressing Like a Tomboy

I did notice one bit of sartorial consistency among the former tomboys I talked to, no matter their gender identity or sexuality.

Almost all of them maintained a certain kind of non-frilly, non-overtly sexy style for the rest of their lives. It wasn't #tomboystyle, necessarily—in fact, few of them had any interest in fashion. But it was a hashtag-less, practical version of it.

Former tomboy Whitney, mom to a six-year-old tomboy now, said, "The way that my tomboy identity persists is in my ongoing choice to not present myself to the world at large with my sexiness up front." She works in tech, a male-dominated field. She dresses how she wants—slacks, flats. "I want to show up with my intellect first, not my sexiness first." Being a tomboy, and dressing like one, gave her the courage and comfort to do that. It showed her that it mattered what she did, not what she looked like—the message many boys receive.

Girls are *still* fighting to wear what they want, to have control over their appearance and the right to reject a look our society deems appropriate for them. In 2014, an eight-year-old Virginia girl, Sunnie Kahle, who was described by her grandfather as "pure, 100 percent tomboy," was strongly encouraged not to return to Timberlake Christian School because of her short hair and penchant for dressing in boys' clothes. The school sent the family a letter that read, "We believe that unless Sunnie as well as her family clearly understand that God has made her female and her dress and behavior need to follow suit with her God-ordained identity, that TCS is not the best place for her future education."[7]

Meanwhile, in 2019, the Supreme Court heard the case of a trans woman named Aimee Stephens, fired for not appearing feminine enough after she transitioned—an issue that affects all women and girls, whether cis or trans.[8] Several other times in 2019 (not 1959!), girls successfully fought to end dress codes that required them to wear skirts. An eighteen-year-old self-identified tomboy named Lacey Henry, who does "not feel super confident in a dress," petitioned her school to allow girls to wear pants to graduation, which worked only after she contacted the American Civil Liberties Union. "The students expect freedom of dress and choice for their body, but instead, their bodies are over-sexualized and objectified," her petition read. It's time "to step into this century and remove these patriarchal standards."[9]

MIRIAM

There were two reasons I wanted to wear pants: My favorite activity was playing on the monkey bars, which was much harder in dresses, and the Chicago winters were frigid.

My mother, who wore pleated pants and sensible shoes, was a freethinker in terms of dress, despite the fact that she was married to a conservative Jewish husband who worked twelve hours a day, six days a week in a factory. He had very old-fashioned ideas, even for the 1950s, about what boys and girls should look like and do. But my mother didn't see anything wrong with my wearing pants. So after I was told that I had to wear dresses to school, my mother protested for the longest time, and kept sending me in pants, particularly in the winter when it was brutally, brutally cold. Finally, she was called in not just to the teachers but to the principal and told that I would not be allowed to go to this school—my neighborhood, public school—if I continued to wear pants.

This was heartbreaking for me. I was a shy child with poor eyesight who felt isolated from my peers, who were mostly Catholic. My only playground pleasure was the monkey bars, which I could no longer enjoy. I tried many times, barelegged, but they were rusted, icy, and painful. After a while, forced to wear that ridiculous attire—dresses—I gave up.

I spent my recesses by myself, incredibly cold in the winter, miserable, and just not being able to do anything at all that was fun in any sort of way. To wear pants was to be free; to wear dresses was to be restricted. It was a lesson I never forgot.

After winning my high school and state science fairs, and being told by my science teacher that there was no place for women in science, I was knocked back for a while but undeterred. I had seen the path that most women had to take, including the outfits, and it was not for me. I continued to essentially live and do well in what was called at that time a man's world. As an adult, I still dress in a masculine style, in slacks and sensible shoes, and have never dressed in a way that would be seductive. I can't remember the last time I wore a skirt. I feel that kind of attire is like putting on a costume.

Chapter 9

PARENTING BETWEEN THE PINK AND BLUE

"There's a land that I see where the children are free
And I say it ain't far to this land from where we are."
—*The New Seekers,* Free to Be, You and Me

Are you having a boy or a girl?

It's almost always the first question we ask someone who's pregnant. Or we don't have to because the parents have already held a gender-reveal party, announcing the assigned sex of their fetus with a pink-icinged cake or a hundred blue balloons.

The first thing we do with a newborn is wrap him or her or them up, often in the ubiquitous Kuddle-Up fuchsia-and-teal-striped receiving blanket disseminated in most hospitals, with a pink-and-blue-striped knit cap on their heads. For most American babies, this is their last—but not always their first—ungendered moment, the last pink *and* blue, gender-neutral thing they'll wear. By the time they leave the hospital, they are usually dressed in a way that announces their gender, or at least their genitals, to the world. We tell children what section they belong in, and enlist others to reinforce the division.

Though I didn't find out the sex of my children before birth, I was adamant that I only wanted girls. Partly I didn't want to make the decision about whether or not to circumcise, and partly I reasoned that it must be hard to find a good man because it's so hard to raise one. Thus, I hoped for, and got, two girls. Cue the pink confetti!

Except I was a mostly pink-free mom the first time around. I dressed my firstborn in dresses because I love them, and because that's what came in the bags of hand-me-downs generously gifted by my childhood friend Katie. But I was careful to avoid Barbies and princess paraphernalia and other super "girly" items, even if I never asked myself what made them girly, or what was wrong with girliness—those questions came many years later, after the reality of how my children differed or aligned with my sex-based expectations became clear. One of them was a tomboy—her word, or the word given her by a classmate, not by me—dressing in boys' clothes, mostly friends with boys for the first few years, interested in sports. The other would have left the house looking like a beauty pageant contestant, in full makeup and a ball gown, if we'd let her.

In some ways, their divergent gender expressions seemed proof that such behavior was innate. But I also treated them differently. The second time around, I was forty years old and exhausted, and didn't have the emotional resources I'd had the first time to erect bulwarks against the relentless pressures of gender—resisting the pink headbands and the princess paraphernalia and the incessant messages about how boys and girls should look and play. My kids have shown me how different people of the same assigned sex can be, but I will never know how much my own attitudes about gender, the gatekeeping and then the lack of it, affected them.

But the efforts to create tomboys in the mid- to late-1800s and the 1970s, to raise girls with the idea that they could and should have access to boys' domains, and subsequent psychological research show that gender attitudes of parents matter tremendously.

The research also shows that parents who think children should be treated equally regardless of sex are more likely to have tomboys, and that those tomboy kids are less likely to gender stereotype and more likely to have career aspirations not defined or limited by gender: Gender egalitarian parents tend to beget gender egalitarian kids.[1] There's even research showing that women who don't learn their baby's sex in utero may have fewer traditionally gendered expectations.[2] If you start with a prenatal sex test, a gender-reveal party, a pink headband, a princess-themed room, you will be more likely to rear a child who is prone to gender stereotyping, to limiting herself to the girl sphere, and imposing limits on others.

Raising Tomboys

Most tomboys I talked to were encouraged or facilitated by their parents. At the very least, they were tolerated.

Allison was raised in the 1990s in Somerville, Massachusetts, with left-wing, activist parents who were more apt to take her and her three sisters to an Amnesty International rally than a Chuck E. Cheese. "Their take on feminism was to raise us to be non-girly-girls," she told me. "Our dad threw the *Berenstain Bears* books out the window once, and actively discouraged play with dolls and the color pink." (The *Bears* books are derided by some people for their cloying gender stereotypes.) Her mom, she said, was less vocal about what choices her daughters should make, less strictly rejecting the feminine. "But she was not the mom that got training bras or showed us how to use mascara."

As a kid, Allison cut her hair short and wore T-shirts and jeans. "No dresses," she said. Her only female friend was a fellow tomboy, who played sports and didn't care about clothes either. Allison, who majored in biology and works at an engineering firm, was the most tomboyish of her sisters, but even they played sports and one went into IT. One of her sisters is my good friend, and the crew has always seemed to be unfussy, well adjusted, and confident.

Which is exactly how a dad named Eric described his nine-year-old daughter Zoey, whom he's currently raising with his wife in Nebraska. From early on, he played football with her, took her cliff-jumping, taught her to skateboard. He and his wife let Zoey get a Mohawk and then shave her head. "She's just adventurous and loves doing crazy stuff," he said. Zoey's older sister was more stereotypically girly, which multiple therapists told me is common in families with more than one girl. Often one is more traditionally feminine, the other more tomboyish, otherwise known as "sibling differentiation": becoming what the other isn't, filling the open role. Zoey gravitated toward athletic shorts and T-shirts because, Eric said, "she knew that she would like to be running around and climbing, and wearing a dress was less functional. And I think for her, she kind of takes after me. I'm a functional type of person. So for me it doesn't really matter what clothes look like or anything, it's just how they work."

Allison and Zoey had natural inclinations, helped along by their parents, and they seemed to take after their dads more than their moms. In fact, dads can loom large in tomboys' minds. When sociologist C. Lynn Carr studied tomboys, she could hardly get a word out of them about their mothers, but they went on and on about their dads. They identified with their fathers and other male role models. They said they were their father's favorites, or that they were or wanted to be "just like" their dads, or that their fathers treated them "as sons," taking them hiking and fishing, playing and watching sports, doing home repair.[3]

One study found that the amount of time spent with dads, or how relatively masculine or feminine dads were, made no difference in how tomboyish a girl was. What made a difference was having a dad who approved of a daughter engaging in "culturally typical masculine behavior" like, say, fishing, sports, home repair.[4] (One study did find that the more time girls spend with their fathers the less likely they are to choose gender-typical occupations.[5] Another noted that child-rearing has a direct effect on later choice of gender-atypical occupation. "Parents' beliefs and behaviors influence children's values, expectations, and interpretations of achievement-related experiences, which contribute to children's goals and self-schemas, and ultimately play a role in occupational attainment," one study noted.[6]) Tomboys tended to have dads with positive attitudes toward girls participating in such activities—though we don't know if their attitudes or their daughters' behaviors came first. Typically, though, fathers have a harder time accommodating gender atypical activity than mothers; after all, they were raised not to transgress gender boundaries themselves.

In some cases tomboys weren't just inspired by their dads; sometimes they were rejecting the model of their moms, or their moms as models, not wanting to walk down the proscribed feminine path. Some tomboys in C. Lynn Carr's study wanted to disassociate themselves from their mothers and used the term "no future" to describe them—that is, there was nothing about their mothers' lives they wanted to emulate. They were more likely to say that they never wanted to be like their moms, seeing them as victims, weak, overly emotional, obedient, overworked, and helpless.

But as much as they adored their fathers and wanted to distance themselves from their mothers, tomboys, research shows, are far more impacted by their mothers, especially if the moms were tomboys themselves. The mothers of tomboys tended to like "boy" toys and activities themselves. And girls in families where the mom was perceived as the "boss"—where the mother managed the money, disciplined the children, planned the activities, and dominated in family disagreements—were more likely to be tomboys: strong mothers, strong girls. This is not such a stretch, that a mother with an interest in both sides of the divide would try to facilitate that same open-mindedness in her kids. But it also confirms that, as much as some aspects of our kids are hardwired, deliberately helping them rebel against gender stereotypes in childhood can have lasting positive effects, as can other ways we treat them.

Many studies reveal how adults treat kids differently because of what they assume their assigned sex to be; that is, how they conflate gender with sex. Most famous is a 1976 study called "Baby X: The Effect of Gender Labels on Adult Responses to Infants,"[7] with a follow-up in 1980 called "Baby X Revisited."[8] These studies looked at how adults interacted with three-month-old babies who were introduced as boys, girls, or without gender information. Not surprisingly, the adults acted completely differently based on what sex they were *told* the baby was. If told the baby was a boy, the grown-ups offered the babies a football or gender-neutral teething ring to play with—especially the men. If told the baby was a girl, the adults were more likely to choose a doll.

Such discrepancies have routinely been recorded; egalitarian parenting is possible, and many of us think we're engaging in it, but there's plenty of evidence that most of us slip into differential treatment and attitudes. One study found that mothers routinely underestimated their daughters' crawling ability, while the mothers of sons overestimated it.[9] Another found that adults interpreted babies' cries differently depending on what they *thought* their sex was.[10] When they thought the babies were boys, adults characterized their cries as distressed based on how high, or "feminine," the pitches were. Parents have been found to speak differently to their infant daughters than sons. Fathers more often play gently with girls and roughly with boys and are more likely than mothers to approve of kids when they select gender-appropriate toys.[11] On and on, unconscious—and sometimes conscious—gender bias for miles, even among progressive people.

What We Got Wrong

The nonsexist parenting movement of the 1970s, inspired by the counterculture and the sexual revolution, was supposed to combat that insidious gender bias. It promoted tomboy styles that became so popular that we didn't even think of them as tomboy styles. Some clothes and toys in that era communicated that girls were not a separate species, and that they need not be kept away from boys' stuff. It was intended to infuse kids with the idea that boys and girls could be and do anything—including being tomboys—but most of these studies about how differently we still treat boys and girls were conducted in the last two decades. The messages didn't take, or were replaced.

The 1970s didn't exactly usher in a wave of all-around gender equality for kids. Most of the era's messages pushed parents to rear girls as tomboys, to make them more like boys, but not the other way around. No conversion chart appeared for girls'-to-boys' sizes in the Sears catalogs in the 1970s. Unisex clothes really meant "masculine" styles that girls could wear. It wasn't that boys could wear pink; *no one* could. The dearth of pink toys and clothes in the 1970s Sears catalog, the boys'-to-girls'-sizes conversion charts, quietly discouraged all kids from reaching for typically feminine things—empowering girls by devaluing traditional femininity. (It was quite effective: The majority of tomboys I talked to, even the most feminine ones, rejected pink; 46 percent of my survey respondents said they didn't like it, and 37 percent liked it only sometimes.) The nonsexist parenting movement may have liberated some girls, and pushed tomboys to the top of the heap, but it discouraged femininity and left out lots of other kinds of kids, especially boys.

It's uncomfortable to claim that boys are disadvantaged by this gender system when girls and women are still so tremendously oppressed. Child marriage for girls is still legal in much of the world; only six countries provide equal work rights to women;

only 33.1 percent of speaking or named characters in 2017 and 2018 films were girls or women; and there are a whole slew of other ways that things are worse for women than men.[12] But nonsexist parenting can't really work unless it liberates boys, girls, and kids who don't fit neatly into either category, equally.

To really make kids free to access both sides of the gender line, those sides must be un-gendered, or less gendered, and doing that requires a lot of creativity, as well as a lot of opening what's marked and marketed as feminine to boys (and to girls, after they leap from loving PFD to internalizing sexism). We focus on getting girls into STEM, but we have a shortage of nurses and teachers, jobs we generally think of as women's work. We should encourage boys to pursue things inaccurately marked that way.

But how to undertake this monumental task? It's up to the next generation.

Baby boomer children were the first to be able to recognize one another's gender by clothes and colors, and some grew up to cast off traditional gender roles and attempt nonsexist parenting. Some of those kids raised in the nonsexist, pro-tomboy era grew up to rear their kids in a hyper-gendered way. Now, as that first hyper-gendered generation procreates, some members of it are casting off the confines of gender for their babies altogether.

Instead, they're giving birth to theybies.

Cool, Fluid Childhoods

Kyl Myers and her partner Brent are perhaps the country's most famous proponents of gender-creative parenting, after an article in *The Cut* recounted their mission. They have kept their child Zoomer Coyote's assigned sex to themselves while chronicling the family's adventures on a blog and Instagram feed and book, to be released in 2020, called *Raising Them: Adventures in Gender Creative Parenting.*

Myers grew up Mormon in rural parts of Oregon and Utah, and while that religion has very strict gender roles for adults, she and her friends were grouped by age, not sex, during early childhood, until they were baptized around age eight. Myers's own home was fairly equitable, despite the hyper-gendered zeitgeist that had taken hold elsewhere. "We wore each other's hand-me-downs; we went to thrift shops. There wasn't hyper-gender in our home," she said. "I just think it was this really cool fluid childhood that I got."

Her family left the church before she hit puberty, but she watched her friends fall into Mormon gender roles as they aged, especially the girls. "No one thought we were going to grow up to amount to anything but mothers and wives," she said. Education and empowerment weren't valued for women. "It all felt like you're biding your time until your husband comes along."

Later, as she worked toward her PhD in sociology and studied feminist and queer theory, Myers was struck by the fact that most health outcomes have gendered roots. Men are more likely to die in accidents, not because of biology or sex, but because of gender: cultural pressures to perform masculinity, to be macho, tough, not cry, not be vulnerable. Women are more likely to suffer from poverty or acute illnesses because they're usually the ones in daycare fields, or home with kids, exposed to sickness. Men have higher homicide rates; women have higher rates of disordered eating. "This is all linked to how we think people should behave and these stereotypes, and we are not going to solve the problem in adult-hood," she said. "We have to change how we are treating kids."

She vowed that she'd protect her own kid from these gen-dered outcomes, the limitations of and stereotypes associated with assigned sex. Thus: Myers didn't assign a gender identity or expression to Zoomer. Instead, she believed Zoomer would iden-tify with a gender in their own time and until then, could have the freedom to explore. To some, this seems a radical approach, but it's not really that much more radical than gendering every moment and activity and object from before a child is born, the constricting imposition of the pink/blue divide.

Zoomer has they/them pronouns (until they declare which pronouns fit them best), and toys and clothes that are marketed to both boys and girls. Zoomer knows their body parts, but not that they correspond to a sex category or gender "because some people with penises may identify as women, and some people with vulvas may identify as non-binary," Myers wrote to me. If the family shops for sneakers, Zoomer is presented with the pink sparkly options and the blue and black options. One month they choose an Elsa toothbrush; the next month it's Paw Patrol. They play with trucks and ambulances, but they construct caretaking stories about the people in the crash. Myers said that 95 percent of what her family does can be replicated by people who still want to assign a gender, or reveal their babies' sex. You don't have to buy a new blue stroller when you're having a boy; keep the old pink one. "They want you to buy two of everything," she said, of marketers. But that leads us to treating kids differently.

Myers has observed over and over how people treat Zoomer dif-ferently based on what they assume Zoomer's sex to be, commenting on "her" appearance if they think they're a girl and calling "him" buddy, treating him like an equal, if they think they're a boy. When people don't know a child's anatomy, they can't stick to the gender script. "If there is a penis, it's a boy. Here's the script. There's the vulva. It's a girl. Here's the script. We don't have scripts for inter-sex kids. We don't have scripts for nonconforming kids," she said. "I just think we rely too much on these two scripts that are really useless in actually being able to connect with a child on what they're really authentically interested in." When she talks to kids who are assigned a gender, she tries not to stick to the script, to not compli-ment a girl on what she's wearing, to deliberately talk to a boy about his emotions.

It's catching on. A Facebook group, Raising Theybies, had more than six hundred members as I wrote this (up two hun-dred members in three months). *Vanity Fair* reported in 2019 that Prince Harry and Meghan Markle would be raising baby Archie with "a fluid approach to gender," and that "they won't be impos-ing any stereotypes." The nursery would be splashed with white and gray, not pink or blue, because, as an HGTV article claims, "gray is the new yellow"[13]—yellow being one of the few colors that was previously available to the sixteen people a year (okay, more like 2 to 45 percent, depending on age of parents) who don't find out the sex of their babies before birth.[14]

For some people, none of this is enough. Del La Grace Vol-cano, an intersex, non-binary artist, calls themself a "part-time gender terrorist" and is raising two kids assigned male at birth with their partner in Sweden. Their kids go to one of the country's many gender-neutral preschools, where differences between boys and girls are de-emphasized; Sweden successfully introduced a gender-neutral pronoun, *hen*, sometime around 2009. What others call a dress-up box to Volcano is a "wardrobe full of possibilities," though not many of them are stereotypically male. Volcano is raising gender revolutionaries—they are white, assigned male at birth, and able-bodied, but, Volcano said, if they identify as men, "they damn well better be the kind of guys I want to hang out with."

Volcano presents somewhat as male, though often wears skirts and makeup. "I go out of my way to model gender nonconformity to my kids," Volcano told me. "Gender-neutral is far too passive for my liking. You have to be proactive, you have to be engaged, and you have to possibly err on the side of excess rather than caution."

After all, the messages about how to be a boy or girl, and that those are the only options, are so pervasive and intense; if you're trying to counteract them, it requires a whole lot of energy, creativity, persistence. It requires fighting a culture that has made a boatload of cash via gendering, with books like *How to Be Your Daughter's Daddy: 365 Ways to Show Her You Care* and the companion book, *How to Be Your Little Man's Dad: 365 Things to Do with Your Son.* Notice the difference: ways to care versus things to do.

Every object, color, activity we gender contributes to the idea of children being profoundly different from birth by way of assigned sex and asks parents to reinforce and perpetuate those differences. "Parents say, 'My little girl didn't want trucks,'" said Volcano. "How much of a real choice did you actually give them?"

Limiting the nursery to gray and yellow is not the same as opening the whole rainbow of colors and possibilities to every child, regardless of assigned sex. Discouraging anybody from wearing pink and pursuing feminine activities isn't the same as valuing sports, dolls, dominance, and nurturing equally, as thinking masculine girls and feminine boys are well within the range of normal.

But we don't usually think that. Once a job or a color or a name is marked as feminine, it becomes very hard for boys and men to partake of it. There are a lot of ways to be girls and still get cultural approval, but the limits of acceptable boyhood remain narrow.

One way to expand them is by talking to kids early and often about gender stereotypes. The 2017 Global Early Adolescent Study found that risky adolescent behaviors are shaped by damaging gender roles, leaving girls around the world prone to things like early pregnancy, violence, and sexually transmitted diseases. Boys are prone to substance abuse, suicide, and shorter life expectancy.[15] Challenge those roles immediately, before they sink in, the report suggests. A 2019 report about the harms of gender stereotypes led to a ban on using them in ads in the UK: No more unhealthily thin bikini bodies. No more women vacuuming while men lie on the couch chugging beer.[16]

But while we're waiting for the media and the culture to catch up, parents might not realize how much they are treating their kids differently and making decisions based on assigned sex, which is one thing the parents of theybies aim to change.

Writing New Scripts

Naturally, there are skeptics, and downright disagreers, people who will cling to "she just likes pink" and "he just likes trucks" and believe that these things are written on the DNA more than in the cultural script, and that it's a losing battle to try to get kids to behave differently than they're biologically programmed to, that to do so is to ignore biology, or reality. Maybe it's a losing battle to try to convert those parents, but it seems clear from tomboy heydays in the 1800s and 1970s that it is possible to steer the big ship of our culture toward more gender-equitable parenting.

There are sometimes reasons to treat boys and girls differently: not because they are different species, but to create equity. If there are fewer girls interested in, or veering toward, STEM activities, it makes sense to have girl-focused classes or games (not pink, necessarily, but girl-focused) revolving around STEM. If boys are more culturally prone to violence, it makes sense to beef up opportunities for them to explore more emotional, less physical play. We can respect the biologically inspired differences while shifting the culturally and capitalistically created ones, to create space for all children—cis, trans, non-binary, intersex, and gender nonconforming—to explore.

We should help children find their passions and proclivities, push and encourage them, resist the sexism and genderism that pressures girls to be excessively feminine and boys to be exclusively masculine, helping each child find a spot on the continuum between them. We don't know what activities children would partake of, or what they'd be like, if there weren't such excessive gender roles, reinforced by marketing and parents and peers, the power of socialization and self-socialization and peer policing, directing them in how and who they're supposed to be.

Until he had a tomboy daughter who was not just willing to do the stuff that Eric wanted to do, but totally into it, Eric hadn't realized how many old-fashioned ideas he'd had—he'd thought all the stuff Zoey wanted to do was boy stuff. "I've had some of those gender biases in my head," he said.

As have I. Once my older daughter started expressing a desire for things culturally marked as "for boys," I stripped whatever vestiges of pink remained out of her wardrobe (and gave them to her little sister). If I hadn't had another daughter, all "girl" items would have likely disappeared from my home. I would have communicated that anything marked "girl" was not for my non-stereotypically feminine kid. But years ago when she requested a crew cut, like little boys were getting, I hesitated before giving in; no little girls around us sported such a look. But why would a hairstyle be a problem for a girl but not a boy?

It isn't. It's a problem for the parents.

Zoey didn't have trouble at school, even in her conservative community. The kids accepted that a girl could have a Mohawk and wear shorts. Some days now Zoey wears a dress. She wears boys' swimming trunks and a swim shirt. "Whether she wants to be girly or more boyish or whatever she wants to do, as long as she is kind and caring and loving towards people and respects herself and others," Eric said, "we are in complete support of that."

Gendering qualities and clothes and activities—it's not only unnecessary, it's damaging. We should get to a point, said Eric, where kids are "not having parents that are slamming down their throat their own gender biases." We should think of the qualities we want our child to embody, not how we want a *boy* or *girl* to be. I wouldn't even call this gender-creative parenting. I'd call it parenting.

"Parents are focused on the gender of their babies because they think it's going to tell them what that child's life is going to be like," Dr. Christia Spears Brown, professor of psychology at the University of Kentucky and author of *Parenting Beyond Pink and Blue*, told me. The sex of our babies has been far more a predictor of how we will treat them, what clothes and toys we'll buy them, what activities we'll sign them up for, what friends we'll encourage them to play with, how we'll speak to them, steer and limit them, and tailor the messages sent to them than of who those babies would instinctively grow up to be.

MIRA

When I was eight, my mom showed me clips from Ellen DeGeneres's TV talk show, and I decided that was the haircut I had to have. It just resonated (though five years later, I have Abby Wambach's shaved-on-the-sides, long-on-top haircut and Megan Rapinoe's pink coloring).

My hair reached past my shoulders at that point, but I told my parents what I wanted to do. Wait a week, they said, just to make sure you still feel the same. I did. I was happy with the haircut, and my parents were supportive. So was my teacher, who had short hair, too. My classmates were a little weirded out, but I handled it. I'd been wearing "boys'" clothes ever since I was allowed to dress myself: hoodies, shorts and T-shirts, and pants and collared shirts for dress-up occasions. They were used to it. People had always used the word tomboy to describe me, which back then I thought meant "a girl that's tough," and that was okay with me.

What I didn't know was that the rest of the world wasn't as encouraging as my parents, friends, and teachers.

There were the bathroom incidents, the grown-ups and teenagers telling me I was in the wrong one. The constant misgendering. When I was ten years old, I was shoved out of a girls' locker room by my own camp counselor because she thought I was a boy. When I was eleven, I went to an all-girls softball camp and was referred to as "he" and "him" for an entire day.

This year, when I got my state-licensed ID at the DMV, I was referred to as "he" while the employee stared at my birth certificate that stated on it, "Sex: Female."

When I'd correct people, especially older women, they'd be apologetic, uncomfortable, but then the women would try to reassure me, saying, "I went through a phase just like that." The obvious implication was that I'd grow out of it someday.

Worse was what kept happening at soccer. Coaches and parents from the opposing teams would say to my coach, "Your team is cheating. You have boys on your team." As my team, which included three other short-haired teammates, won more games, it happened even more. The opposing coaches would demand to see the rosters, which had gender markers—and they still wouldn't believe us. Sometimes they'd ask for birth certificates.

At camp one day when I was ten, a boy asked me, "So you like boys' clothes?"

"I like *my* clothes," I told him.

"So you like boys' hair?" he asked.

"I like *my* hair," I said.

Every once in a while, I'd second-guess myself. Is my hair worth the trouble?

Every time I'd decide, yes, it was worth it. Because it wasn't about hair. It was about the fact that I am happy with who I am, and nobody gets to decide that but me.

My look was not a phase. The thing that has changed is my feeling about the word "tomboy." I don't like being called a wannabe boy. I'm proud to be a girl.

III

Tomboys, All Grown Up

Chapter 10

WHAT HAPPENS TO TOMBOYS WHEN PUBERTY HITS? (A BRIEF INTRODUCTION TO A GIANT QUESTION)

"The age of the tomboy is what makes her adorable if she is under twelve, interesting in early adolescence, problematic in late adolescence, and downright dangerous in adulthood."

—*Renée Sentilles,* American Tomboys, 1850–1915

Connie didn't wear dresses. She wore shorts, T-shirts, and sneakers, and idolized her brother, who was five years older. She rode bikes around the neighborhood with him, played toy soldiers, made model airplanes and lit them on fire, ran through creeks and woods, engaged in mock wars in the strip of concrete they called a backyard. A lot, but not all, of her friends were boys.

At puberty, she got more feminine—not with clothes, necessarily, but with how she played, did her hair, presented herself. Maybe it was the pressure to fit in, the different and unequal set of expectations we have for pre- and post-pubescent girls, the pressure to pack tomboyism away once "Aunt Flow" comes visiting. Or maybe it was that in seventh grade she developed her first crush on a boy. The people she'd been palling around with for ten years suddenly became potential dates.

Many studies show that tomboyism often desists at puberty. They chalk it up mostly to social pressure.[1] Prepubescent girls may get props looking cute in their overalls and spiky hair, mucking it up with the boys, but masculinity in adult women has historically garnered far less praise than it has social punishment.

"I think when people stopped calling me a tomboy, they just didn't call me anything," said Robin Dembroff, an assistant professor of philosophy at Yale who writes extensively on gender. Dembroff was called a tomboy throughout their childhood by adults who explained their penchant for short hair and boys' clothes with the word. No one took it as a sign of a future sexual orientation or gender identity. "It didn't go any deeper than that," they said. Having been homeschooled in a very conservative Christian community in California's Central Valley in the 1990s, Dembroff accepted the word because "I didn't know of any of the alternatives."

The alternative Dembroff uses now is genderqueer—an identity outside the male-or-female binary—but that didn't exist when they were going through a traumatic puberty. They went from belonging to a recognized, and recognizable, gender category to someone whose gender was unintelligible and unacceptable to cisgender people: an "other."

"There wasn't a label," they said. "I was just 'weirdo.'" Neither Dembroff nor their family nor community had a conceptual framework for understanding their experience. Dembroff very much wanted to be a boy, and had, in some ways, been living as one; at puberty that option evaporated.

"It's Not a Perpetual Tomboy We're Trying to Produce"

Prepubescent boys and girls are not terribly different from one another in their hormonal profiles in early childhood. One pediatric endocrinologist told me that androgen and estrogen levels are so low in young children that they are virtually undetectable. After the hormonal surges in utero that differentiate genitalia and reproductive organs (and the brain, if you're going that route), and another shortly after birth, both boys and girls experience a modest increase in androgen levels in middle childhood, from ages five to nine. At puberty the brain's hypothalamus directs the releasing of hormones that further masculinize or feminize the body, to start menstruation or the production of sperm. (I speak of what happens generally, for *most* kids, but of course there are exceptions.)

In other words, hormonal differences postnatally are minor in childhood but become major at puberty. We become extremely sexually differentiated, both due to societal expectations and at the corporeal level.

Puberty's physical changes may contribute to girls turning their backs on tomboyism—not just because those changes can cause emotional and physical suffering, from periods to breast growth to sudden-onset male leering—but because a postpubescent girl breezing across the football field shirtless, while legal in the city where I live, just isn't a thing. A tomboy is no longer in the protective shield of a prepubescent body, deciding how masculine or feminine she wants to be, and no longer in control of whether the world sees her as male or female. It's a protection that many tomboys told me they never felt again. It was the end of a certain kind of privilege.

While puberty can cause depression and anxiety for any kid, for some trans kids, or those who identify outside the gender binary, it can also be when gender dysphoria sets in if it hasn't already. Gender dysphoria is known as "a marked difference between the individual's expressed/experienced gender and the gender others would assign him or her"—or them. It can cause "clinically significant distress or impairment in social, occupational, or other important areas of functioning."[2] (I cover this in chapter 12.) Some kids are insistently, consistently, and persistently trans from a young age. Some come out at puberty. Some even later.

For tomboys of all kinds, puberty can be a tough time because they will likely be giving up more, changing more, than girls who were already floating down the feminine stream. But from the beginning of the embrace of tomboyism in this country, it had a condition: It had to stop at puberty.

As the father of the playground movement, Joseph Lee, wrote in 1915, "a girl should be a tomboy during the tomboy age, and the more of a tomboy she is the better." The tomboy age was eight to thirteen, and he warned "of adhesions to a passing phase. It is not a perpetual tomboy we are trying to produce."[3]

Why not a perpetual tomboy? For social control. As mentioned in chapter 1, from the time the word "tomboy" first became positively attached to young girls, in the mid-nineteenth century, it was connected to eugenics, a project of raising healthy white girls to become successfully procreating white women. Girls had to stop being tomboys so they could take up their rightful duties as wives and mothers, and be neither masculine nor lesbians nor identify as men. Though the word is no longer steeped in racism, the expectation of femininity after puberty remains.

Almost all the tomboys I talked to felt pressure to stop being one after puberty, from their parents, their peers, the culture. Most of them made some kind of attempt at stereotypical femininity—pearl earrings and pink sweatshirts—and for many of them it felt like a performance, as if they were walking around in the world in costume. What they did after depended on how much freedom they had, what language they could access, how they understood themselves, and how much support they received. But almost all of them felt their childhood tomboyism affected their adulthoods in positive ways and stayed with them.

For instance, Deborah grew up a tomboy in the 1950s in Detroit. She had a Hopalong Cassidy outfit and a two-gun holster that she'd wear to bed—her mother had to sneak it off her when she was asleep, to wash it. She hated dresses, and pink, and still doesn't like frills. Her mom had been a rebel, run away from home in Brooklyn at thirteen, and didn't care about gender norms. "I wanted to be Hopalong Cassidy or Roy Rogers or maybe Perry Mason, but I had a mother who kept telling me that short of a physical disability, I could do anything I wanted to do—anything, if I could put my mind to it. And she was right." It was her dad who had a harder time, expecting her to relent at puberty. "He had a design for me," she said, which meant that her tomboyism would stop and she'd follow the path he'd carved out for her—but she refused. "There was no way I was going to go to college, get a BA, work for a year, marry the kid who belongs to the same country club, have children, do charity work, and die. I'm out of here."

Deborah left home, went on to marry a man, have children, become a co-CEO of a family-owned business. Her sexuality and gender identity were just what her father expected of her; her behavior was not.

Many former tomboys I talked to went on to male-dominated fields, like finance or tech. Many continued to wear comfortable, functional clothes that didn't accentuate their bodies. Almost all had an inner comfort and a self-confidence that seems to come with the tomboy territory. But for many tomboys, puberty was tough.

It took Dembroff years to find the language for their identity, and now they spend a lot of time trying to give others access to that language, to make living between or outside traditional genders an acceptable place to be. "I write the things that I wish I had had to read," they said.

As for Connie, though she feminized—physically and culturally— some aspects of her tomboyism remained. She has to wear professional clothes to work as a lawyer, but they are as tomboyish as she can make them. "I don't wear dresses to work," she told me. "I don't wear skirts mostly because I don't find them very comfortable. I just prefer to wear slacks. I don't wear high heels." She does not light model airplanes on fire or run around with her shirt off, but she is comfortable with herself, and comfortable in both a man's and woman's world.

The idea that there are just two kinds of tomboys, the "sometimes" or "feminine" tomboy and the "always" or "masculine" tomboy, rather than a wide variety seemed to me simplistic and reductionist: another binary, instead of a more inclusive prism. But many LGBTQ+ people I spoke with said "tomboy" *didn't* feel like the properly inclusive category. They divided tomboys into those who were cisgender and straight, and those who were trans, non-binary, bi, pansexual, or gay. They acknowledged the spectrum of both gender and sexuality, but also felt there was some kind of breaking point, a line that they crossed.

The research shows us that there are correlations, but not necessarily a clear path, between being a certain kind of tomboy and a certain kind of adult. Childhood tomboyism is fertile ground for all kinds of later possibilities—as long as the seeds planted then are allowed to grow into whatever shape they need to. A lot of the tomboys I talked to had similar childhoods. But what happens to a tomboy after puberty?

As we will see in the coming chapters: It depends.

KATE

I was not an angel. The nuns told me so.

I grew up a strict Catholic in the 1950s in Paterson, New Jersey, and went to Catholic school. My mother was a homemaker, my father a school administrator, and they were fully doing the 1950s Ozzie and Harriet thing. But I wasn't. I was a tomboy. I was a butchy little girl.

My father was more accepting, but my mother was more cautious, worried, hoping I would be like my sister, studious and toeing the feminine party line, a nice Catholic girl.

But I played basketball every day after school, and sported a Davy Crockett hat and a holstered gun, and played with trains. I was a little daredevil. When my dad told me I couldn't take my bike to the beach because it wouldn't fit in the car, I took it apart myself, held the wheel on my lap, and put it all back together again when we got there. I didn't take no for an answer.

I didn't want to wear girls' hats, except at Easter, opting instead for a motorcycle hat or an admiral's hat. Sure, I had to wear the standard Catholic schoolgirl uniform, but outside of school, it was all jeans and sweatshirts and my favorite sweater, black-and-red striped with a crewneck collar, which I called my "beatnik sweater." Nobody said much about my clothes—it was the 1950s, and there were some tomboy styles around for kids. It was within the range of normal.

But some of my behavior fell outside that range.

In first grade, I adored my teacher, Sister Joan. But then the incident happened.

Every afternoon, the boys and girls would scoot out of their desks, the kind where the seat and the desktop are attached, to line up to go to the bathroom. One day, just before Christmas, the nuns told the girls to walk like "little angels, going to see Jesus" on their way. The boys were told to "walk like shepherds," which most of them interpreted as license to jump over their desks rather than step around them. And since I was always doing what the boys did, I grabbed the top of my desk and flung myself over it, too.

Sister Joan was not pleased.

"Kathleen," she said sternly. "Little angels going to see baby Jesus don't jump over the desk."

I was both humiliated and scared. Would I never see baby Jesus? Would Sister Joan reject me? Would I never be an angel now? Had I done something horribly, irrevocably wrong? I got a message loud and clear that little girls who want to be angels don't jump over their desks.

But it was also a moment of revelation, of the limits of tomboyism and the unfairness of the world, its unequal treatment, its lopsided rules. I was being chastised for doing a boyish thing, a tomboy thing, that the boys always did. I felt like I was being picked on.

I didn't extrapolate much from my behavior, or my preferred way of dressing, until after college, when one of my friends said, "Oh Kate, you dress so unisex." They kind of knew I was different, but I hadn't grown up around gay people, hardly knew what it was, or that it applied to me. Almost nobody was openly gay. There were no out gay characters on TV. So even if they knew I was different, they didn't think I was gay. I didn't know myself.

Chapter 11

I USED TO BE A TOMBOY. NOW I'M A FULL-GROWN LESBIAN.

"Many a parent feared that a Tomboy daughter might grow up
to be a Lesbian. Female gym teachers were always suspect."
—*Bitches, Bimbos and Ballbreakers: The Guerilla Girls'*
Illustrated Guide to Female Stereotypes[1]

In the beginning, it had nothing to do with sexuality. It was the 1970s,
and Karleen Pendleton Jiménez was growing up in a mostly Mexican
L.A. suburb, with no out gay people around, no gay role models on
TV—she only knew the word "gay" as an insult. "I didn't know any-
thing about the gay stuff," Jiménez, associate professor of education at
Trent University, told me. "I only knew about the gender stuff."

That is, Jiménez knew she was not acting like most of the other
little girls around her. She was strong and athletic, good at math
and not so into reading and writing, a soccer lover. To her sixth
birthday party, she invited only boys. She had short hair and wore
boys' clothes, except when her mother forced her to wear dresses
to visit family or go to Sunday school.

"It was unbelievable torture and we'd have these horrible fights," she said, but otherwise, her parents were pretty accepting. People asked her constantly if she was a boy or a girl, so much so that years later she would write a children's book called *Are You a Boy or a Girl?* and, later still, make an animated film, *Tomboy*, based on her experiences. "I couldn't do the girl thing—the feminine girl thing," Jiménez said.

That was all fine in elementary school. The word "tomboy" explained her behavior and her family filed it under normal. She had two older brothers who simultaneously took her under their wings and made fun of her. In the closed world of boys to which she had access, she heard how they disparaged girls and girliness and knew both that it wasn't for her, that she was "born masculine," as she put it, and that she had to distance herself from the feminine. "In my case it was quite biological, but then the part that is socialized was getting all that crap, that anti-girl stuff," she said.

Things got tougher in junior high, when she was, as a cruel joke, nominated queen of the dance, but for the most part, her classmates accepted her. She'd run with the same ragtag group of boys since first grade. She had her crew. She was okay.

Then Jiménez's mother got her into the high school on the other side of the tracks—the whiter, wealthier side—and life got harder. Not only did she come from the mostly Mexican town, but there, people had grown up with Jiménez's way of being, had understood it. In the new school, it was a liability.

At first, she tried fitting in, donning a pink sweater, wearing earrings, but it just felt wrong. She found respite in the marching band, where she could wear masculine uniforms, play the French horn, and hide out among the other misfits in the band room. Being masculine after puberty was a whole other ballgame, when the word "tomboy" no longer applied and when being feminine enough to secure male approval was what counted.

"I definitely felt like I was unattractive because I was 'like a guy' and guys wouldn't want me," she said. "I thought to be sexual you had to be with guys. It didn't occur to me that there was another option."

It wasn't until she went to college at Berkeley in the early nineties that Jiménez was even aware that lesbians existed, let alone that she was one. In fact, she was butch. The word once referred to a man's haircut and later to a lesbian with a masculine appearance, though it can mean different things to different people—like all things to do with gender, it's complicated, and fraught.[2] I've seen "tomboy" used to connote a lesbian who's not too butch but definitely not femme—which is used to mean "feminine-presenting lesbian" and refers to sexuality, not gender (or sexuality in addition to gender). But many tomboys-turned-queer folks I interviewed rejected that butch/femme binary in favor of gay, lesbian, queer, pansexual, and, as one former tomboy put it, "bisexual, but men are really disappointing."

The gradations of female sexuality, and the arguments around them, are well beyond the scope of this book. Suffice it to say that "butch" is not super in vogue today but was very much so when Jiménez was in college in the 1990s. The masculinity Jiménez had learned and practiced as a tomboy and had not relinquished at puberty, combined with her sexuality, conferred upon her a preferred status. "When you come out, oh my god, there's so many women that like you for looking like a guy," she said.

Gender identity and sexuality are not the same thing. Educators like to break it down this way: Sexuality is about whom you go to bed *with* and gender identity is about who you go to bed *as*. But research, and the experience of many, would show us that childhood gender-atypical behaviors *can* be precursors to homosexuality.

There must be some kind of connection, otherwise there wouldn't be so many T-shirts emblazoned with the phrase "I Was Once a Tomboy, Now I'm a Full-Grown Lesbian."

Secret Loves of the 1800s

Most tomboy literary and cinematic tales assure us that even if the protagonist is sporty or defiant after puberty, she's plenty heterosexual. Tomboys from Jo March to Jesminder Bhamra in *Bend It Like Beckham* are "tamed," their stories tied up with the love of a man.

Tomboyism was promoted in the nineteenth century partly because it was expected to relent at puberty, when, in the theory of that time, sexuality began. But Victorians had some fairly scandalous ideas about love among their strict, gendered mores. After all, Louisa May Alcott may have become famous for writing *Little Women*, changing the way we see girls and girlhood and tomboyism forever, but until its publication she made her living writing sensationalist crime fiction with titles like *Pauline's Passion and Punishment*.

Still, many men in that era thought women had little sexual appetite, and proper girls were expected to remain virgins until married. As a doctor named William Acton wrote in an 1857

British medical textbook, "the majority of women (happily for them) are not very much troubled by sexual feelings of any kind."[3]

Au contraire. One result of the era's separate spheres philosophy was that women spent a lot of time alone together, allowing deep feelings to develop. Women were exchanging rings and vows, leaving one another property, having sexual relationships, making jewelry out of one another's hair.[4] Passionate love between women was plenty common.

Suffragist and temperance leader Frances Willard, who cut her hair short, championed her tomboy identity, and called herself Frank, reported just such passionate love for her best friend Mary Bannister (who would go on to marry Willard's brother). Once-tomboys like Harriet Goodhue Hosmer, known as the first professional female sculptor, or the great actress Charlotte Saunders Cushman, known for playing both male and female roles, lived openly with same-sex partners. Alcott herself once said, "I have fallen in love with so many pretty girls and never once the least bit with any man."[5]

These women likely didn't identify as lesbians, since the word was hardly in use at the time, and since that kind of social identity—lesbian as a human classification—was not yet common. Remember that sex (as in bodies), gender, and sexuality were largely still thought of as one intertwined thing then; the end of the century was the beginning of unraveling them. Thus, people began to link gendered behaviors to sexuality more than they had before,[6] while recognizing that some women might cross-dress to gain power or access, or to disguise themselves as men so that they could maintain relationships with women.

For early sexologists, homosexuality had as much to do with atypical gender behavior as it did sexual attraction. Freud saw attraction to women as a masculine trait, so lesbians had a masculine psychology.[7] At the end of the century, Havelock Ellis published the first English medical textbook on homosexuals. He called them "inverts"—males with feminine gender traits or females with masculine gender traits; his book was titled *Sexual Inversion*. Female inverts had a "dislike and sometimes incapacity for needlework and other domestic occupations, while there is often some capacity for athletics." Thus, the first inkling of the lesbian/gym teacher stereotype. Male inverts never married or never smoked, and were "entirely averse to outdoor games." Karl Heinrich Ulrichs, a nineteenth-century sexologist and supporter of gay rights, called such people—men born with women's spirits, women born with men's—third sexes.[8]

Another late nineteenth-century sexologist, Richard von Krafft-Ebing, believed that "inverts" contained the soul of the opposite sex—that is, in fact, how Alcott described herself, as having a "man's soul," because of her love of women. Many female inverts had been tomboys, and though Krafft-Ebing didn't propose that tomboyism caused sexual inversion, he noted a correlation.[9]

Tying Tomboyism to Lesbianism

As these connections were being dissected, the rise of mass media and the philosophies of popular psychologists, sexologists, and psychiatrists married childhood experiences to adult sexuality. While deeply problematic, and often sexist and homophobic, their theories acknowledged women's sexuality, despite often categorizing lesbianism as aberrant.

The connection between tomboyism and lesbianism became stronger in the twentieth century. According to Ohio State literature professor Michelle Abate, the emerging lesbian and gay rights movements of the mid-twentieth century, and Alfred Kinsey's 1948 bestseller *Sexual Behavior in the Human Male*, which showed that homosexuality was not so uncommon after all, led to the rise of lesbian pulp fiction. Such books linked tomboyish behaviors with sexuality—even amid the outright bigotry, intolerance, and sexual repression of the mid-century.[10] In 1952, the first *Diagnostic and Statistical Manual of Mental Disorders*—a sort of bible for mental health professionals—listed homosexuality as a "sociopathic personality disturbance," yet at the same time, the gay liberation movement grew.[11]

These pulp paperbacks, with titles like *Odd Girl Out* and *Stranger on Lesbos*, were somehow both subversive and popular, and full of characters who made the tomboy-lesbian connection explicit. "Any female character who was even remotely tomboyish was also, ultimately, a lesbian," wrote Abate in her book *Tomboys: A Literary and Cultural History*.[12] In mainstream literature, tomboys were still depicted as innocent, and acceptable, children. In their underground pulp depictions, tomboys were disordered, but alluring, butch women. A connection between gendered childhood behavior and adult sexuality was sowed, but it was also a *reconnection*: The word "tomboy" had, soon after it was coined in the sixteenth century, meant a lascivious woman with a male-like sexuality.

That tomboy-lesbian stereotype isn't universal. Childhood tomboys, unlike feminine boys who are often seen as proto-gay, aren't always assumed to be lesbians, perhaps because girls are allowed and encouraged to behave boyishly far more often than boys are allowed and encouraged to be girlish. But by the twentieth century's end, with the rise of LGBTQ+ activism and a rash of lesbian indie movies, most people knew of the tomboy-lesbian stereotype—and that it's also often a truism, backed up by research.

Some studies found that anywhere between two-thirds and three-quarters of lesbians reported having been tomboys in grade school, compared to between a fifth and a third of heterosexual women.[13] Retrospective studies can be problematic because, as Proust reminds us, "Remembrance of things past is not necessarily the remembrance of things as they were." But there are many famous examples of childhood tomboys who grew up and came out: Kristy McNichol. Jodie Foster. Hannah Gadsby.[14] Anne Lister, often described as the "first modern lesbian" and subject of HBO's *Gentleman Jack*, described herself as an "unmanageable tomboy" growing up.[15] Cultural anthropologist Esther Newton, a pioneering founder of queer studies, told me, "I was a tomboy from as far back as I can remember. That was an issue for me before my sexuality was really settled."

Studies from the late 1990s and early 2000s (when the butch/femme binary was more common and easier to study) asserted that butch women showed more gender atypical childhood behavior (aka tomboyism) than women who were more femme. They tended to figure out their lesbian sexual orientation earlier than more femme women—in their teens instead of their early twenties, on average—and come out earlier. Their tomboyism, their masculinity, as the world insists on calling it, was always with them, early and consistently, and, in retrospect, felt like a preview of who they would become.[16] Even if the pink/blue divide was largely a social construct, they had always stuck to the blue side. It was simultaneously an illusion and an organizing principle of their lives.

The word "tomboy" is so enmeshed with lesbianism now that it has come to define a kind of butch lesbian throughout Asia—though in some cases it refers to a trans man, too, showing the fuzziness of those boundaries. (Some people claim butch as a gender identity all its own.) There are websites and even beauty and talent contests dedicated to Asian tomboys, with thousands of adoring fans, and dozens of Facebook groups. A Tumblr site called *BUTCH. TOMBOY. BUTCH. TOMBOY. LESBIAN* shows how, to some, the words are interchangeable.

One participant in sociologist C. Lynn Carr's 2007 study of tomboys outlined a natural progression: tomboy, jock, lesbian, butch—it's one of the people a girl might become if her tomboy ways don't recede. "You don't call a 25-year-old a tomboy," the participant said. "You call her a lesbian or a dyke."[17]

"Nobody was surprised I was gay," said Laurel, a twenty-eight-year-old middle school humanities teacher who identifies as a butch lesbian. She wore athletic gear for her whole childhood. She had some female friends but a big group of guy friends. "When I came out, my dad said, 'I've known since you were three.'" Laurel, who coaches middle school sports (pretty close to the lesbian gym teacher trope), is the walking embodiment, she said, of "old school lesbian stereotypes."

Tomboys Like Him Are Different

Lesbian tomboys may, in some cases, have fundamentally different experiences than heterosexual tomboys. Jack Halberstam, who has at various times identified as "queer, lesbian, dyke, butch, transgender, stone, and transgender butch,"[18] suggested that some traditional tomboys with ponytails and scraped knees are pre-straight. "There were girl-girls who wanted to play sports and be a bit more active in the world, but they were all heterosexual," he said.

Tomboys like him are different: pre-LGBTQ+. They may not feel the urge, either to become feminine (though of course there are feminine lesbians) or to win the favor of boys, to become some kind of sexual object.

Halberstam was conjuring the two types of tomboy idea, marking a line between cisgender-heterosexual tomboys and transgender-homosexual tomboys. Remember that when sociologist C. Lynn Carr studied tomboys, she found they tended to divide along two lines. There was plenty of overlap, but there were those who were primarily "choosing masculinity" versus those who were both "choosing masculinity" *and* "rejecting femininity."

The latter category distanced themselves from everything to do with being female and feminine. They hated dresses and pink but also expressed distaste for feminine gender roles and the stereotypical need for male protection. According to Carr's work, these girls *were* more likely to be lesbian or bisexual than those former tomboys whose primary association had been with reaping the benefits of the boy side of the line: being proud of how fast they could run or how far they could jump, being treated as "one of the guys," and so on.

Jiménez was on the rejecting femininity side of the spectrum. "Anything that was girl, I wasn't going to do," she told me. She had heard her brother's relentless unkindness toward girls, his misogyny, which, she realized later, she had internalized. "Girls seemed like nasty things that people would hurt and make fun of and just try to use up, and it just seemed really awful," she said. The sexism that six-year-old girls start internalizing as they strip off their PFD in favor of pants can mutate into different shapes as girls age.

All of that affected Jiménez because no matter how masculine she was, she was in a female body—she was guilty by association. "I was with the boys and I knew what the boys thought of the girls and I didn't want to be a girl because that's what they thought of the girls, but I kind of knew I was, too," she told me. She laughed. "It'll be a lifelong thing of trying to sort that out."

This raises a host of bigger questions about masculinity: Does it depend somehow on disparaging the feminine? Does proto-lesbian tomboyism, in these cases, set girls on the same path as heterosexual, cisgender boys who are taught to reject everything from pink sparkles to the idea that women have scientific minds, yet still be attracted to women later? Does being socialized with boys, or in some basic sense drawn to be with them and do what they do, connect to later sexuality? And do tomboys learn to devalue the feminine during this process?

Some tomboys continued to reject pink and dresses in adulthood, maintaining their masculine tomboy behavior and appearance but no longer rejecting women. It's just that we live in a world that doesn't promote and support female masculinity, so being a masculine woman, butch, a grown-up tomboy, whatever you want to call it, is harder and rarer than being a prepubescent tomboy. It's harder to feel you're doing gender right. Jiménez told me that she spent so much time navigating gender as a kid, correcting the pronouns people used and their misgendering, that now she's indifferent to what pronouns people use for her. "It's like, what do you see?" she said. "If you see she, good on you. If you see he, good on you." Though she knows that for many people misgendering is deeply painful, she went through that pain as a tomboy child already. She's comfortable now.

For Laurel, cutting off her long ponytail in her twenties—the thing that revealed to the world that she was assigned female at birth—and getting a haircut she describes as "what a Republican senator would have," is what made her feel that she'd gotten not just her sexuality right but her gender right. It made everything in her life more complicated to have a masculine presentation, a female body, and a butch lesbian sexual orientation. It confused the world, which wanted to fit her neatly into a box. But it also had so many advantages, especially in communing with her students. "I have a sense of what it feels like to exist outside of certain social pressures, or what it's like to be different," she said.

For Jiménez, being a butch lesbian and being a tomboy "came from the same place. I felt like, when I came out, I had returned to being that kid," she said. "In terms of gender, that I could just be a tomboy now. That was more honest and true to who I was."

ALEX

I grew up in rural Maine, where even the girly-girls with long hair and earrings drove their family's backhoes on the weekend; that kind of behavior was perfectly acceptable for non-tomboys, too.

Nobody thought ill of my love of sports and my insistence on wearing boys' clothes or short hair. Older women would say, kind of wistfully to me, "When I was your age, I was a tomboy, too." And they would sort of express it as "That was a time in my life where I was free."

"Tomboy" was a positive word, both for me and those around me, but it was also a way to make sense of how I was different, even from the other backhoe-driving girls. I hated to wear dresses because I was a tomboy and I would never wear makeup because I was a tomboy and my best friends were boys because I was a tomboy and it let me say, *Ick, I would never do that*. It gave me permission to do or not do certain things. I felt a lot of validation because of that word.

But there were clues that my gender was more complicated than "just a tomboy." In third grade, a new boy at school asked me if I was a boy or a girl. Before I could even think I answered, "I'm a boy." In that moment, I realized, "Oh my god, I just said I was a boy because I am, I think I am, and I let the truth slip out." But I kept that truth inside, not being able to name it or understand what it was, and it sat there, germinating inside the label of tomboy.

In sixth grade, my teacher brought k.d. lang's *Absolute Torch and Twang* to school. On the cover, k.d. lang stands proudly, looking into the distance with a wheat field behind her, a cowboy hat in her hand, a leather jacket over a jean jacket, her short hair blowing in the wind. The teacher said to the class, "I think I found a picture of a girl who looks more like a boy than Alice does." (I don't mind people knowing my birth name.) I stared at that cover and thought, *I can grow up and look like this person. It's possible.*

k.d. lang, a butch lesbian icon, was the first adult version of tomboy that I came across—not someone who was tough or sporty, necessarily, but she looked like a boy. That's what I wanted.

Except, I wanted more than to look like a boy. I *was* a boy. But it took me a while to understand. "Lesbian" was the first word I found. That was the best I could do at the time. That was the best way to explain myself. If I could have lived as a butch lesbian, I would have been delighted to do that. I have tons of friends who are super butch and, in some ways, I envy their identity. It seems so cool to me but that's not who I am. You know, I'm a trans masculine person. I'm a trans guy.

I finally figured that out in college, when I became Harvard's first out transgender student in 1996. Now I give lectures around the world about gender and I've written two novels, *Revolutionary* and *Continental Divide*, both featuring transgender characters.

Chapter 12

WAR OF THE WORDS: TOMBOY OR TRANS BOY?

"That's the surprise. I'm a girl. But now I'm a boy too and I can do anything and anything and anything."

—*Ernest Hemingway*, The Garden of Eden[1]

In 2017, after I wrote an op-ed for the *New York Times* about adults in my child's life assuming, sometimes insisting, she was trans—and how I will support her if she is—there was a lot of pushback on social media and in the press. Or, in millennial-speak: I was canceled, called a transphobe, a cisnormative ass, and a child abuser. As a supporter of trans rights, I was mortified but also inspired to talk to some of my critics and learn what they thought I'd gotten wrong.

Some of the kerfuffle was based on an essay I had written four years before the *Times* piece for *Parenting* magazine, about my conflicting feelings around having a daughter who dared to be different (even though she wasn't different on purpose; she was following her own lead, and we were facilitating it). I wrote that she expressed in subtle and direct ways a desire to be a boy, but that wasn't true, either. At the time I was fully buying the pink/ blue divide, and interpreting a request for short hair and blazers as a desire to leave girlhood behind. In the piece I wrote, "Dressing like a boy? Cool. Thinking you actually *are* a boy? Way more complicated." It was published as "My Daughter Wants to Be a Boy!" though that was a misrepresentation of the piece.[2] Writers don't choose their own headlines. In actuality, the piece was about my philosophical struggles with nonconformity, even though I come from a long line of nonconformists: Wanting her to be exceptional but fit in. Wanting her to not need approval, but be able to get it. This piece, uploaded without being edited on the day the magazine closed, caused no upset at the time.

I didn't give it another thought until after the *New York Times* published my op-ed, with yet another attention-grabbing but misleading headline: "My Daughter Is Not Transgender. She's a Tomboy." For one thing, *I* didn't call her a tomboy. I called her a girl, which is what she called herself—though at the time I hadn't presented her with other options. I acknowledged that someday she might identify as trans, but my point was that in our zeal to affirm trans kids, we might be confusing cisgender girls with stereotypically masculine interests with those who needed to transition, socially or medically—and in the process telling them that they're not actually girls, and thus narrowing that category.

In the uproar that followed, I found myself in the middle of a war I hadn't known existed: a war that was about both language and being, about who was a tomboy and who was trans, and what those words mean. While the piece expressed full support of trans kids, to many, the op-ed smacked of transphobia and ignorance.

Critics pointed to the title of the *Parenting* piece as proof that in fact I had a son and that if I didn't transition him, he'd kill himself. They said I blamed adults' narrow views of gender on the increasing visibility and acceptance of trans people.

About that last part they were partly right: I have since learned, after two years of study, that conflating a young child's desire for a haircut or a football with gender identity was very much the fallout from hyper-gendering childhood.

A widely read opposition piece by an ACLU lawyer named Chase Strangio, whose perspective was that of "a white, transmasculine person who identifies outside the gender binary," homed in on my assertion that my daughter was not gender nonconforming but gender *role* nonconforming. "She does not fit into the mold that we adults…still impose upon our children," I wrote, suggesting that we didn't need a separate category for such girls, just because they're not acting how we expected them to, based on their body parts.

Strangio wrote in response, "What is the difference? What is gender if not the role and behaviors that we ascribe to it?"[3] He asserted that I had a fundamental misunderstanding of gender, and gender nonconforming, and of what it meant to be trans.

He was right. I didn't understand any of those words, especially not as he did. So I set out to do so.

Decoding "Gender Nonconforming"

First, I looked into Strangio's assertion that there was no difference between "gender *role* nonconforming" and "gender nonconforming," or GNC. To me, gender role nonconforming had meant not living up to society's stifling sex-based expectations, and thus not a condition requiring a separate category but rather what all humans should aspire to.

But most of the definitions I read categorized GNC as a broad adjective describing anybody who doesn't hew to societal expectations based on assigned sex, or who exhibits behavioral, cultural, or psychological traits commonly associated with another gender. Columbia University sociologist Tey Meadow, author of *Trans Kids: Being Gendered in the Twenty-First Century*, told me that GNC people don't necessarily socially transition, but are "doing what people around them read as inconsistent with their gender category." That's what tomboys do—they don't act the way society dictates that girls should act, ignoring the line that adults make between boy and girl stuff. "Tomboy" may be an unpopular term now, but GNC is increasingly popular as a term of self-identification—and unlike tomboy, it can include anyone of any gender, doing gender in all kinds of ways. According to University of New Hampshire's "Bias-Free Language Guide," the word tomboy is "problematic/outdated," and should be replaced by "Children who are gender nonconforming, Children who are gender variant."

Teacher and author Alex Myers, who is transgender, works with teenagers at a private school in New Hampshire. There, he sees "gender nonconforming female-bodied individuals who were raised as girls," he said, "but there's nothing about them that's particularly masculine. There's nothing about them that would ever make you say they're a tomboy. They're not athletic. They're not even particularly masculine-looking and they really don't want he/him/his as pronouns, they use they/them/theirs. But really what they feel is: *I'm not a girl. I don't want to be a young woman. That's not for me.*"

These kids are proud to be gender nonconforming. It's not some kind of scarlet letter slapped on them, or a diagnosis, but a declaration of leaving the restrictive pink/blue divide behind. "I don't see gender nonconformity as necessarily implying either transgender or tomboyishness," Myers said. "I see kids occupying that as a different category now that wasn't available because that term and that category just didn't exist in my adolescence." That is, the resistance I felt to the term is a by-product of being raised in a tomboy heyday and as a member of an older generation; to many people today, tomboy and GNC functionally mean the same thing.

The Many Meanings of Trans

In theory, gender nonconformity refers to behaviors, as tomboy does, and trans is about identity: having a gender identity that differs from the one associated with sex assigned at birth; it's about one's internal sense of self as a man or a woman or neither or both. Meadow put it to me this way: "There's a difference between having a core gender identity that is trans and then doing or saying or being in the world in some way that is inconsistent with what people think your gender category is."

Strangio explained to me that trans and gender nonconforming can be synonymous, but they aren't always. "You can identify as trans and physically transition all the way to the other side of the gender binary, and be a very gender conforming trans person," he said. That is, you may comply with gender norms after transition, sticking faithfully to the opposite side of the pink/blue divide. Or you can be trans and identify anywhere in between the binaries, and/or not physically transition at all. You can identify as transgender and have no distress, no need for hormones or surgery, no sense of "being trapped in the wrong body" as it's often described in the mass media, but is not everyone's experience.

"You can still be trans even if you're fine with your body," Diane Ehrensaft, director of Mental Health at UCSF's Child and Adolescent Gender Center, told me. "Trans is not about body. It's about gender identity." Some people change nothing about their bodies. Others "go through radical transformations in the body. And all of those people count for trans," she said. There is an enormous diversity of trans experiences and identities.

To Strangio, the terms "trans" and "transgender" mean the same thing, but that's not always the case. Kate Bornstein, the author of numerous books including *Gender Outlaw* and *A Queer and Pleasant Danger*, and who identifies as transgender, told me that "transgender," among people of her generation—she was sixty-nine when I talked to her in 2017—was "an umbrella term for anybody who was messing around with gender." This included people who called themselves "transvestites, cross-dressers, butch women, sissy men, chicks with dicks, she-males…and what we were calling transsexuals: people who were assigned male at birth, transitioning to female, or assigned female at birth and transitioning to male." That is, transsexual was about changing sex, the physicality of gender. And transgender was about everything else, the gender role, the social construction of gender.

She stopped to say that people frown on her using the word "umbrella."

"Why?" I asked.

"As if it was a protection," she said. Now the word is "inclusive." "I get it. Okay, inclusive, language changes."

In this vernacular, trans means what transgender once did, including behaviors, physical characteristics, and identities, and transgender means what transsexual once did, pertaining to bodies and binaries. Transsexual is now usually considered offensive—perhaps because it originated in the medical and psychological communities that historically preyed upon and mistreated trans and GNC people (more on that below), or because it medicalizes the experience of being trans, which is much broader than just making physical changes.

But there's little consensus about language, even among many people steeped in it. The World Professional Association for Transgender Health (WPATH), a nonprofit devoted to transgender health, defines "Transsexual" as a noun meaning "individuals who seek to change or have changed their primary and/or secondary sex characteristics through feminizing or masculinizing medical interventions (hormones and/or surgery), typically accompanied by a permanent change in gender role." Transsexual is still commonly used in medical literature. WPATH says transgender is an adjective for "a diverse group of individuals who cross or transcend culturally defined categories of gender. The gender identity of transgender people differs to varying degrees from the sex they were assigned at birth."[4]

Susan Stryker, a professor and author and who indentifies as trans, defined transgender in her book *Transgender History* as: "People who move away from the gender they were assigned at birth, people who cross over (trans-) the boundaries constructed by their culture to define and contain their gender."[5] That's GNC *and* trans *and* non-binary (see chapter 13) *and* tomboy.

Tomboy? Trans Boy? GNC?

Because tomboy, GNC, and trans *can* all mean the same thing, or manifest the same way in a human being, it's hard to distinguish between who is crossing societal gender boundaries, and needs the space to be different/themselves, and who needs medical or mental health care. Gender identity and gendered *behavior* aren't the same thing, even if they can and often do overlap. As psychologist Sheri Berenbaum told me, "Identity is not synonymous with our external manifestations of gendered characteristics. A girl can engage in sports and boy-typical activity. She can dress in overalls and she can have her hair cut short and she can still say 'I'm a girl.'"

Perhaps because these definitions are so overlapping and amorphous, there is confusion, and fighting, about who is gender nonconforming, who is a tomboy, who is trans, and who is some combination. Some of that confusion, I believe, has to do with tomboys not being common characters for an entire generation overtaken by Girl Power girls. So some people assume that any women or girls dressing as or acting like men or boys, looking masculine in the past or doing so now, were or are trans. Many articles posit that famous tomboy figures, real and fictional, were actually trans, from Anybodys in *West Side Story* to Louisa May Alcott, who once said, as mentioned earlier, "I am more than half-persuaded that I am a man's soul, put by some freak of nature into a woman's body."

That absolutely could be—Jos March and Polniaczek, Amelia

Earhart and Joan of Arc, might well have chosen Mx or Mr. over Ms. (or Miss or Mrs.) and identified any number of ways other than as women. But Alcott said that because she had fallen in love with many women, and she lived in a time when gender identity, sexuality, and sex assigned at birth were not separated in people's minds. So we can't know.

The point is, the retroactive imposition of transgender identities on famous tomboys, the rewriting—or righting—of history is one facet of the culture war. On the opposite side is another facet: adult cisgender women claiming too many "just tomboys" are being "transed"—convinced that they need to transition and receive treatment.

Yet another facet is trans boys being told that they *don't* have gender dysphoria, or are not really trans. They're told they don't need hormones or surgery or new names or pronouns, and their experiences are questioned or denied or discredited because they are "just tomboys." Fights break out on social media when an adult cisgender former tomboy declares that she would have met the criteria for gender dysphoria in adolescence—that she would have come out as or been told she was trans had such words been available—but has since grown out of it. Therefore, other tomboys certain that they are trans will, too. In this way, the word "tomboy" gets weaponized against young trans boys.

Jack Halberstam, author of *Female Masculinity*, was called a tomboy and begrudgingly accepted it. "Tomboy was not necessarily a word that I was super happy with because I definitely just wanted to be a boy," he said. When people called him a tomboy, they were setting boundaries, telling Halberstam he shouldn't cross them. He could play soccer, but not for the school, which didn't have a girls' team. He could wear shorts, but not to proper events. "The tomboy category at the end of the day was being used to discipline me, not to encourage me." And it allowed people to not see who he really was. As he once wrote, "If I had known the term 'transgender' when I was a teenager in the 1970s, I am sure I would have grabbed hold of it like a life jacket on rough seas."[6]

But if trans and GNC can be separate, and cover different territory—core identity versus behavior—"TGNC care" is a common term, lumping together transgender and GNC for medical and mental health care. This includes people who need the full checklist of medical interventions, like hormones and surgeries, and those who require none. So many parents try to figure out if there is a dividing line between the T and the GNC, and where their kids fall. Thus, the plethora of articles asking some version of "Is being a tomboy the same as being transgender?" as a 2010 Planned Parenthood article did. (Short answer: no, though it can be.)

Quora is full of posts asking versions of the same thing.

- "How do you know if you are transgender or a tomboy?"
- "Am I actually trans or just a tomboy?"
- "Were all trans men tomboys?"
- "Am I androgynous, genderqueer, or just a tomboy?"
- "Can someone be a trans woman and a tomboy?"
- "I'm a girl who is a tomboy. Are there any signs of being trans?"
- "What is the difference between a tomboy and a trans female?"
- "Am I a tomboy with a girl streak or something more like genderfluid?"

Ehrensaft has fielded many versions of these questions. Sometimes the answers are clear—or clear-ish. Sometimes the kid is saying, " 'Look, I'm fine with who I am in terms of whatever label I got right after birth, but I do not like your rules for gender here. I want merely the freedom to do it differently,' " she said.

Other times, children are expressing a core gender identity that doesn't align with their sex assigned at birth, and sometimes that causes extreme distress. One thing that stood out between the cisgender, heterosexual tomboys and those who identified somewhere on the LGBTQ+ spectrum was the extreme discomfort some in the latter group felt at being forced to present as a girl (though the cisgender tomboys definitely weren't psyched about it).

The criteria for gender dysphoria include "significant distress or impairment in function" or "insistence that one is the other gender."[7] How you dress or whom or what you play with—that stuff alone doesn't add up to gender dysphoria. But there is a long and complicated history of that diagnosis, and what gets categorized as normal and abnormal, variant versus deviant. The medical and psychiatric establishment pathologized not only transgender identities but gender nonconformity, for years.

A Brief History of GID and GD

Psychiatrists and psychologists use the *Diagnostic Statistical Manual*, known as the *DSM*, to classify and diagnose mental disorders. In the 1960s, transvestitism—sexual arousal from cross-dressing—and homosexuality were listed under "sexual deviations" in the *DSM-II*, along with pedophilia and exhibitionism. Each of those was seen as similarly disordered, ills that needed treating.[8] The psychiatrists and psychologists who wrote the *DSM* failed to realize that not every man who wears women's clothes does so for sexual pleasure. And even if they did, what makes that *disordered*? Somehow the sexual revolution didn't reach those hallowed halls.

Homosexuality was removed from the *DSM* in 1973—now a difference, not a disorder, thanks in part to activism after the 1969 Stonewall riots and a growing body of research that showed gay people weren't psychologically disturbed, and that homosexuality was common. Obviously, the entire country didn't get on board—homophobia is pervasive, and we continue the homophobic practice of not dressing boys in pink, communicating that they should be masculine, cisgender, and straight. But it was huge progress.

Then in 1980 a category called "gender identity disorder" was added to the *DSM-III*, which included three diagnoses: gender identity disorder of childhood (GIDC); transsexualism (for adolescents and adults); and psychosexual disorder not elsewhere classified.[9] The latter category caught all the "residual" people with "psychological disturbances not covered by any of the other specific categories in the diagnostic class of Psychosexual Disorders." An example: a person with "marked feelings of inadequacy related to self-imposed standards of masculinity or femininity." In other words: feeling like you're doing gender wrong. Is that a psychological disturbance or the nature of existence in a world powered by outdated and oppressive gender roles?

GIDC's criteria were slightly different for boys and girls,

presumably because we have different expectations of normalcy. For female children, they included:

A. Strongly and persistently stated desire to be a boy, or insistence that she is a boy (not merely a desire for any perceived cultural advantages from being a boy)

B. Persistent repudiation of female anatomic structures, as manifested by at least one of the following repeated assertions

    1. that she will grow up to become a man (not merely in role)

    2. that she is biologically unable to become pregnant

    3. that she will not develop breasts

    4. that she has no vagina

    5. that she has, or will grow, a penis

C. Onset of the disturbance before puberty

For boys:

A. Strongly and persistently stated desire to be a girl, or insistence that he is a girl

B. Either (1) or (2)

    1. Persistent repudiation of male anatomic structures, as manifested by at least one of the following repeated assertions

        a. that he will grow up to become a woman (not merely in role)

        b. that his penis and testes are disgusting or will disappear

        c. that it would be better not to have a penis or testes

2. Preoccupation with female stereotypical activities as manifested by a preference for either cross-dressing or simulating female attire, or by a compelling desire to participate in the games and pastimes of girls

C. Onset of the disturbance before puberty

Note the major differences: First, there's an assumption that there are no cultural advantages to being a girl—a boy would never *want* to be a girl unless he were disordered, whereas a girl might want to be a boy because there was good stuff on the blue side of the pink/blue divide. And it was categorized as a disturbance, even if only the adults with narrow ideas of gender normalcy were the ones who were disturbed.

Second, boys could either repudiate their anatomy *or* be preoccupied by "female stereotypical activities." Playing with girls or dolls was given as much weight as wanting to have a penis removed or insisting that one was a girl. In theory, girls could still be tomboys, or masculine, but feminine boys had a "disorder," which required treating, whether they felt themselves to be girls, whether they were in distress, or not. We largely invented this pink/blue divide and then diagnosed as disordered and disturbed those who crossed it.

Some researchers over the years dismissed "androgynous tomboyism" as a normal variant of the "feminine role," and diagnosed "masculine tomboyism" as gender identity disorder—they were breaking down girls into some version of "always" and "sometimes" tomboys, and the always tomboys were problematic, even pathological, and the sometimes tomboys were fine.[10]

Some psychologists and psychiatrists thought that life would be so hard for feminine boys and masculine girls whom they saw as future transsexuals, as they were then called, that it would be better to try to "correct" their trajectories or cure them, so they could lead happier lives with typical psychosexual development. At a loss to change the culture, to make it more accepting of non-conformity, they tried to make, or "help," children conform, run interference in childhood to cut the "illness" of being differently gendered off at the pass. This is now known as conversion therapy and is illegal in eighteen states and the District of Columbia. Because some childhood gender atypical behaviors can be precursors to homosexuality, critics asserted that the mental health establishment had found another way to pathologize being gay: GID was seen as "a backdoor maneuver to replace homosexuality" in the DSM.[11]

In 1987, concurrent with the onset of hyper-gendered childhoods and the receding of tomboys in the media, the *DSM-III* was updated to the *DSM-III-R*, and added to the criteria for GIDC in girls was "persistent marked aversion to normative feminine clothing and insistence on wearing stereotypical masculine clothing, e.g., boys' underwear and other accessories." Boys' behavior alone could still qualify them, but a girl not wanting to wear dresses or wanting to wear boys' underwear was now among the criteria.

The revision included "persistent and intense distress" about either being a boy or a girl, so dysphoria became part of the diagnosis. Kids couldn't just be treated for being tomboys and sissies, for behavior that made parents or schools or society uncomfortable; their own discomfort was key.

GIDC was added to and altered, objected to by people who asserted that their proclivities and senses of selves, their behaviors and identities, were not disorders. Forms, not failures. Variations, not deviations, just as was the case for gay and lesbian people.

Phyllis Burke's 1997 book *Gender Shock* gives gruesome details of many of the boys, and occasionally girls, who were diagnosed with GIDC and shamed for their inclinations, by way of "treatment." Some of the men, and sometimes women, who worked for decades on these diagnostic criteria were homophobic; a prominent proponent and practitioner of the diagnosis, antigay activist Dr. George Rekers, was discovered in 2010 to have traveled with a male escort from Rentboy.com, so he may have been gay and suffering from internalized homophobia, and perhaps victimizing others because of it.[12] In the name of GIDC, mental health professionals experimented on children with gender-atypical behavior. They started from the presumption that there was something either morally or psychically wrong about being gay or an effeminate boy or a masculine girl or transgender, even though many of these kids didn't need treatment, but rather support and freedom. The kids' suffering came mostly from parents wanting them to change and society not accepting them, from being bullied, rejected, humiliated. At least several times there were disastrous results; Rekers's former patient, Kirk Murphy, committed suicide, which his family attributed to Rekers's "sissy boy experiments."[13]

Finally, in 2013, GID was changed to "gender dysphoria" in the *DSM-5*: "significant distress and/or problems functioning associated with this conflict between the way they feel and think of themselves (referred to as experienced or expressed gender) and their physical or assigned gender," per the American Psychiatric Association.[14] This was a huge win for trans, non-binary, and gender nonconforming people. Maintaining a listing in the *DSM* meant continued medical care for those who needed a diagnosis to access treatment like hormones or surgeries, but with less stigma. "Replacing 'disorder' with 'dysphoria' in the diagnostic label is not only more appropriate and consistent with familiar clinical sexology terminology, it also removes the connotation that the patient is 'disordered,'" the APA explained.[15]

In addition, gender dysphoria was no longer housed in the *DSM-5* under Sexual Dysfunctions and Paraphilic Disorders ("transvestic disorder" is still there, along with pedophilia and exhibitionism, though consenting and non-consenting behaviors are divided into two sections). The dysphoria is what's tended to, not the behaviors themselves, not the identities. Rather than try to "treat" kids so they move away from being trans, the mental health community has largely moved toward supporting them, normalizing them, facilitating transition, in what's now called "gender affirming" treatment. Not a disorder. Just a difference.

Tomboy Versus Trans Boy Fights

Curiously, gendered behaviors are *still* listed in the criteria for Gender Dysphoria, which include:

1. A strong desire to be of the other gender or an insistence that one is the other gender
2. A strong preference for wearing clothes typical of the opposite gender
3. A strong preference for cross-gender roles in make-believe play or fantasy play

4. A strong preference for the toys, games or activities stereo-typically used or engaged in by the other gender
5. A strong preference for playmates of the other gender
6. A strong rejection of toys, games and activities typical of one's assigned gender
7. A strong dislike of one's sexual anatomy
8. A strong desire for the physical sex characteristics that match one's experienced gender

Everything but 7 and 8 are quite common for tomboys and/or gender nonconforming people. Even "a strong desire to be of the other gender" is common, so it's easy to see why there is still confusion. Many cisgender tomboys I talked to *did* want to be boys at some point during their childhoods. Some said they ached to until age four, or wanted to in an abstract way. Some craved "the perks of masculinity" like going topless or nabbing a spot on the baseball team, which used to have quotas for how many girls could play.

Remember that psychologist Randi Ettner found that those childhood tomboys who stated they *were* boys were far more likely to transition than those who stated they *wanted to* be a boy. Now that's an option, one those assigned female at birth increasingly go for: England's National Health Service reported in 2017 that twice as many girls as boys were seeking gender identity treatment, a complete swap from ten years earlier.[16] (One article attributed the shift to tomboyish characters like Katniss Everdeen from *The Hunger Games*, Tris Prior from *Divergent*, and Eleven from *Stranger Things*, gutting my argument about the retreat of tomboys in the media—but even if it were true that such tomboy characters were coming back, that should teach girls that they can be masculine and female, not that they need to transition to be tough.[17])

We've arrived at this cultural moment, in which trans kids are finally starting to be accepted, at least in the more progressive corners of the country. It's a beautiful moment of widening our range of normal, increasing acceptance of people who have historically been abused and marginalized, giving them the recognition, care, and protection they deserve. But the moment is also confusing for some parents who are uncertain about what is gender behavior and what is gender identity, since there is so much overlap, about who needs treatment and transition and who just needs less pressure to do gender a particular way. They want to know what's going on with their kids, and how best to help them.

When boys want to wear dresses or play with girls or be princesses, people ask Ehrensaft, "What's wrong with that little boy? And before trans it was *He must be gay*," she said. Now she gets more of "*Oh that's a trans girl*. And all we know is it's a boy in a dress." Some parents tell trans boys that they are "just tomboys," but she's also seen adults jump to the conclusion that a football-playing girl is a trans boy. Many parents have written to me wondering if their daughters are trans or need to socially or medically transition because the kids asked for short hair or chose swim trunks from the boys' section of the Gap. "How do you know?" Ehrensaft asks such parents. "You just saw a girl who wants to wear a football uniform."

Yes—how do you know?

In some cases, it's fairly clear. If your kid is dysphoric or in distress over their gender, or is insistent, persistent, consistent about

217

being another gender, tend to their gender health, with therapists and/or doctors who specialize in gender, said Ehrensaft. That's different than a kid who exhibits preferences for clothes or playmates or toys that don't match up to what you'd imagined for them based on their assigned sex. Maybe that gender nonconforming kid will be trans. Maybe not.

When a young child makes statements like "I'm a boy," Kate Bornstein said to me, "we're crediting that child with an adult's nuanced understanding of gender." We should reply with: " 'Okay, what does being a boy mean to you? Let's explore that, and let's hold on to the possibility that you can always be a girl if that's what you want, too. Anybody can be a boy, anybody can be a girl and you don't have to be either, sweetie, you can make your own way in the world.'... That's a response that allows the kid more possibilities."

Ehrensaft suggests shifting the goal from knowing unequivocally whether a child is "just a tomboy or trans" to "getting your child's gender in focus," as she calls it—trying to understand who they are and what they think and feel, and why. It may not be immediately clear but could unfold over time. We should try to make peace with the fact that we might not be able to satisfy our need to classify, to map, to make patterns, and to place children in a gender box, no matter how many boxes there are. Take a cue from Kyl Myers and others doing some version of gender-creative parenting, and allow these kids access to both sides of the pink and blue divide, room to explore.

Ehrensaft said to listen to kids, to be comfortable with ambiguity, prepare and research. If you think professional help is needed or welcome, partner up with mental health or medical professionals who won't push too hard in any specific direction. Every pathway is possible, she said, "so we just have to leave them all open and not shove our kids down one or another or shut a door on them."

Selin Gülgöz, assistant professor of psychology at Fordham University, works with the TransYouth Project, a longitudinal study of three hundred socially transitioned transgender children in affirming families. Among the research subjects are cisgender and transgender tomboys alike. "There are many different ways to be a boy and a girl, and many different ways to be transgender and many different ways to be cisgender," Gülgöz told me. "That can be disturbing to some people because as humans we like clarity. But there's also comfort to be taken from how complex and varied these identities appear to be. All of these identities are valid and there's no one way for anyone to be."

Welcome to the Trans Family

A headline that declared "My Daughter Is Not Transgender" was based on a very specific idea of trans as a person with gender dys- phoria, who needs to physically transition—it made sense that so many trans people objected to my article when that headline was followed by a description of a kid that, to many people, fit neatly within the trans category. Bornstein noted that, by her definition, my kid wasn't trans because that's an identity that a kid lays claim to him- or her- or themself. But, she said, my kid was "trans fam- ily." Whatever the terms that I or others use, that my daughter claims now or will claim later, Bornstein suggested that having a kid like mine, who is constantly misgendered, "puts you square in the middle of all the same shit that trans people have to deal with. It doesn't make you trans," she said, "but you're sure as fuck family." Thus, a headline that positioned my family's experience as outside of, or in opposition to, what trans folks face felt like an insult. I wish I'd posed a question as to how we can all hold space together for these different kinds of kids. However mine identifies, she is gender fluidity personified—a term I hadn't heard until a reader introduced me to it in a kind but critical email after the *Times* piece came out, and to which I was resistant then, but no longer.

Maybe trying to figure out how to expand one box without narrowing another assumes too much of a divide between boxes. Maybe boxes are the wrong way to go. Maybe definitions of trans, tomboy, and gender itself are so ambiguous that trying to find direct correlations between words and experiences is an adult's preoccupation that doesn't always serve the interests of children. "Tomboy" once offered a temporary, protective bubble of ambiguity, even if it came with a long list of conditions. But the search for clarity is perhaps the wrong quest—maybe we should search for the power to be comfortable with ambiguity, to create more protective bubbles of it.

I talked to my daughter and her good friend Jude, a ten-year-old tomboy, about how people react to them, and their identities.

"People are so interested in like, Are you a boy? Are you a girl? I think they're so interested because they just *need* to know," said Jude. "I don't think people can accept the fact that, like, you're transgender or you're gender nonconforming or, like, you're a tomboy." She paused. "What's a girl that likes boy stuff?"

"A person!" my daughter exclaimed. Then she announced that she identifies as girl, human, or rainbow banana. My kid knows her sex assigned at birth. And now she knows the bevy of options available to her, in identities, in medicine, in pronouns—as well as clothes, toys, behaviors, personality traits, and colors. And that right now, she has the privilege of not having to reject any of them.

The only way to do gender wrong, I've come to believe, is to tell someone else that they're doing it wrong—something trans people, and even some masculine cisgender girls, are constantly told. Though I've spent most of my life thinking about the invisible, and visible, forces encouraging me to be a certain kind of girl, and leaving me with the self-esteem of roadkill because I couldn't measure up to those standards, I'd never thought about the forces encouraging me to *identify* as a girl. I never questioned my gender identity, not even when I wondered about my child's, even though I am often loud and aggressive and pushy and brash and embody a host of qualities culturally branded as masculine. But certainly I had internalized the feeling that I was doing gender wrong, as far back as I can remember.

The point isn't just to have the power to do gender however you want or need to. It's about *self*-identification and *self*-determination—that's what many people are fighting for, to declare who they are, not have labels forced upon them. For a new generation—a genderation, some call it—gender nonconforming, or trans, or transgender are not worst-case scenarios, not some parent's nightmare, not some diagnosis of mental illness. They're authentic, acceptable, totally normal, and often fabulous chosen terms of pride that apply to a broad swath of people, some of whom are dysphoric and some of whom are not. With the ever-widening definition of trans, whatever lines there are will likely move, boxes will shift, and we will have a much larger and broader trans population going forward.

In that *New York Times* piece, I said my daughter's hair and clothing choices were just a look, but I was wrong about that, too. When a kid straddles or ignores the pink/blue divide, she or he or they have a different experience than conforming kids; it changes the trajectory of their lives. It's not just a look; it's a way of being.

CLARK

I grew up a tomboy in a rural area outside Washington, DC, in the 1990s. I had short hair and wore boys' clothes, played with my older brother's friends, ran shirtless, roughhoused, played with LEGO bricks. I didn't like sports because I didn't like competitiveness, but I really liked more silly things like climbing trees and going on hikes. My tomboyism was about being outspoken, loud, confident, goofy. Other girls weren't like that. They weren't running down the hallways screaming, chasing each other. They were, like, in the bathroom hanging out and chatting.

I know that confidence, physical activity, outspokenness shouldn't be the domain of just boys. Women can be confident. Women *should* be confident. But I think at its core that sort of innate confidence that is built up by the people around you is more of a masculine trait because men aren't constantly tearing each other down the way that women do a lot of the time. Or not tearing each other down—having society tear them down. But it was also the reality: Girls were one way and boys another. And I was like the boys.

I didn't get my period until I turned fifteen, which allowed me a longer grace period with the acceptable tomboy phase. But having a period, growing breasts, was a nightmare, a visceral sensation of *this should not be happening to my body*. I went on birth control to stop my periods, telling my mother I couldn't take the cramps.

In some ways, surrendering the identity of tomboy was most traumatic because that word made my gender expression acceptable. After puberty, girls teased me for continuing my tomboyish ways, being rough-and-tumble, a masculine girl. I attributed my growing unease to sexuality: I made this excuse that I was a lesbian.

That would have been fine, except that I liked boys, too, but I thought boys wouldn't like me back because I looked like a boy myself.

When I went to a small, liberal arts school in upstate New York, I met trans and gender nonconforming people who helped me realize that I didn't have to wear tight clothes or accentuate certain parts of my body, to cling to anything that was culturally coded as feminine. My freshman year, I changed my very feminine given name to Clark. I came out as genderqueer and, after college, identified as a man for a year before getting hormones and top surgery.

I don't know if I'd had the choice of having a male puberty back then whether I would have taken it, if it would have been better to skip my late-bloomer tomboy phase and go straight to man. Nobody knows. I'll never know. But I think in a lot of ways being raised as a strong, competent, independent woman has been extremely helpful for me as a man to not engage in toxic masculinity. I would have loved to have been spared the years of agonizing, of not understanding who I was, of thinking I was gay just because of the way that I like to dress and things I like. But you know, I would be a totally different person now.

I was a tomboy. And it was a huge part of figuring out who I was as a person.

Chapter 13

BREAKING THE BINARY

"I was a kid that you would like, just a small boy on her bike riding topless, yeah, I never cared who saw."

—*Dar Williams, "When I Was a Boy"*

Until they were in fourth grade, Phoenix, who then went by Phoebe (and doesn't mind people knowing their birth name), seemed like most little girls. They weren't super girly, and their mom, Stefanie, shied away from the traditional objectifying pink princess stuff anyway. But they were happy in dresses and skirts—or at least skorts—and willing to put on earrings to please their grandmother. Then it started to seem to Phoenix that the boys and girls were veering in wildly separate directions, and with the boys was where Phoenix belonged. Sort of. Mostly the draw was kickball.

Phoenix's parents assumed they were a tomboy, a word leftover from their own youths, even if they saw few kids like Phoenix around. But by the time Phoenix got to middle school, that word didn't seem to fit. "I don't feel like a girl and I don't feel like a boy," Phoenix told their mom, but neither of them knew of a word that represented that feeling.

Phoenix had been taking LGBTQ+ books out of the library, and Stefanie would read them after. Most of the narratives seemed narrow to her, reinforcing the pink/blue binary: someone assigned male at birth who, in addition to having a strong core identity as female, liked pink and sparkles, or someone assigned female at birth who *didn't* like pink and sparkles, but wanted short hair and sweatpants. "It was such an uncomplicated view of gender," said Stefanie. "It's not interrogating the categories of gender at all; it's just switching sides." Phoenix had made it clear that they didn't identify with people at either gender pole.

In 2019, at the end of seventh grade, Phoenix read a book called *The ABC's of LGBT+*, which gave dozens of options of gender identities and labels, from genderqueer to demigirl (someone who partially identifies as female, regardless of sex assigned at birth). The word *non-binary* leapt out at them. "It was in-between or outside," they said. "Not strictly male or female, boy or girl." They came out as non-binary, changed their name, and requested they/them pronouns. Phoenix hadn't much minded when people misgendered them as he/him, but it made them uncomfortable to be read as a girl. Now they had an identity, a pronoun, and a name that communicated their authentic gender to the world.

The Blooming of Non-binary

Mere Abrams, a therapist and clinical researcher at the UCSF Child and Adolescent Gender Center, who identifies as trans non-binary, defines non-binary as "both male and female, somewhere in between male and female, or something different than male and female." As their website says, "Nonbinary gender creates space for each person to acknowledge and celebrate the masculine and feminine without being defined by either one."[1]

Related words are finding their way into the lexicon, like genderfluid (not having a fixed gender) and bigender (two genders), and non-binary is becoming a more standard option—on official forms and in the public mind. As of this writing, Washington, DC, and New York City, along with fourteen states—including more conservative ones like Arkansas and Utah—offer non-binary options on driver's licenses.[2] Hollywood is seeing more actors identifying outside the binary, like Nico Tortorella, genderfluid actor; Ruby Rose, genderfluid actor and model; Indya Moore, non-binary actor and model; Rain Dove, non-binary model and activist; Rose McGowan and Rhea Butcher, non-binary actors; and Jill Soloway, non-binary creator of *Transparent*. Using they/their/them as singular pronouns is now accepted by writer style guides such as the AP, MLA, and the *Chicago Manual*; in some places, it's celebrated.[3] As the *New York Times* gushed in 2018, "They are the new beautiful people and their pronouns are they, their and them. Fashion courts them. Publishers pursue them. Corporations see in them the future of consuming, as generations come of age for whom notions of gender as traditionally constituted seem clunkier than a rotary phone."[4]

Diane Ehrensaft, Abrams's colleague at UCSF, started seeing an uptick in non-binary young adults, teens, and children around 2013. Google Trends recorded a sharp increase in the term's usage starting that year, in all states but the Dakotas and Wyoming, peaking in March 2019 when singer Sam Smith came out as non-binary.[5] At the Ackerman Institute for the Family, a New

York City therapy clinic specializing in gender, at least a quarter of the children seeking treatment at the Gender and Family Project identified as non-binary in 2019.

Further evidence of the explosion of this identity: Google added non-binary emojis in 2019. Mostly, they seem to have shaggy Beatles mops instead of recognizably masculine or feminine hairdos, but non-binary identity does not have to have anything to do with physical appearance, with physical androgyny or looking or playing a specific part. Non-binary people may change their looks, bodies, pronouns, and/or names—or not. It's an identity that allows people access to both sides of the line; they are not beholden to any expectations associated with sex.

The word "non-binary" articulated the feeling that had been rumbling inside Phoenix for years. Phoenix was happy and well adjusted, with friends and good grades. They didn't have gender dysphoria or need to change their body—at least not yet, though they could later. They needed to change their name, their pronoun, the way they labeled themselves, and the way others labeled them. They needed to declare themselves independent of the gender divide.

Beyond the Binary Boundaries

Non-binary gender, while a new concept for many Americans, is actually ancient. There have always been people who were somewhere between or outside of man and woman. That includes India's *hijra*, an acknowledged third gender known for bright saris, joyous dances, and heavy makeup. *Hijra*, an Urdu word, roughly translates to "eunuch," and while most *hijra* are assigned male at birth, some are intersex.[6] Samoa's *fa'afafine* are assigned male at birth but tend to show female-typical behavior in childhood.[7] They have distinct, feminine gender roles and are often androphilic—meaning, attracted to males. (Homosexuality is stigmatized and in some cases illegal in Samoa.[8]) An interactive map on the PBS website shows thirty-six genders outside the man/woman binary around the world, both modern and ancient, from the *waria* in Indonesia to the Incan *quariwarmi*. These third genders, more common in Eastern cultures, are sometimes marginalized but are usually recognized.[9]

In America, long before the European settlers got here, some First Nations or indigenous tribes had, and some still have, people who occupy distinct genders outside the binary. They could be male, female, or intersex, but in traditional native cultures they drew from both masculine and feminine gender expressions, roles, norms, and activities in their everyday lives, and were almost always thought of as a third gender. If males and females were referred to with separate terms, there were four genders. Early Europeans called such gender norm–flouting people *berdache*.

But rather than learning from First Nations peoples about the natural expansiveness of gender, the Europeans opted to map their moralistic and restrictive binary onto their cultures—not that this plan fully succeeded. In 1990, the term "two spirit" was adopted at the Inter-tribal Native American, First Nations, Gay and Lesbian American Conference in Winnipeg, as a self-chosen term across all tribes, also known as a pan-Indian term.[10] There are many two spirit people today, and annual local and international two spirit gatherings.

In historical accounts, two spirits may have had same-sex relations (or not), and a special status was sometimes bestowed upon them. As the Indian Health Service writes, "Two spirit identity was widely believed to be the result of supernatural intervention in the form of visions or dreams and sanctioned by tribal mythology. In many tribes, two spirit people filled special religious roles as healers, shamans, and ceremonial leaders." Rather than pariahs, outcasts, people who were doing gender wrong, sometimes two spirit people were seen as exceptional, as gifts.

When Mere Abrams came across a photograph of a two spirit person in 2011, it was life-changing. Abrams had had a fairly happy tomboy childhood, even if they coveted their little brother's superhero underwear—and his clothes, toys, boys only sports teams, and the way people saw and understood him, the comfort he seemed to feel in his own skin. But Abrams's puberty was full of anxiety, confusion, questioning. In college, they came out as "a kind of queer, nonconforming woman," but that didn't feel quite right, either. It wasn't about sexuality. It had something to do with identity, but the words weren't there. Abrams knew gender-conforming trans people, who transitioned from one side of the binary to the other. But in the modern Judeo-Christian American culture in the early twenty-first century, we didn't have a commonly accepted name for an experience outside this construct.

Reading about two spirit people changed Mere's world. "There was this double affirmation that happened of: *Yes, this is real and has always been real.*" As a white person, Abrams didn't adopt the term two spirit, but understood that indigenous communities, often erased by white European colonization, can play a huge role in helping those colonizing cultures understand the vastness of gender. In 2012, Abrams came out as non-binary—a word hardly in play then—and eventually became a leading educator on the topic.

Abrams identifies both as trans (not identifying with their sex assigned at birth) and non-binary (not exclusively male or female), but some non-binary people, like Phoenix, don't identify as trans. In fact, many kids who would have been called tomboys when I was young may identify as non-binary today—as long as they have family or community that facilitates or supports their identity, and as long as they have access to the language. In a 2015 US survey by the National Center for Transgender Equality, almost a third of nearly twenty-eight thousand transgender respondents identified as non-binary; 80 percent of them were assigned female at birth.[11] And some people who *did* identify as tomboys come out as non-binary as adults, after becoming aware of the option, the word, the idea.

Jessie, a non-binary book publicist in Portland, Oregon, was a hard-core tomboy growing up in Washington, DC, in the late 1980s, short-haired and shirtless, whom people mistook for a boy, to their delight, most of the time. They were less "butch jock girl" than "nerdy boy girl": reading a lot, caring for wounded baby animals, playing a dangerous game called Military School with the boys, throwing rocks at each other while running on the beach.

"By the time I was an adolescent, I was really open to trying out things and not nervous and really brave," they said. In some ways, puberty contributed to their sense of inner strength. "I think that there was that superpower that came with having big breasts and being female and liking being a really sexual person. I think probably my sexuality, in terms of wanting sex, is probably kind of male as well." They knew they wanted children, and the ability to reproduce felt like a superpower of sorts, too. They embraced their femaleness, even if they didn't exactly feel like a woman, or feminine. "I never felt like a man," Jessie said. "I felt like a boy."

When a friend formerly known as Claire transitioned to Foster in 2018 (they don't mind people knowing their birth name, and still use it professionally), the proverbial lightbulb went off. "I had heard the term [non-binary] before, but Foster was the first person I felt similar to and connected to who identified this way," they wrote to me. "That word...is what I am."

I asked Jessie if they would have identified as non-binary as a kid, had the phrase been around. "I am nearly positive that I would have," they said. When I asked if they weren't a tomboy then, they answered, "I always assumed non-binary and tomboy were the same thing."

For Jessie, there was no distinction between tomboy and non-binary; tomboy was simply the incomplete, unfulfilling word that we used before this more accurate and gender-neutral one came into play. For them and many others, the word "non-binary" is providing much of the same psychological relief gifted by taxonomy that tomboy once did but is more inclusive and expansive. There are still girls like Mira, who once proudly claimed the title of tomboy and now proudly rejects it in favor of girl. But there will likely be more kids identifying outside the binary in the future.

Which doesn't mean that all adult non-binary folks reject their tomboy childhoods. "I still strongly identify as a tomboy," Abrams told me. "But I don't believe that I was a tomboy who turned out to be non-binary. I believe that I was always non-binary from the get-go."

The Challenge of Non-binary Medicine

Jessie hasn't needed to alter anything about their body, and Phoenix hasn't yet but may still, but some non-binary people do. This presents a conundrum for the medical community. Protocols for transgender medicine have largely been based on helping someone transition from one side of the binary to the other, to pass as cisgender. "That's not my goal, so these protocols don't apply to me," Abrams said. What does it look like to physically transition from a woman, but not to become a man?

Abrams had to figure it out on their own, chart their own path—something they could do because they were educated, had resources, and worked in the world of gender medicine and mental health. They addressed their gender dysphoria by requesting a lower-than-normal dose of testosterone, to deepen their voice but not grow an Adam's apple or much facial hair, and to leave their fertility unaffected in case they wanted to have children later. They had a bilateral mastectomy, known as top surgery. The body changes, Abrams said, were "about feeling that maleness and masculinity" without becoming a man. In some ways, the changes rendered them a permanent tomboy.

"We have a number of gender non-binary kids coming to the clinic, asking for, for example, a touch of testosterone. They would just like to have a little bit of a deeper voice and a little bit of peach fuzz and then stop the testosterone. Because once you get that deeper voice you don't undo it, right? It's a one-way street," Ehrensaft told me. "We have some young adults saying, 'I just want my breasts removed. They don't match who I am. I'm not a man. But I'm not a woman either and I'm gender non-binary and I don't want breasts.' And we've had to really look at our own biases about it. Why is it okay [to have top surgery] if someone says, 'I'm a man'? They could get their breasts removed, but if they say 'I'm neither,' you think, 'Oh I don't think so.'"

When Ehrensaft was initially called on to make recommendations about medical interventions for non-binary kids, she found her first instinct was to say no, to see these kids as confused, not landed yet, stuck in the middle. But eventually, after talking to enough of them and watching their trajectories, she realized that they *had* landed; they had landed at this middle place. That was where they wanted to be.

"I have kids as young as four or five saying, 'Look, I'm not either. I'm not a boy. I'm not a girl. I'm a boy-girl or I'm just a rainbow kid,' and they really don't think of themselves as one or the other. It's really that I'm any-and-all rather than either/or." Being confronted by a generation of children declaring themselves neither boys nor girls, Ehrensaft said, "just shakes the foundations of what we think gender is."

Ehrensaft had grown up a tomboy herself, and told me that she and another former tomboy friend of hers realized that they might have identified as non-binary when they were kids, "because of how we didn't put our gender together in any binary way," she said. She was good at math, playing poker, riding bikes, doing ballet, dressing femininely when she had to. "It was mostly about what we did. Not that kind of, who I know myself to be inside, but we just didn't fit into the girl box well at all. I think we're just changing the lens in which we see all of this, but it's always been there."

Identities and Stereotypes

In Ehrensaft's example, not fitting in the girl box because you play poker and are good at math is an indication of how small the box is, too. Some people believe that girl is only a social category, not a biological one, but it has become so narrow, so pink-hued, heart-and-rainbow-slathered, and sparkly, that only a select few can fit inside it. The feminist in me couldn't help questioning why we couldn't widen that girl category to accommodate people like Jessie or Phoenix or Mere. Did it have to be abandoned in order for people to feel free to be themselves?

Historian Jo B. Paoletti, who charted the rise of the pink-and-blue divide in kids' clothes over the last century, felt very supported in her 1950s tomboy childhood. "When I was a little kid, I could fantasize about being a cowboy when I grew up and pretend to name myself John when I played cowboys and Indians with my brother," she said. "Because I was a girl, and being a tomboy was culturally okay, that was fine. I didn't have to redefine myself as something other than a girl in order to do that." A little girl who does the same thing after the hyper-gendering of the 1990s, she said, is "getting a really strong message of 'a boy is this,' and 'a girl is this.'"

That is, in some cases there is actually *less* latitude within masculinity and femininity, within the girl category and the boy category, so we created new categories with all the latitude in the world. But I kept wondering how much some non-binary folks are embracing a separate gender identity and how much they are rejecting gender stereotypes, or still somehow beholden to them.

Some of Jessie's ideas about what it meant to be a girl seemed similarly conflated with stereotypical femininity. "I was really tan and really strong. I remember that feeling of flexing my arm muscles and really liking the way that looked. So that idea of not feeling like a girl," they said. Most of their best friends are women, but they relate more to men. "I'm aggressive and I have a lot of masculine qualities," they said, like "mansplaining" or interrupting, or wanting to be a boxer or wrestle. "I often prefer to talk to men because I like a very straightforward conversation with interrupting and I just don't really back down very easily."

What, I wondered, does being assertive, playing military school, having short hair, running on the beach, being brave, being sexual, have to do with being male? Why is it "like a man" to interrupt and be straightforward? Shouldn't we already know, by way of separating sex and gender, and by seeing so many females who embody those qualities, that traditional femininity and masculinity are not mutually exclusive or the domain of one sex?

Well, sex and gender may be separate, but they're still tethered. Many people today seem not to differentiate between masculine and feminine—society's stereotypes of what boys or girls *should* look like and do—and male and female, as in bodies and biology, or man and woman or boy and girl, as in gender or social identities. Even Abrams's description of non-binary includes masculinity and femininity—not just bodies and identities but cultural expressions. "Explaining the sensation of being non-binary is very difficult without using gendered stereotypes because we don't have the language for this," Jessie wrote to me.

The recent hyper-gendering of childhood has strengthened this connection between sex and gender. After gender-coding toys, clothes, personality traits, and colors as masculine and feminine, perhaps we have shrunk the categories of male and female with them. Maybe it's impossible to assign sex without assigning gender, too. It's as if all those words and ideas have been superglued, so the one way to break them apart, to be free of gender stereotypes, is to get rid of the boxes and blow up the gender binary altogether, to smash it to bits. Maybe the explosion of the gender binary is fueled by people feeling those words and their associations have gotten too narrow to accommodate them. Gender is such a powerful force that this is what it takes to push back. Binaries in general are so limiting: girl/boy; homosexual/heterosexual; trans/cis; good/bad.

Phoenix told me that when they were a girl, they had to dress like a boy so people wouldn't misgender them. "Now that I'm non-binary, I just dress like myself," they said—which translates into a lot of tie-dye, and purple hair. That is, they don't have to overcompensate for their assigned sex; their pronouns, their non-binary identity, communicates and confirms who they are. It is not about expression or stereotypes, my non-binary interviewees assured me. It is about a core sense of self.

I asked Ehrensaft what all this uprooting of the binary, and the language around it, may lead to. "We may have a world in front of us that is not based on gender categories or just very loosely," she said.

"As these children declaring themselves non-binary march into the world saying, 'I reject your notion of gender,' what does the world have to do?" I asked.

"I think the world has to loosen up their own sense of gender and certainly dispense with gender in two boxes and recognize what I call gender infinity," she replied. "Ask itself: Why do we need to categorize by gender at all? We're much more open to the possibility of a gender non-binary status in life and aware that it's not our job to police that but facilitate it."

When I asked the writer and gender theorist Kate Bornstein, who identifies as trans and non-binary, about how to open more people's minds to these ideas, she said, "What is a man, what is a woman, who says we have to be one or the other?" She drew a circle in the air for me. For eons, she said, that circle was divided in half, with men on one side and women on the other, and you had to transgress that line to get something you wanted from the other side. Many people want to erase that line altogether. Sure, some people will hew to the binary edges, but everybody else will be mixed together in gender soup, able to grab any ingredients they want from around the circle. Rather than see the in-between place as a no-man's—no-person's—land, see it as a legitimate, healthy, respectable spot.

Ehrensaft describes it as "poetry in motion."

KERA

I grew up in the seventies in Chicago, Illinois, the daughter of Jewish liberals who had very traditional ideas about gender. My mother really wanted me to conform, enrolling me in ballet classes, putting my short hair in floral barrettes, even getting me a Schwinn bike with a floral motif, and practically crowbarring me into dresses.

I wasn't interested in playing with dolls, or the horses and unicorns and Barbies that other girls liked, or the toys that would mold me into a future homemaker. I wanted the *Star Wars* action figures that had taken over the toy world. I liked LEGOs. I liked running around outside. I liked creative projects. My collection of favorite endeavors were neither male nor female. But mostly the boys were doing the things I liked to do.

I had an androgynous bowl cut and wore clothes that could easily look right on boys or girls. And dress-up? Well, my dad had been a pilot in the navy and had his flight uniform—a onesie with zippers and compartments—and pilot helmet with a mouthpiece and adjustable visors. There's no comparison—a negligee versus that? I always chose the boys' clothes. They were more comfortable, more kid-friendly, and I wanted above all to be a kid, not pretending at some antiquated notion of femininity. I was just an in-between, really gender nonconforming; but of course we didn't have that vocabulary in the 1970s and early '80s. If I were a child today, I'd likely be non-binary.

I was able to pull that in-betweening off until I got closer to puberty, when my body's decisiveness to feminize befell me. So when my best friend announced one day, when I was ten, that we were going to the mall to pierce our ears, I felt like she was kind of testing me: *I am making a decision to declare that I am female.* Which I wasn't sure I felt quite ready to do. But I did.

It wasn't until a few months later, when *Newsweek* magazine featured gay men on the cover—one of whom was wearing earrings—that I discovered that earrings weren't the sole domain of women. Media and pop culture played a huge role in making me feel it was okay to be me. Performers like David Bowie and Prince were androgynous and sexy and genius and beloved. The first time I saw Annie Lennox and Boy George on MTV: That was such a breathtaking moment. That was a game changer.

It wasn't until I was older, when I came out as a lesbian in my teens, that I reckoned with my femininity, with my female body in general.

Chapter 14

IS IT TIME TO RETIRE THE WORD "TOMBOY"?

"I never quite understood why a girl who climbed trees, clung to the tail-end of carts, and otherwise deported herself as a well-conditioned girl should not, was called a tomboy. It always seemed to me that, if she was anything she should not be, it was a tomgirl."

—*Jeannette Gilder,* Autobiography of a Tomboy, *1900*

When Karen Michelle opened her online clothing retail site HauteButch in 2013, which sells bespoke formal wear, bowties, rainbow bracelets, and athleisurewear, she initially had trouble picking up traffic.

"When we started out, everything we had on the website was butch, butch, butch," she said. "And we noticed that the word 'butch' was not being searched for like tomboy. The word 'tomboy' was being searched for like crazy." She added the keyword all over the website, so now HauteButch is a "fierce fashion and lifestyle brand offering a one stop shop for butch + tomboy" and is "designed by and for Butches, studs and tomboys."

Traffic picked way up. "We got a gold mine with the keyword," she said. "It's all about the word 'tomboy.'"

There has been, over the last 180 years or so, since it was first applied to young girls in a positive way, a lot of arguing over the word "tomboy." Likely the first declaration that the word should be retired was in 1898, when *Harper's Bazaar* published "The Passing of the Tomboy." It happened again in 1917, when a widely read essay also called "Passing of the Tomboy" suggested: "Either the genus has unhappily ceased to exist or the characteristics have become so common that they have ceased to be distinguishing." Tomboy had become a "useless term."[1] And in 1926 an article called "The Passing of Tomboys" announced: "There aren't any Tomboys anymore. Standards have changed."[2]

Throughout the twentieth century, this same pronouncement was made. "Tomboy label wears out," "The term 'tomboy' is as passé as a slingshot," "'Tomboy' slips into world of yesteryear," and "Tomboy term nearly obsolete" read headlines from a syndicated column in the 1980s.[3] In 1993, sociologist Barrie Thorne asked, "Why call a girl a quasi boy just because she likes to dress comfortably, play sports, climb trees, go on adventures, or have boys as companions?"[4] In 2016, *Bustle*, *Babble*, and the *Huffington Post* each published articles by mothers demanding that the world stop referring to their daughters as tomboys.[5]

"When we label sporty, adventurous girls as boyish, we're reinforcing the idea that certain behaviors or interests are better suited to boys and men, while the rest are for girls," wrote developmental psychologist Dr. Andrea Bastiani Archibald in an April 2019 Girl Scouts blog post, "It's Time to Stop Calling Her a Tomboy." Over and over the same argument was invoked: Using a word with "boy" in it to describe a girl who loves action and adventure is reinforcing gender stereotypes, not bucking them, and we should nix it.

Over the course of my research, many people told me that the word had rightly receded because we have evolved enough to know that boys' stuff isn't just for boys. Standards, they noted almost a hundred years after this point had been made, had changed. This sentiment was expressed to me mostly by upper-middle-class, white former tomboys who had been successful in male-dominated fields like geology and television production, had reaped the benefits of being socialized with or like boys, been treated with equality by their parents, or were perhaps naturally driven to the "boy" side of the line, and accepted there. They were women for whom gender had not been limiting, so they figured it wasn't limiting others.

Jack Halberstam, Columbia University professor of gender studies and English, told me that girls have so many different options and representations in the media now, and are excluded from so few "boy things" that we don't need a word for a girl who transgresses into the land of boys. Look at all those ponytailed girls blazing across the soccer field, and all those girls kicking ass in STEM, the incredible gains they've made in the past few decades. "I think that the tomboy category is somewhat anachronistic," he said. "I wonder if we'll eventually end up thinking of the tomboy category as a twentieth-century category not a twenty-first-century one."

Even those who don't know of the word's problematic history—its connection to eugenics, or the fact that it once referred to a boisterous boy or an adult woman's sexuality—know it has been problematic. As Emma McIlroy, cofounder of the feminist fashion company Wildfang told me, "Tomboy is a polarizing word."

McIlroy grew up in Ireland in the eighties and nineties, sporty and proudly claiming the title of tomboy, but she understands its complexity. "There are a lot of people who love it and own it," she said, and then others who hate the idea of describing a fort-building, fast-running girl with a double-masculine word, or feel that it's only for cisgender women, excluding people elsewhere on the gender spectrum.

While Karen Michelle was happy about the uptick in traffic on HauteButch, she doesn't care for the term, or that she had to subjugate the word "butch" to promote the company. "Tomboy is such a watered-down, vanilla term," she said. But she approved of what tomboys stood for: their independence, their confidence, their courage, running shirtless in a world that tells them to cover up. "The characteristics of a tomboy, the behaviors—that's the stuff we love," she said.

Fashion writer and entrepreneur Lizzie Mettler shuttered her fashion blog *Tomboy Style* in 2015 partly because some readers objected to the word "tomboy" itself—even though it had been a hit with the press when she started the blog in 2012. "Thoughtful, smart commenters said, 'I don't understand why this blog is not just called 'Cool Women,'" Mettler told me. "Why did I have to label it with this antiquated word?"

Nevertheless, Tomboy Persisted

But tomboy, while at the very least outdated and to many offensive, is a zombie: No matter how many times it's pronounced dead, it springs back to life. Case in point: Wildfang's graphic TOMBOY T-shirts were so popular that Forever 21 knocked them off. (Forever 21 also hocked a graphic "tomboy tube top," despite the fact that the phrase seems oxymoronic.)

The word has given solace, meaning, to many. Adults used it for almost two centuries to make sense of and accept girls who played more like boys did. It provided a sanctuary, a safe passageway over the line, freedom for girls to explore, often without the condemnation of their peers or community, and sometimes with their approbation. It made misfits feel understood. In many ways, it was language doing good taxonomic work, to explain and affirm and acknowledge, to quell fears and answer questions, to help parents understand children and children understand themselves.

Thus, famous women from Clara Barton to Dolly Parton proudly, nostalgically recalled their tomboy childhoods, as their way of saying that they were nonconformists, confident, doing what they wanted regardless of the direction the rest of their peers veered in. It's still conjured up in song, in a multitude of musical genres, and there's even a Portland-based, David Bowie cover band of female-identified musicians called Major Tomboys.

Princess Nokia's 2017 "Tomboy" is an anthem to her own gender independence and kick-ass sexuality: "*With my little titties and my phat belly, I could take your man if you finna let me,*" she raps.

There's Destiny Rogers's 2019 "Tomboy," in which she sings: "*My mama said, 'Marry a rich man.' And I was like, 'Mama, I am that rich man.'*"

Miranda Lambert croons, "*Tomboy in between, dirt in her nails and holes in her jeans, she'll destroy all your dreams, and ride out like a rodeo queen,*" in her 2016 song "Tomboy." In these examples, tomboy seems more about young women claiming the power to define and design their own destinies and sexualities than about riding a bike shirtless across the field.

In the fashion and entertainment industries, tomboy still works—as a keyword and as a hashtag. As noted earlier, there are millions of #tomboy posts on social media, often featuring sexy, androgynous, or masculine women or non-binary folks with high style and sex appeal, in #tomboystyle duds. There's very little awareness of the word's past, or even its application to children. So when moms detail their offense at the word's application to their daughters, I wonder: How often does that even happen anymore?

What Should the New Word Be?

These parents who object to the word "tomboy" believe that the category of girl has deepened and widened enough to make the word obsolete. I understand their stance. Even after all this research, I wonder why we must slap a sticker on kids whose behaviors diverge from grown-ups' narrow range of what's acceptable. But I believe the opposite has happened: We've created many new categories, dozens of gradations, rather than broadening girl into a complex one that can encompass many behaviors, expressions, and traits. Humankind has apparently not created protective bubbles of ambiguity. Rather, it has taken the urge for classification to new heights, in the hope that this will lead to gender freedom in the way the constricting boy/girl binary and the pink/blue divide never could.

As mentioned in chapter 12, many people who would scoff at

the word "tomboy" proudly call themselves, or their kids, gender nonconforming. Michele Yulo, founder of Princess Free Zone, delivered a great TED talk on parenting a gender nonconforming child, but also created an internet meme that says "Not a tomboy. Not a girl who likes boy things. Not a girl who isn't girly. Just a girl." For her and many others, gender nonconforming and girl are not in opposition, but rather easily overlap. GNC? A-Okay! Tomboy? No way!

Here's the conundrum: For others, especially former tomboys, this new terminology is equally problematic. Writer Lizzy Acker noted in *Willamette Week* in 2016 how proud she was when she was a kid and her best friend told her, "My mom said we're tomboys." "It was a pretty magical moment of mutual and self-identification, and I just don't think I would have felt the same way if she'd said to me, 'My mom said we're gender nonconforming,'" Acker wrote. "Isn't calling something 'nonconforming' or 'variant' still assuming there is one way to correctly express gender anyway?"[6]

Originally, the word "tomboy" was a way to break free of gender roles. Later, it came to perpetuate them. These days, Generation Z and its steadily increasing band of non-binary and genderfluid kids are disrupting gender in a way that the word "tomboy" never could. The language of gender changes: We have flight attendants instead of stewardesses. We have council people and firefighters and police officers. We successfully wove Ms. into the lexicon during the feminist 1970s, instead of just Miss and Mrs., and now we have gender-neutral Mx. on the wax. We're getting new words, but not everyone feels that labeling a kid who would once have been called a tomboy a "child who is gender variant" is better, and those who loved the word "tomboy" don't love the clinical sound of these new terms either, or want to let tomboy go; some trans women identify as tomboys, too. We still haven't found terms that work for everyone. So as we add new words, and expand definitions of male and female and man and woman, I'd like to see us expand our ideas of masculine and feminine, too—or maybe nix those words altogether. They're so poorly applied.

I love the vision that the word "tomboy" receded because our culture became enveloped in a cloud of equality, in which nothing is off-limits for girls—or boys, intersex, trans, and non-binary kids—and that we have achieved freedom from the constraints of gender. But I don't think the word "tomboy" retreated because equality has been achieved.

I think we found cleverer and more pernicious forms of sexism to keep people, especially kids, in their gender-segregated lanes. One reason the word "tomboy" is still around is that we're still dividing the stuff of childhood into girl and boy sections, so we still need a name for those who want to visit the section that's not for them. The mission of equality is not complete.

Carrie Paechter, director of the Nottingham Centre for Children, Young People and Families in the UK, conducted a study on tomboys and girls' play, and how children conceive of what is acceptable for them based on assigned sex. She found that what she calls "active girlhood" is still not the norm. In the UK, some girls' secondary schools have very little playground space; they even get the message from the *physical* environment that they shouldn't be sporty and playing "like boys." And certainly there's a message from the cultural environment.

"I think society tells them that they shouldn't be active," she told me. "You get to a certain age as a girl and you think, *That's what all the girls are like. That's what adult women are like. We shouldn't do it.* And in fact one of our tomboys said, 'You know, apparently you're not allowed to run around when you get to year six.' I think there's quite a lot of social pressure." Of course, yes, there are still sporty girls who have short hair and wear sweatpants. These are the ones, said Paechter, who still identify, or are identified, as tomboys. They probably don't describe themselves as gender variant, but they're still an exception.

To me, focusing on the word "tomboy" is missing the point. It's not just that the word is improperly gendered. It's that childhood is overly gendered—there would be no need for the word if less of childhood were divided into pink and blue. So go ahead, say goodbye to the word. I'm not attached to it either way. What I'm attached to is creating a culture in which children feel welcome to explore activities and items, in which we stop marking them as "for boys" or "for girls."

But I'm also attached to giving tomboys their due. Without tomboys—the people, the idea, the word, the privilege that some girls were lucky enough to exercise for almost two centuries, which made space for gender diversity—American girls and women would likely not have some freedoms they have today. In fact, there would likely be no Girl Scouts without tomboys. "The Girl Scouts were part of a movement to give girls organizations akin to those of their brothers," wrote historian Renée Sentilles. The organization was birthed in 1912 on the heels of the Victorian tomboy movement that professed the radical idea that raising girls similarly to how boys were raised would make them into the best women, the best citizens.

What if, instead of arguing over the word, we look at tomboys' long history of success, of social acceptance, of confidence that continues into adulthood, and use that as proof that gender is indeed a spectrum, or a sphere, or some other shape besides just two dots, and that the happiest and most self-actualized children are those whose lives are not limited by the gendered expectations of adults? What if we create *more* room, *more* flexibility, label *less*, open more possibilities?

Possibilities—that's what tomboys have always been about anyway.

Conclusion

THE PINK PONYTAIL

"Gender's a hoax. I mean, you see it from far away and then
when you're close to someone, all you see is skin."

—*Tig Notaro,* One Mississippi

"I got that, darlin'," the man said to my daughter, lifting the booster
seat from her hands and setting it on the luggage rack on the Avis
bus. She and I exchanged a look, followed by a spurt of laughter.
Darlin'.

For the six years before this, strangers had been referring to
her as "buddy," or "fella," less likely to take a piece of luggage from
her than encourage her to carry it herself. She'd had short hair,
and had been wearing boys' clothes—loose athletic shorts or track
pants, T-shirts—and looked 100 percent like a boy (per current
cultural standards). Thus, she had been referred to as one, and
treated like one, by strangers.

This was fine with her. She knew who she was, and as a kid
who had begun to skirt between male and female friend groups,
who played baseball but was fine playing with/destroying Barbies,
too, she used she/her but truly didn't care what pronoun anyone

else used. The great bulk of tomboys I spoke to either enjoyed when strangers thought they were boys or didn't care. The boy/girl divide was not something that applied to them. That was the way grown-ups organized the world, not them. Some were offended by it, proud to be girls who did their own thing—not a boy thing, but their own thing. Some were trans and identified as boys, so the "misgendering" actually made them feel good; what made them feel horrible was being misgendered as a girl.

During fourth grade, my daughter decided to grow her hair out into a Beatles mop, to dye a section of it fuchsia, and to put it in a front ponytail known around our parts as a unicorn horn (both my daughters pointed out that the hairstyle, if not the coloring, was quickly adopted by her male friends). Nothing about her changed other than her hair—same ratty shorts and T-shirts, same traditionally boyish posture and energy. But the way strangers treated her—that changed *a lot.*

The first time it happened, we were buying a $5 sun hat at a sidewalk cart in Manhattan's Chelsea neighborhood. "It looks good on her," the man said as she settled the straw fedora over her pink mop.

As we walked away, she said, "That was the first time anybody got my gender right." She was surprised, but pleased. But that was just about pronouns. She hadn't realized yet that with that pronoun would come a completely different set of interactions. By the time we were at the airport, on the way to visit grandparents, she had seen how people treated her differently, the assumptions they made about her physical abilities, about what kind of toothbrush—the pink princess over the blue bear—she'd prefer, and about how they would speak to her: darlin' versus pal, an object of affection versus a peer. She was living the research that shows how adults speak differently to kids, treat them differently, based on what they assume their sex to be.

From younger people, there were other assumptions. One night we were at a concert in the park after my daughter's baseball game. Earlier in the day, the annual Mermaid Parade at Coney Island had taken place, and next to us sat two intoxicated twenty-something women in bright wigs and iridescent outfits. They looked at my daughter, who was wearing her blue baseball uniform and her pink hair, and said, approvingly, "We got a little non-binary situation going on here?"

To which I replied, "No." It was a slightly defensive response, a vestigial unwillingness to let go of my twentieth-century gender-binary belief system, even though I had spent the entire year working to free myself from it. As my husband said in my defense: It's difficult to learn a new language in middle age. A more appropriate response might have been "We'll see!"

I suppose the assumption strangers made that a child's gender *identity* would be located in the sport she chose and the color she dyed her hair caught me off guard. Even for the generation that was exploding the binary and redrawing the gender maps, there seemed to be a vague infrastructure of gender stereotypes powering the revolution.

Still, the problem with my objection is that most of us, unless we are raising theybies, assume our kids will be cisgender, and use the pronouns associated with their anatomic sex—we're already making all kinds of assumptions about our kids because of their bodies. "I don't want people being like, 'Are you sure you're not a boy, are you sure you're not a boy?' to my kid, but she's getting a lot more 'you're a girl'—just because of her natal sex," the ACLU lawyer Chase Strangio told me. "We should take stock of those invisible forces that are encouraging us to be heterosexual, non-transgender people."

It's hard to know how to create room for kids to explore and still operate within the sex-gender system, the gender beliefs, around which our society is organized. That's why so many people are objecting to them.

Most people I talked to associated their tomboy days with freedom. Many spoke of running with their shirts off or engaging in rough-and-tumble play, and for a long time I thought that's what they meant by freedom—physically running free. But now I realize that it was freedom from the pressures of gender: physical, cultural, and psychological. It was freedom from gender stereotypes, and adults' imposition of them. It was freedom to be who they were. That gender freedom is a good thing. Our children should have more of it.

"But what's the problem with girls liking pink?" a mom asked me at the playground by our school. She was in charge of selling the fundraising merch, the T-shirts and baseball caps with our school's name, and I'd made a semi-obnoxious comment when she'd discussed supplying those things in "boys'" and "girls'" colors. She had never considered where she'd gotten the idea that colors could be gendered, and certainly didn't know about the homophobia behind keeping boys out of pink. "What's wrong with dressing little girls in skirts and dresses?" she asked.

Nothing at all. I have absolutely no problem with skirts and dresses and pink and sparkles and hearts and unicorns and rainbows. Love them. There are, however, real structural problems with girls' clothes and the kinds of activities they curtail (pockets, people! shoes with treads!), and a lot of toys that encourage girls to focus on their appearance and boys on their skill sets. What I object to is the hyper-gendering of childhood, and to the gender stereotypes that direct what we expose our children to because those stereotypes have enormous impacts on both physical and mental health, for children and the adults they grow into.

There are some common biological differences between boys and girls, small ones in things like fine motor skills (girls tend to develop theirs sooner) or self-control (some boys' may develop later) that get exacerbated by the separate, gendered streams in which we swim. But much of the way we've gendered childhood is a construction, *not* rooted in biological differences between sexes. Still, what is constructed becomes reality, so much so that we abide by the divisions of our invention as if they are unassailable truths. And the problem is: Many children's experiences don't match up with the "truths" about gender that adults believe. Those gender beliefs lead to discrimination, abuse, violence, lost opportunity, myopia, depression, suppression.

One of the biggest surprises for me, as I set out to write a book about tomboys, was how necessary it was for me to talk about *all* kids, including boys. Among the most powerful things I read was an op-ed by the children's book author Shannon Hale, creator of the kick-ass *Princess in Black* series. When she arrives for a reading, the school librarian announces, "Girls, you're in for a real treat. You will love Shannon Hale's books. Boys, I expect you to behave anyway."[1] The *school librarian* says that, setting kids' expectations, a gender-divided normalcy laid out. Hale travels around the country and hears from adults that boys will not be interested in her books because they star a girl. But evidence, in the form of enrapt boys in the audience, even if they're forced to be there, who ask to buy the books after only to be told by their parents or teacher that they are not for boys, has shown her that all kids, including boys, are plenty interested in tales of a princess with a monster-battling alter-ego.

This message to boys is, ultimately, that they should not be sissies—not feminine, not gay, not interested in girls or feminine kids of any kind—and it is ubiquitous. The British gender equity advocacy group Let Toys Be Toys found boys' T-shirts from *Big Hero 6* or *Avengers* with only the male characters on them, and the re-released twelve classic *Star Wars* action figures with two Luke Skywalkers but no Leia.[2]

Why all boys and no girls? We default to the masculine: *Guys* means both men and women, but *gals* sure doesn't. Girls can wear boys' clothes, but not the other way around. A girl named Jo or Sam or Frankie? So cute! A boy named Jennifer, Lisa, or Sarah? Not a thing. Girls will want to watch stuff about either boys *or* girls, the thinking goes, but only girls will watch girl-centric stuff. I suspect there's a reason that J.K. Rowling used her initials instead of her first name, Joanne—so boys would buy the books because we believe that they won't cross a gender line into something associated with femininity.

This is what men and boys are told, and what they are pressured to feel. We assume that boys won't want to play with or watch or wear anything to do with a girl, but in reality we're telling them that they *shouldn't* want to, that they *shouldn't* be interested in girls, in their worlds, their books, their toys, their colors, their clothes, or what we have codified as feminine: empathy, kindness, gentleness, the love of beauty. That if they have those tendencies, those interests, they should squelch them because they are *not for boys*, and thus are less valuable.

Because we label colors and play and personality traits as masculine and feminine, nearly half of society feels cut off from them. "If boys are steered away from dolls and soft toys, they're missing out on the opportunity to learn communication and nurturing and empathy skills," said Jess Day of Let Toys Be Toys, "and if girls are steered away from construction toys and physical activity, then they'll miss out on the chances to develop those skills."

I am not suggesting that all parents name their little boys Jennifer and Julie and send them to school in pink gowns and tiaras—though I fully support those parents who want to and will. But I am suggesting that by not letting them access things marked as for girls, play with them, read them, dress up in them, parents are sending boys on a path that can lead to dark places.

"What happens to a boy who is taught he should be ashamed of reading a book about a girl? For feeling empathy for a girl? For trying to understand how she feels? For caring about her? What kind of a man does that boy grow up to be?" Shannon Hale asks.

Well, according to ethnographer Dr. Maria do Mar Pereira, author of *Doing Gender in the Playground: The Negotiation of Gender in Schools*, boys who feel pressure to adhere to gender stereotypes become adults who drink too much, suppress their feelings, engage in low-level—and sometimes high-level—violence, and suffer from anxiety. And while tomboys have had way more leeway, dressing in boys' clothes or having boys' names or playing their games, the great bulk of girls absorb the extreme pressure to be thin, explaining why as many as 5 percent of girls have eating disorders and around 60 percent are on diets.[3] Even some girls who like sports avoid them because they seem unfeminine— yet we know just how important sports are to mental and physical health. According to the Women's Sports Foundation, girls drop out of competitive sports at twice the rate of boys by age fourteen, in part because of the lack of positive role models and because of gender-related stigma.[4] As Dr. do Mar Pereira's study concluded, "This constant effort to manage one's everyday life in line with gender norms produces significant anxiety, insecurity, stress and low self-esteem for both boys and girls, and both for 'popular' young people and those who have lower status in school."[5]

A myriad of other studies draw similar conclusions. One showed that girls taught for longer than a year by teachers with traditional views of gender perform worse on math and verbal tests, and it gets worse the longer they're with those teachers.[6] Another revealed that girls between ages ten and fifteen fared worse in grades and on tests when they'd internalized the message that women are supposed to be sexually attractive to men.[7] Childhood gender stereotypes leak into adulthood, into what we chastise or reward, into money and power. Male-led startups raise five times more funding than female-led startups.[8] The World Economic Forum reported in 2019 that it will take *208 years* to attain gender equality in the United States.[9] And the Organisation for Economic Co-operation and Development estimated that wasted potential, caused by gender discrimination, costs the global economy up to $12 trillion each year.[10]

There are more numbers and statistics I could gather, but they all add up to something fundamental: shame. The regulatory power of shame. It's such an easy, basic way to exert control, to make someone feel they're not doing gender right. It's something children learn so young, to form alliances and impose sanctions for not adhering to the rules, no matter how arbitrary those rules of gender may be. And the failure to do gender right is something that almost everybody feels. It's equal opportunity shame.

How awful it must be to be told that your desires, your way of being in the world, is wrong. Here I speak of cisgender boys, but if you add up all the trans and non-binary kids who are told that they are not real or valid and who live in far more fear and danger and discomfort than cisgender people generally do, and if you add all the kids like mine told that they're not doing "girl" right—well, it's just about everybody. Gender nonconformity should be our goal, and, eventually, our default.

When Karleen Pendleton Jiménez went around Canada leading writing workshops about gender with schoolchildren in fourth through twelfth grades, she found that everybody had broken rules around gender and everybody was feeling anxiety about gender, that they were doing it wrong, that they weren't free to be themselves. The cisgender, masculine, straight men felt pressure to be manlier, were teased for their interest in horseback riding or dance or having "girl knees." The cisgender girls were told that they shouldn't play sports or were picked last for teams or found that no boys passed them the ball. They were told that they should dress more femininely and not speak up. "This gender policing stuff is just everywhere," Jiménez said. "Everybody had these really deep experiences with gender and not feeling like they're doing it competently."

Gender stereotypes are not benign. Neither is shame.

I do think we are correcting course in many long overdue,

creative, and exciting ways. A week after the "darlin'" incident, we were on the plane heading home when the United States women's national soccer team scored the winning goal of the Women's World Cup. The entire plane erupted in cheers. They were still cheering when we disembarked. The next day I saw an op-ed about how many little boys were wearing soccer jerseys with women's names and numbers on the back.[11] Progress! Megan Rapinoe haircuts all around!

Groups like Let Toys Be Toys are successfully pressuring toy manufacturers to include both boys and girls in toy advertisements (I look forward to seeing some boys on those LEGO Friends packages). The Toy Industry Association nixed the categories of "boy toy" and "girl toy" in its Toy of the Year Awards in 2017, after a concerted effort and petition by parents who objected to the categories, and there's been a small uptick in dolls marketed to boys.[12] Target and Amazon have removed the "boy" and "girl" toy categories on their sites. You can get an Easy-Bake Oven in black and silver now thanks to a New Jersey teen's activism on behalf of her brother.[13] Those are officially boy colors, but surely some girls and intersex and non-binary kids will like them, too. Barbie herself has an impressive line of diverse dolls, including a Muslim fencer and some whose physical proportions are vaguely human, and there's a Ken doll with a man bun. Barbie's maker, Mattel, introduced genderfluid dolls in 2019.

There are improvements in the world of kids' clothes, too. The British clothing company John Lewis announced in 2017 that it would remove "boy" and "girl" labels (not without withstanding some criticism).[14] In 2018, a nine-year-old girl convinced Steph Curry to stop selling his sneakers in only "boy" sizes, and in 2019

Old Navy offered girls' shirts with slogans like "Be Fearless" and "Hear Me Roar."[15] There are many emerging brands of gender-neutral clothes, like Free To Be Kids' pink shirts with unicorns for boys *and* girls (rather than boys' or girls' sections, they have "inspired by boys" and "inspired by girls"). Such clothes tend to be more expensive and niche, like the $25 boys' pink shirt with ice cream scoops and bulldozers from Boy Wonder, which also makes pink and purple boys' T-shirts with unicorns, rainbows, and sparkles. They are cool, but costly, and a complete turnaround from the time when it was *more* expensive to wear heavily gendered clothes, at least feminine ones. Still, these shifts contribute to the project of creating more freedom, at least in purchasing power, and much of it is inspired by consumers pushing back, voting with their dollars, and pressuring big corporations to do better.

It's even happening in employment. One study found that women filled almost a quarter of typically male-dominated jobs, from CEO to chemist, between 2009 and 2017. And a bit more than a quarter of typically female-dominated jobs, from cook to pharmacist, were held by men.[16]

Many people are rethinking their gender beliefs. In 2019, the woman credited with inventing the gender-reveal party eleven years before, Jenna Karvunidis, announced to the world, via a Facebook post, that she had changed her mind about the trend. "Who cares what gender the baby is?" she wrote. "I did at the time because we didn't live in 2019 and didn't know what we know now—that assigning focus on gender at birth leaves out so much of their potential and talents that have nothing to do with what's between their legs." And then she made a new reveal: that daughter, who was announced to the world via pink icing eleven years before, is now a short-haired girl who wears suits. A kid who fits the definition of "a child who is gender nonconforming, a child who is gender variant"—in expression, if not in gender identity.

In other words, Karvunidis's daughter grew up to be quite different from the person she'd imagined when she'd made a cake with pink icing. But, contrary to what most of the media reported, what really alerted Karvunidis to the misguidedness of gender-reveal parties, of the expectations we set when we have them, was when her younger daughter got a "boys'" LEGO set at Christmas, and cried because it wasn't pink. "She came to that conclusion: *If it's pink, it's for me and if it's not pink, it's not for me.* This is a situation that we have to get away from," Karvunidis told me.

At the same time, when Karvunidis announced that she disavowed the trend she'd created, she received international media coverage, mostly from outlets assuming that her suit-wearing daughter was non-binary, and even printing that she was until Karvunidis corrected them. The focus was on her pronouns and identity, not gender stereotypes. People misinterpreted Karvunidis's note about not "assigning focus on gender" and thought she meant "not assigning a gender." But the media obsessing over her daughter's pronouns is not the same as lessening the focus. That's just focusing on a different aspect of gender.

It is not radical to suggest that we focus less on gender, as Karvunidis—who, in high school, both wore a tie and was head cheerleader—said, or that in some fundamental way we treat kids more alike, that we don't assume a pink ponytail means a girl can't carry her luggage. Or, for that matter, that short hair and a baseball uniform mean a kid needs a new name, pronoun, or identity.

The need to know, the ache to classify—that's from adults imposing their experiences, their labels, onto children. If we really want to be grown-ups, maybe we could try learning to embrace ambiguity. In my house, we have a sign that says "Be comfortable being uncomfortable." I'm terrible at it, but it's my goal.

Many young people today already have a far more expansive view of gender than those who came before. A 2019 Pew poll showed that 35 percent of Generation Z and 25 percent of Millennials (as opposed to 16 percent of my own, woefully behind-the-times Generation X) personally know someone who uses gender-neutral pronouns.[17] One poll found that half of millennials see gender more as a spectrum than a binary.[18]

But not everybody is ready to reimagine the entire sex/gender system, or swap out their gender beliefs. Several times when people read drafts of this book, they asked me to address parents of tomboys who have some anxiety that their kid may be trans. These are probably cisgender parents with little experience with trans people who have heard the stories of violence, high suicidality, lack of acceptance, nightmares navigating health insurance, battles that start locally and lead to the Supreme Court. This is foreign territory for them, and they are nervous. They want answers. They want to know what label is right for their child, what their identity will be, how to be supportive, and how to make sure their kids don't make a life-altering wrong decision.

I can't tell you if your child is "just a tomboy" or who they will grow up to be—only your kid can. If your child is in serious distress over their gender, they're not experiencing the freedom that tomboys generally do. But this book has many stories of very successful, smart, happy, and well-adjusted trans and non-binary people whose lives do not reflect the statistics about depression and suicidality because they found support and got the help they needed. They navigated that distress and successfully got to the other side. Life isn't perfect for the people I talked to, but it is not ruled by gender dysphoria. Some people went through traumatic periods and, without transitioning socially or physically, came out on the other side, too. And I talked to many parents of masculine young daughters who never felt any distress or dislocation with their gender, even if the parents did; every experience is possible.

Tey Meadow, the Columbia sociologist who studies trans kids and their families, believes that some kids are consistently trans from an early age and will always be trans. For many other kids, both gender conforming and nonconforming, the outcome is less clear. Gender can be "an emergent feature of somebody's life that changes, that mutates, that is full of ambivalence and contradiction," Meadow told me. "We don't know where that second category of kids will land, so all we can do is cultivate openness, without putting too much of our own anxiety onto them, to let things evolve."

I think it's important for parents, and kids, to understand how sex, gender, and sexuality have been understood in different eras, to see that the way we are experiencing and understanding them now is part of the evolution, and that we've still got so much more to learn. More people now see aspects of gender, of masculinity and femininity and identity, as fixed, and see the body as mutable—the opposite of what many used to believe. But the biological and the cultural are in a constant dance; sex, gender, and sexuality are independent *and* interdependent. What's most natural, I believe, is diversity in all three.

Gender is very important to kids—and to grown-ups. It's the first way we learn to divide and make sense of the world. According to the researchers I talked to, there are no cultures without gender, and none in which children don't divide by sex or gender at some point, in some way. We don't need to ignore or deny it, but neither do we need to exploit it. I suggest that we partition less of childhood into boy-and-girl sections. Stop marketing pink as a girls' color. Sign more girls up for baseball and more boys for ballet. Don't use the words "feminine" and "masculine" to describe personality traits. Let kids dress up in whatever the heck they want. Don't make gender the major focus of their lives. Don't make sex a major criterion in decision-making. Don't let it have so much power over children and childhood.

Changing the culture means more short-haired girls and more boys in pink. It means adapting to new meanings of old words, and for some of us, learning a new lexicon. It means fewer sex-segregated activities for young children, and more space for trans and non-binary and intersex kids, along with gender nonconforming kids who prove how many points along the spectrum or dots along the axes there are, not just between boy and girl, but also between masculine and feminine. Invoke the old-fashioned tomboy, whatever word you may use, and straddle the line, or explore, without shame, what's on either side of it, or stomp on it until it disappears.

Maybe it seems extreme, but from my perspective, it's less extreme than the hyper-gendering of childhood that's already happened.

Research shows that facilitating and supporting kids in their gender—whether that be expression or identity or both—greatly reduces mental health risks.[19] Often discussed are the *fa'afafine* of Samoa, an acknowledged—though sometimes marginalized—third gender, not usually prone to the kinds of mental health problems many trans kids face here because they are facilitated. "There is no compelling evidence that cross-gender behaviors or identities, in and of themselves, cause distress in the individual," one study concluded.[20] Thus, it's not the condition of being trans or nonconforming or non-binary, or even a tomboy, that puts a child at risk; it's the lack of familial and societal acceptance. Along with decreasing the amount and extent of gendering in childhood, we can increase acceptance for all kinds of gender identities and expressions.

"Nobody talks about just the sheer pleasure when you get your gender right," Jiménez told me. Maybe, in the emerging age of pansexuality and gender-independence—the age of self-determination—when, the advertising research group J. Walter Thompson Intelligence reports, 56 percent of Gen-Z knows someone who uses gender-neutral pronouns and only 48 percent identify as exclusively heterosexual, more kids will feel free to express and explore their complex genders and sexualities.[21] I hope so. The lesson from these studies and stories seems less about lines between childhood behaviors and adult outcomes and more about leaving room for kids to explore without the pressure to define themselves in some way that appeases adults and their persistent need for classification.

"Every young person should be exploring gender identity in some way, shape, or form," Mere Abrams, the therapist and educator, who is trans non-binary, told me. "Even cisgender people. Gender identity development is a part of human development for everyone, and all the concepts should be explored for everyone, and where you land is where you land."

As for my kids, I plan to be open and supportive, loving and accepting, no matter who they turn out to be and how they identify. I discuss the complexity of gender with them—the many ways to be a girl and the options beyond that identity.

I once heard a Juilliard professor on the radio, talking about the various pearls of wisdom he'd acquired over decades of teaching. Try not to be too attached to any one outcome, he cautioned. When you make a mistake, lift your hands in the air and cry, "How fascinating!" Instead of worrying about the future, look to it and say, "It will be interesting to find out what happens."

And if you ask me about my children, that's what I'll say. I will wonder. And I will worry. I will try to be comfortable being uncomfortable. And I will love them so much it aches.

But about their futures? It will be interesting to find out what happens.

ACKNOWLEDGMENTS

So many people helped me with this project, whether they wanted to or not. Thank you to my kids, who had to yell "Stop talking about gender, Mama!" at least twenty times during the research and writing process. You make me feel like I won the lottery, every single day. And the hugest of thank-yous to my kind and hilarious husband, Alex, who took on so much to provide me with time and space to write.

Tremendous gratitude for my kids' six grandparents, who contributed in so many ways to the impossible task of being a mother and a writer at the same time: Helaine Selin and Bob Rakoff, who also edited and gave feedback; Peter Davis, Beverly Lazar Davis, Susan Sherwin, and Martin Sherwin, whom I also thank for the writing advice—I put in some short paragraphs for you! And thanks to my siblings, Adrienne Davis, Ben Davis, Lisa Sanditz, and Tim Davis, just for being the super-cool, supportive, and talented bunch that you are.

Thank you to my agent, Eve Attermann—this probably would not have happened if it weren't for you, and you've been a tremendous advocate and at times a human Xanax. Thank you to Deborah Tannen for connecting us. Thank you so much to my editor, Krishan Trotman, for being able to see the potential in this project and pushing me in all the right ways to reach that potential, and her assistant, Carrie Napolitano, for all your hard work. Thanks to the rest of the stellar Hachette team: Sarah Falter, Michael Barrs, Cisca Schreefel, and Lauren Ollerhead.

So many people were incredibly generous with their time, talents, and tales. Most people featured in this book, including my kids, were given the opportunity to review the chapters in which they appeared, and any other portions of the book they wanted, and make or suggest edits (and, yes, my kids had plenty of edits). I tried to make the process of writing this book as inclusive and collaborative as possible, and to account for many different viewpoints and gender belief systems. My interviewees donated their time, not only to be interviewed, but to read what I'd done with those interviews after. I am deeply grateful to all of you who participated in the project of this book. Thank you to all who told me their stories, or granted me interviews, even if I didn't have room to weave them in.

Thank you to the dozens of people I roped in to reading parts of this manuscript or in other ways supporting me, or just having long conversations about gender with me. I am sure I'm forgetting a few people, but here goes: Lizzy Acker, Gretchen Aguiar, Sheana Ahlqvist, Celeste Alexander, Laura Allen, Sami Allen, Jeff Allred, Jenee Anzelonee, Reagan Arthur, Katherine Ayers, Caspar Baldwin, Cris Beam, Dave Beaudry, Ulla Berg, Jennifer Block, Kera Bolonik, Ellen Bonjorno, Bobbi Booker, Amy Brill, Christia Spears Brown, Megan Butler, Sara Clemence, Connie, Suzanne Cope, Lisa Savoy Davis-Ross, Sarah DiGregorio, Diane Ehrensaft, Eric and Zoey, Randi Ettner, Stephanie Feuer, Mia Gaudin, Jean Gazis, Sarah Gee, Jessica Glenn, Elizabeth Gold, Amy Goodman-Kass, Susan Green, Malwina Grochowska, Pamela Grossman, Jack Halberstam, Sarah Jaffe, Karleen Pendleton Jiménez, Dylan and Elie and Samantha, Jude, Mitra S. Kalita, Jenna Karvunidis, Joshua Kendall, Erin Kiernon, Gabby Kirschberg, Soren Kisiel, Carolyn Kogan, Carlyn Kolker, Annie Kunjappy, Chuck Loesner, Judy Lotas, Georgia Lowe, Tris Mamone, Mary Stuart Masterson, Anne McDermott, Tey Meadow, Lizzie Mettler, Karen Michelle, Megan Milks, Kyl Myers, Esther Newton, Jenni Olson, Robert Ostertag, Penny and Nikki, Alissa Quart, Nancy Rawlinson, Allison Ray, Glenis Redmond, Roz Rita, Kate Rope, Sarah Sachs, Joshua Safer, Lauren Sandler, Leonard Sax, Liesl Schwabe, Michele Yulo, Deborah Soh, Jennifer Soto, Lisa Tolin, Luisa Tucker, Tali Vardi, Del La Grace Volcano, Kate Walter, Lorin Wertheimer, and the Wilde family. Special thanks to Melissa Onstad and David Mizner for your marathon, last-minute readings. Thank you to Sarah Palma and Kate Frost Mastrangelo for allowing me to mine our childhood photos.

Thank you to Karen Herskowitz, who suggested, when my daughter was in kindergarten, that we come up with a stock refrain for when kids were confused about her gender. You have helped my family so much over the years.

Thank you to the academics, writers, and experts who not only granted me interviews but looked over the chapters in which they were featured, especially Carol Martin and Sheri Berenbaum, along with C. Lynn Carr, Mario DiGangi, Lise Eliot, Dr. Anne Fausto-Sterling, and May Ling Halim. The historical research of Renée Sentilles and Michelle Abate, who have both written books on tomboy history, was invaluable, as was the incredible research and writing of Jo Paoletti and Elizabeth Sweet. Thank you to Monica Bell and Jane Ackermann for research assistance. And to Lisa Kenney of Gender Spectrum for your time and encouragement to come to the Gender Spectrum Conference.

Acknowledgments

My deepest gratitude to Alex Myers and Mere Abrams, who shared not only their stories but their expertise, and reviewed the manuscript for sensitivity. I learned so much from them. And to Kate Bornstein and Chase Strangio, for allowing me so much of your time and expertise, too.

Thank you to Amy Farley, Mike Woodsworth, Susie Kravets, and Sarah Boriello for so much last-minute childcare, and thank you to my running partner, Janene Licata, who had to listen to me talk about this project almost more than anyone else. And thank you to Hannah Purdy and Betsy Nichols for putting me up/putting up with me.

And thank you to the people who tolerated me talking non-stop about this subject. Good news: We can talk about something else now!

BIBLIOGRAPHY

Abate, Michelle Ann. *Tomboys: A Literary and Cultural History*. Philadelphia, PA: Temple University Press, 2008. https://www.jstor.org/stable/j.ctt14bt346.

Abrahams, Mitra. "Gender Stereotypes in Kids Clothing—A Data Blog," July 5, 2019. http://mitraabrahams.co.uk/gender-stereotypes?fbclid=IwAR3Q2JRo7 _HTkHFHZWk7VyiIoGvtWh5X1EkL84-t_Q6ofX92QdsEyAO1Le8AAPF.

Abrams, Mere. "Mere·Their." Accessed October 25, 2019. https://www.meretheir .com/.

Acker, Lizzy. "Lady Things: The Plight of the Modern Tomboy." *Willamette Week*, January 26, 2016. https://www.wweek.com/arts/2016/01/26/lady-things-the -plight-of-the-modern-tomboy/.

African American Policy Forum. "Black Girls Matter: Pushed Out, Overpoliced and Underprotected," December 30, 2014. http://aapf.org/recent/2014 /12/coming-soon-blackgirlsmatter-pushed-out-overpoliced-and-underprotected.

Ahlqvist, Sheana, May Ling Halim, Faith K. Greulich, Leah E. Lurye, and Diane Ruble. "The Potential Benefits and Risks of Identifying as a Tomboy: A Social Identity Perspective." *Self and Identity* 12, no. 5 (September 1, 2013): 563–81. https://doi.org/10.1080/15298868.2012.717709.

Alan, Sule, Seda Ertac, and Ipek Mumcu. "Gender Stereotypes in the Classroom and Effects on Achievement." *Review of Economics and Statistics* 100, no. 5 (July 16, 2018): 876–90. https://doi.org/10.1162/rest_a_00756.

Alcott, Louisa May. *Little Women*. Penguin, 1989.

Alexander, Gerianne M. "An Evolutionary Perspective of Sex-Typed Toy Preferences: Pink, Blue, and the Brain." *Archives of Sexual Behavior* 32, no. 1 (February 2003): 7–14.

American Civil Liberties Union. "R.G. & G.R. Harris Funeral Homes v EEOC & Aimee Stephens." Accessed October 25, 2019. https://www.aclu.org/cases /rg-gr-harris-funeral-homes-v-eeoc-aimee-stephens.

"The American Tomboy: She Often Becomes a Woman That Men Admire and Worship." *San Francisco Call*, August 2, 1891.

Bibliography

APA. "What Is Gender Dysphoria?" Accessed August 6, 2019. https://www
.psychiatry.org/patients-families/gender-dysphoria/what-is-gender
-dysphoria.

Bainbridge, Jason. "Beyond Pink and Blue: The Quiet Rise of Gender-Neutral
Toys." The Conversation, June 5, 2018. http://theconversation.com/beyond
-pink-and-blue-the-quiet-rise-of-gender-neutral-toys-95147.

Baron-Cohen, Simon. "The Essential Difference: The Truth About the Male
and Female Brain," 2003. https://www.researchgate.net/publication/2324
30614_The_Essential_Difference_The_Truth_About_The_Male
_And_Female_Brain.

Bartlett, Nancy H. "A Retrospective Study of Childhood Gender-Atypical
Behavior in Samoan Fa'afafine." *Archives of Sexual Behavior* 35, no. 6
(December 2006): 659–66. https://doi.org/10.1007/s10508-006-9055-1.

BBC News. "Kim Jong-Un's Sister: 'Sweet but with a Tomboy Streak.'" BBC
.com, February 7, 2018. https://www.bbc.com/news/world-asia-36210695.

Bem, Sandra L. "Beyond Androgyny: Some Presumptuous Prescriptions for a
Liberated Sexual Identity." In *The Psychology of Women: Future Directions
in Research*, 1–23. New York: Psychological Dimensions, 1978. https://
scholar.google.com/scholar_lookup?title=Beyond%20androgyny%3A%20
Some%20presumptuous%20prescriptions%20for%20a%20liberated%20
sexual%20identity&author=S.%20L..%20Bem&publication_year=1978.

Berenbaum, Sheri A., and J. Michael Bailey. "Effects on Gender Identity of
Prenatal Androgens and Genital Appearance: Evidence from Girls with
Congenital Adrenal Hyperplasia." *Journal of Clinical Endocrinology &
Metabolism* 88, no. 3 (March 1, 2003): 1102–6. https://doi.org/10.1210
/jc.2002-020782.

Berenbaum, Sheri A., Kristina L. Korman Bryk, and Adriene M. Beltz. "Early
Androgen Effects on Spatial and Mechanical Abilities: Evidence from Congenital Adrenal Hyperplasia." *Behavioral Neuroscience, Hormones and
Cognition: Perspectives, Controversies, and Challenges for Future Research*
126, no. 1 (February 2012): 86–96. https://doi.org/10.1037/a0026652.

Blakemore, Judith E. Owen, and Renee E. Centers. "Characteristics of Boys'
and Girls' Toys." *Sex Roles* 53, no. 9 (November 1, 2005): 619–33. https://
doi.org/10.1007/s11199-005-7729-0.

Blaszczyk, Regina Lee, and Uwe Spiekermann. *Bright Modernity—Color, Commerce, and Consumer Culture*. Accessed October 17, 2019. https://www.google
.com/books/edition/_/-qUyDwAAQBAJ?hl=en.

Blum, Robert W., MD, MPH, PhD. "Achieving Gender Equality by 2030: Putting
Adolescents at the Center of the Agenda—Global Early Adolescent Study,"

Bibliography

June 2019. https://static1.squarespace.com/static/54431bbee4b0ba652295db6e
/t/5c87bd9ea4222fba7f4f2444/1552399776334/Bellagio_Report_030419.pdf.

Blum, Robert W., Kristin Mmari, and Caroline Moreau. "It Begins at 10: How Gender Expectations Shape Early Adolescence Around the World." *Journal of Adolescent Health* 61, no. 4 (October 1, 2017): S3–4. https://doi.org /10.1016/j.jadohealth.2017.07.009.

Blyton, Enid. *Third Year*. New York: Hachette Children's, 2016.

Boag, Peter. *Re-Dressing America's Frontier Past*. Berkeley: University of California Press, 2012.

Bureau of Labor Statistics. "Employment Characteristics of Families—2018," April 18, 2019. https://www.bls.gov/news.release/pdf/famee.pdf.

Byand, Penn Bullock, and Brandon K. Thorp. "Reporters Find Tragic Story amid Embarrassing Scandal." CNN.com, June 10, 2011. http://webcache .googleusercontent.com/search?q=cache:JPo3F35KLLYJ:www.cnn.com /2011/US/06/08/rekers.sissy.boy.experiment/index.html+&cd=1&hl=en &ct=clnk&gl=us.

Carr, C. Lynn. "Tomboy Resistance and Conformity: Agency in Social Psychological Gender Theory." *Gender and Society* 12, no. 5 (1998): 528–53.

———. "Where Have All the Tomboys Gone? Women's Accounts of Gender in Adolescence." *Sex Roles* 56 (April 5, 2007): 439–48. https://doi.org/10 .1007/s11199-007-9183-7.

Chalabi, Mona. "How Many Parents-to-Be Want to Know the Baby's Sex?" FiveThirtyEight, July 22, 2015. https://fivethirtyeight.com/features/how-many -parents-to-be-want-to-know-the-babys-sex/.

Chandler, Charlotte. *I Know Where I'm Going: Katharine Hepburn, A Personal Biography*. Simon and Schuster, 2010.

Clemence, Sara. "The Gender Divide in Preschoolers' Closets." *New York Times*, August 28, 2018. https://www.nytimes.com/2018/08/28/well/family /the-gender-divide-in-preschoolers-closets.html.

Connors, Catharine. "I Refuse to Call My Daughter a 'Tomboy.'" *Babble*. Accessed October 20, 2019. https://www.babble.com/parenting/i-refuse-to -call-my-daughter-a-tomboy/.

Culp-Ressler, Tara. "Forcing Kids to Stick to Gender Roles Can Actually Be Harmful to Their Health." ThinkProgress, August 7, 2014. https://thinkprogress .org/forcing-kids-to-stick-to-gender-roles-can-actually-be-harmful-to-their -health-34aef42199f2/.

de Beauvoir, Simone. *The Second Sex*. New York: Vintage Books, 1952. https:// www.google.com/books/edition/The_Second_Sex/OgMbKqJMzxcC?hl =en&gbpv=1&dq=%E2%80%9CTo+be+feminine+is+to+show+oneself+a

s+weak,+futile,+passive,+and+docile.%E2%80%9D&pg=PA335&printsec
=frontcover.

Drescher, Jack. "Out of DSM: Depathologizing Homosexuality." *Behavioral Sciences* 5, no. 4 (December 4, 2015): 565–75. https://doi.org/10.3390/bs5040565.

Duffey, Eliza Bisbee. *What Women Should Know: A Woman's Book About Women, Containing Practical Information for Wives and Mothers.* J.M. Stoddart & Company, 1873.

Eckert, Penelope, and Sally McConnell-Ginet. *Language and Gender.* Cambridge University Press, 2013.

Edwards, Tanya. "Store Removes Boys and Girls Labels from Kids Clothes." September 3, 2017. https://www.yahoo.com/lifestyle/uk-retailer-john-lewis -removes-boys-girls-labels-kids-clothes-155813055.html.

Endendijk, Joyce J., Marleen G. Groeneveld, Marian J. Bakermans-Kranenburg, and Judi Mesman. "Gender-Differentiated Parenting Revisited: Meta-Analysis Reveals Very Few Differences in Parental Control of Boys and Girls." *PLOS ONE* 11, no. 7 (July 14, 2016): e0159193. https://doi.org/10.1371 /journal.pone.0159193.

Ettner, Randi, Frederic Ettner, Loren Schechter, Tanya Friese, and Tonya White. "Tomboys Revisited: A Retrospective Comparison of Childhood Behavioral Patterns in Lesbians and Transmen." *Journal of Child and Adolescent Psychiatry* 1, no. 1 (May 30, 2018): 1. https://doi.org/10.14302/issn.2643-6655.jcap-18-2086.

Flores, Andrew R. Jody L. Herman, Gary J. Gates, and Taylor N. T. Brown. "How Many Adults Identify as Transgender in the United States?" The Williams Institute, June 2016. https://williamsinstitute.law.ucla.edu/wp-content /uploads/How-Many-Adults-Identify-as-Transgender-in-the-United-States .pdf.

Formanek-Brunell, Miriam. *Made to Play House: Dolls and the Commercialization of American Girlhood, 1830–1930.* Baltimore, MD: JHU Press, 1998.

Fox, Florence Cornelia. *The Indian Primer.* American Book Company, 1906.

Freud, Sigmund. "The Psychogenesis of a Case of Homosexuality in a Woman." 1920. Accessed October 26, 2019. https://psycnet.apa.org/record/1999-04164-001.

Good, Jessica J., Julie A. Woodzicka, and Lylan C. Wingfield. "The Effects of Gender Stereotypic and Counter-Stereotypic Textbook Images on Science Performance." *Journal of Social Psychology* 150, no. 2 (April 2010): 132–47. https://doi.org/10.1080/00224540903366552.

"Googles-Ideological-Echo-Chamber.Pdf." Accessed October 30, 2019. https:// web.archive.org/web/20170809220001if_/https://diversitymemo-static .s3-us-west-2.amazonaws.com/Googles-Ideological-Echo-Chamber.pdf.

Bibliography

"Google Trends." Accessed October 10, 2019. https://trends.google.com/trends /explore?date=all&geo=US&q=non-binary.

Halberstam, Jack. "Toward a Trans* Feminism." *Boston Review*, January 18, 2018. http://bostonreview.net/gender-sexuality/jack-halberstam-towards-trans -feminism.

Hale, Meredith. "Don't Call My Daughter a Tomboy." HuffPost, January 11, 2016. https://www.huffpost.com/entry/dont-call-my-daughter-a-tomboy_b _8950530.

Hale, Shannon. "What Are We Teaching Boys When We Discourage Them from Reading Books About Girls?" *Washington Post*, October 10, 2018. https://www.washingtonpost.com/entertainment/books/parents-and -teachers-please-stop-discouraging-boys-from-reading-books-about -girls/2018/10/09/f3eaaca6-c820-11e8-b1ed-1d2d65b86d0c_story.html.

Halim, May Ling, Diane N. Ruble, and David M. Amodio. "From Pink Frilly Dresses to 'One of the Boys': A Social-Cognitive Analysis of Gender Identity Development and Gender Bias: Changes in Gender Identity and Gender Bias." *Social and Personality Psychology Compass* 5, no. 11 (November 2011): 933–49. https://doi.org/10.1111/j.1751-9004.2011.00399.x.

Hedreen, Siri. "The Dangers of Gendered Jobs." *Business News Daily*, August 14, 2019. https://www.businessnewsdaily.com/10085-male-female-dominated -jobs.html.

Henry, Lacey. "Change Cumberland Polytechnic High School Graduation Dress Code c/o 2019 and After." Change.org, 2019. https://www.change .org/p/daniel-krumanocker-change-cumberland-polytechnic-high -school-graduation-dress-code-c-o-2019-and-after.

Hicks, David. *Ritual and Belief: Readings in the Anthropology of Religion.* Lanham, MD: Rowman Altamira, 2010. https://books.google.com/books ?id=hdW-AAAAQBAJ&pg=PA319&lpg=PA319&dq=Hijra+roughly+tran slates+to+eunuch+in+Urdu&source=bl&ots=G7Z4fn-caq&sig=ACfU 3U2Oe8aURRIsxjo_YPwpFQfkGdR1fQ&hl=en&sa=X&ved=2ahUK EwjvheyHlbrlAhWpiOAKHUHUAaQQ6AEwCXoECAcQAQ#v=one page&q=Hijra%20roughly%20translates%20to%20eunuch%20in%20 Urdu&f=false.

Hiestand, Katherine, and Heidi Levitt. "Butch Identity Development: The Formation of an Authentic Gender." *Feminism & Psychology* 15 (February 1, 2005): 61. https://doi.org/10.1177/0959353505049709.

Higham, Charles. *Kate: The Life of Katharine Hepburn.* New York: W. W. Norton & Company, 2004.

Bibliography

Hilgenkamp, Kathryn D., and Mary Margaret Livingston. "Tomboys, Masculine Characteristics, and Self-Ratings of Confidence in Career Success." *Psychological Reports* 90, no. 3, Part 1 (June 2002): 743–49. https://doi.org/10.2466/pr0.2002.90.3.743.

"Homogenizing Fashion." Accessed October 17, 2019. http://users.rowan.edu/~mcinneshin/5120/wk13/fashion5.htm.

Houlihan, Jane, Sonya Lunder, and Anila Jacob. "Timeline: BPA from Invention to Phase-Out." EWG, April 22, 2008. https://www.ewg.org/research/timeline-bpa-invention-phase-out.

Hughes, Kathryn. "Gender Roles in the 19th Century." The British Library, May 15, 2014. https://www.bl.uk/romantics-and-victorians/articles/gender-roles-in-the-19th-century.

Hughes, Sarah Anne. "Family of Kirk Murphy Says 'Sissy Boy' Experiment Led to His Suicide." *Washington Post*, June 10, 2011. https://www.washingtonpost.com/blogs/blogpost/post/family-of-kirk-murphy-says-sissy-boy-experiment-led-to-his-suicide/2011/06/10/AGYfgvOH_blog.html.

Hyde, Janet S., B. G. Rosenberg, and Jo Ann Behrman. "Tomboyism." *Psychology of Women Quarterly* 2, no. 1 (September 1, 1977): 73–75. https://doi.org/10.1111/j.1471-6402.1977.tb00574.x.

INSA. "How Common Is Intersex? | Intersex Society of North America." Accessed October 31, 2019. https://isna.org/faq/frequency/.

Johnson, Richard. "Iowa's Pink Visiting Locker Room: 6 Things to Know." SBNation.com, September 23, 2017. https://www.sbnation.com/college-football/2017/9/23/16320460/iowa-hawkeyes-pink-locker-rooms.

Kanze, Dana, Laura Huang, Mark A. Conley, and E. Tory Higgins. "Male and Female Entrepreneurs Get Asked Different Questions by VCs—and It Affects How Much Funding They Get." *Harvard Business Review*, June 27, 2017. https://hbr.org/2017/06/male-and-female-entrepreneurs-get-asked-different-questions-by-vcs-and-it-affects-how-much-funding-they-get.

Kinsey.org. "Prevalance of Homosexuality Study." Accessed October 25, 2019. https://kinseyinstitute.org/research/publications/kinsey-scale.php.

Koss, Maddie. "Madison Girls Soccer Team Bristles at Critics Who Say Players Are Boys."*Milwaukee Journal Sentinel*. Accessed October 25, 2019. https://www.jsonline.com/story/news/2017/08/05/madison-girls-soccer-team-bristles-critics-who-say-players-boys/459741001/.

Kotila, Letitia E., Sarah J. Schoppe-Sullivan, and Claire M. Kamp Dush. "Boy or Girl? Maternal Psychological Correlates of Knowing Fetal Sex." *Personality and Individual Differences* 68 (October 1, 2014): 195–98. https://doi.org/10.1016/j.paid.2014.04.009.

Laughlin, Shepherd. "Gen Z Goes Beyond Gender Binaries in New Innovation Group Data." JWT Intelligence, March 11, 2016. https://www.jwtintelligence.com/2016/03/gen-z-goes-beyond-gender-binaries-in-new-innovation-group-data/.

Lawson, Katie M., Ann C. Crouter, and Susan M. McHale. "Links Between Family Gender Socialization Experiences in Childhood and Gendered Occupational Attainment in Young Adulthood." *Journal of Vocational Behavior* 90 (October 1, 2015): 26–35. https://doi.org/10.1016/j.jvb.2015.07.003.

Lee, Joseph. *The Playground.* Executive Committee of the Playground Association of America, 1919.

Lee, Nancy. "Focusing on Diversity." Google, June 30, 2016. https://blog.google/topics/diversity/focusing-on-diversity30/.

Lemish, Dr. Dafna, and Dr. Colleen Russo Johnson. "The Landscape of Children's Television in the US & Canada." The Center for Scholars & Storytellers, April 2019. https://static1.squarespace.com/static/5c0da585da02bc56793a0b31/t/5cb8ce1b15fcc0e19f3e16b9/1555615269351/The+Landscape+of+Children%27s+TV.pdf.

Ling Halim, May, Elizabeth Dalmut, Faith K. Greulich, Sheana Ahlqvist, Leah E. Lurye, and Diane N. Ruble. "The Role of Athletics in the Self-Esteem of Tomboys." *Child Development Research* 830345 (September 19, 2011). https://doi.org/10.1155/2011/830345.

Linton, E. Lynn (Elizabeth Lynn), Sallie Bingham Center for Women's History and Culture, NcD, and Leona Bowman Carpenter Collection of English and American Literatur, NcD. *The Girl of the Period: And Other Social Essays.* London: Richard Bentley & Son, 1883. http://archive.org/details/girlofperiodothe01lint.

Marcus, Sharon. *Between Women: Friendship, Desire, and Marriage in Victorian England.* Princeton University Press, 2007. https://press.princeton.edu/titles/8259.html.

Martin, Carol Lynn, and Lisa M. Dinella. "Congruence Between Gender Stereotypes and Activity Preference in Self-Identified Tomboys and Non-Tomboys." *Archives of Sexual Behavior* 41, no. 3 (June 2012): 599–610. https://doi.org/10.1007/s10508-011-9786-5.

McKenney, Sarah J., and Rebecca S. Bigler. "Internalized Sexualization and Its Relation to Sexualized Appearance, Body Surveillance, and Body Shame Among Early Adolescent Girls." *Journal of Early Adolescence* 36, no. 2 (November 3, 2014): 171–97. https://doi.org/10.1177/0272431614556889.

McNamara, Mary. "It Was Her Defining Role: Life." *Los Angeles Times,* July 1, 2003, sec. A.

Bibliography

Miller, Allison. *Boyhood for Girls: American Tomboys and the Transformation of Eroticism, 1900–1940*. New Brunswick, NJ: Rutgers University, 2012.

Mondschein, Elaine, Karen E. Adolph, and Catherine S. Tamis-LeMonda. "Gender Bias in Mothers' Expectations About Infant Crawling." *Journal of Experimental Child Psychology* 77, no. 4 (2000): 304–16. https://doi.org/10.1006/jecp.2000.2597.

Money, John, and Anke A. Ehrhardt. *Man and Woman, Boy and Girl: Differentiation and Dimorphism of Gender Identity from Conception to Maturity*. Oxford, England: Johns Hopkins University Press, 1972.

Morgan, Betsy Levonian. "A Three Generational Study of Tomboy Behavior." *Sex Roles* 39, no. 9 (November 1, 1998): 787–800. https://doi.org/10.1023/A:1018816319376.

Muskus, Jeff. "George Rekers, Anti-Gay Activist, Caught with Male Escort 'Rentboy' [UPDATE: Escort Says Rekers Is Gay]." *HuffPost*, July 5, 2010. https://www.huffpost.com/entry/george-rekers-anti-gay-ac_n_565142.

National Eating Disorders Association. "Statistics & Research on Eating Disorders." February 19, 2018. https://www.nationaleatingdisorders.org/statistics-research-eating-disorders.

Newspapers.com. "Newspapers.com Search." Accessed October 30, 2019. http://www.newspapers.com/search/.

Newton, Esther. *My Butch Career*. Durham, NC: Duke University Press, 2018. https://www.dukeupress.edu/my-butch-career.

Nordberg, Jenny. *The Underground Girls of Kabul*. New York: Crown Publishers 2014. https://www.penguinrandomhouse.com/books/213715/the-underground-girls-of-kabul-by-jenny-nordberg/9780307952509/readers-guide/.

O'Dell, Larry. "Christian School Pressured 'Tomboy' Not to Come Back | The Spokesman-Review." Spokesman.com, March 30, 2014. https://www.spokesman.com/stories/2014/mar/30/christian-school-pressured-tomboy-not-to-come-back/.

Okahana, Hironao, and Enyu Zhou. "Graduate Enrollment and Degrees: 2006 to 2016." September 28, 2017. https://cgsnet.org/ckfinder/userfiles/files/CGS_GED16_Report_Final.pdf.

O'Neil, A. Kathleen. "Childhood Tomboyism and Adult Androgyny." *Sex Roles* 34, no. 5 (n.d.): 419–28.

Orenstein, Peggy. "What's Wrong with Cinderella?," *New York Times*, December 24, 2006. https://www.nytimes.com/2006/12/24/magazine/24princess.t.html.

Ostertag, Bob. *Sex Science Self: A Social History of Estrogen, Testosterone, and Identity*. Amherst: University of Massachusetts Press, 2017. https://

Bibliography

www.amazon.com/Sex-Science-Self-Estrogen-Testosterone-ebook/dp /B07CHB9B7Y.

"Our Daughters—Tom-Boys." *Lancaster Examiner,* March 16, 1859.

Paoletti, Jo Barraclough. *Pink and Blue: Telling the Boys from the Girls in America.* Bloomington: Indiana University Press, 2012.

Parachini, Allan. "Tomboy Label Wears Out." *Berkshire Eagle,* May 1, 1988.

"Passing of the Tomboy." *Evening Star,* August 27, 1898.

"The Passing of Tomboys." *Wilkes-Barre Times Leader, The Evening News,* July 20, 1926. http://www.newspapers.com/clip/31372987/wilkesbarre_times _leader_the_evening/.

Perlman, Merrill. "Stylebooks Finally Embrace the Single 'They.'" *Columbia Journalism Review,* March 27, 2017. https://www.cjr.org/language_corner /stylebooks-single-they-ap-chicago-gender-neutral.php.

"Pocahontas | Biography, History, & Cultural Legacy." Britannica.com. Accessed October 21, 2019. https://www.britannica.com/biography/Pocah ontas-Powhatan-princess.

Pollard, Josephine. *Freaks and Frolics of Little Girls & Boys.* New York: McLoughlin Bros, 1887. https://ufdc.ufl.edu/UF00055359/00001/6j.

Pope, McKenna. "Petition · Hasbro: Feature Boys in the Packaging of the Easy-Bake Oven." Change.org, 2012. https://www.change.org/p/hasbro -feature-boys-in-the-packaging-of-the-easy-bake-oven.

Prather, Jane E. "When the Girls Move in: A Sociological Analysis of the Feminization of the Bank Teller's Job." *Journal of Marriage and Family* 33, no. 4 (1971): 777–82. https://doi.org/10.2307/349451.

Ragoonanan, Simon. "Star Wars: Where Is Princess Leia?" Let Toys Be Toys, May 4, 2015. http://lettoysbetoys.org.uk/star-wars-leia-toy-marketing/.

Reby, David, Florence Levréro, Erik Gustafsson, and Nicolas Mathevon. "Sex Stereotypes Influence Adults' Perception of Babies' Cries." *BMC Psychology* 4 (April 14, 2016). https://doi.org/10.1186/s40359-016-0123-6.

Reitman, Erica. "10 Gender-Neutral Nursery Decorating Ideas." HGTV's Decorating & Design Blog. HGTV.com. Accessed October 25, 2019. https://www.hgtv.com/design-blog/design/10-gender-neutral-nursery -decorating-ideas.

Rekers, George. "Treatment of Gender Identity Confusion in Children: Research Findings and Theoretical Implications for Preventing Sexual Identity Confusion and Unwanted Homosexual Attractions in Teenagers and Adults." University of South Carolina School of Medicine, 2009. https://www.genesisce.org/docs/IdentityConfusion.pdf.

"Researching for LGBTQ Health." Accessed October 25, 2019. https://lgbtqhealth
.ca/community/two-spirit.php.

Rowland, Carolyn (Caz). "What Is the Netflix Special Everyone Is Talking
About?" CAZINC. Accessed October 27, 2019. https://www.cazinc.com.au
/home/2018/7/20/what-is-the-netflix-special-everyone-is-talking-about.

Ruble, Diane N., Leah E. Lurye, and Kristina M. Zosuls. "Pink Frilly Dresses
(PFD) and Early Gender Identity," Princeton: Princeton University, 2011.

Rush University Medical Center. "How Gender Affects Health." Accessed
October 10, 2019. https://www.rush.edu/health-wellness/discover-health
/how-gender-affects-health.

Sanbonmatsu, Karissa. *The Biology of Gender, from DNA to the Brain.* TED
Talk. Accessed October 25, 2019. https://www.ted.com/talks/karissa
_sanbonmatsu_the_biology_of_gender_from_dna_to_the_brain
/transcript?language=en.

Sax, Leonard. *Why Gender Matters, Second Edition: What Parents and Teachers Need to Know About the Emerging Science of Sex Differences.* New York:
Doubleday, 2005. https://www.amazon.com/dp/B01N1OOJ0L/ref=dp-kindle
-redirect?_encoding=UTF8&btkr=1.

Schilken, Chuck. "Girl with Short Hair Kicked Out of Soccer Tournament:
'They Only Did It Because I Look like a Boy.'" *Los Angeles Times,* June
6, 2017. https://www.latimes.com/sports/sportsnow/la-sp-girl-disqualified
-soccer-20170606-story.html.

Seavey, Carol A., Phyllis A. Katz and Sue Rosenberg Zalk. "Baby X: The Effect
of Gender Labels on Adult Responses to Infants." *Sex Roles* 1, no. 2 (n.d.):
103–9.

Sentilles, Renée M. *American Tomboys, 1850–1915.* Amherst and Boston:
University of Massachusetts Press, 2018. https://muse.jhu.edu/chapter
/2242189.

"Shortchanging Girls, Shortchanging America: Executive Summary: A Nation-
wide Poll That Assesses Self-Esteem, Educational Experiences, Interest in
Math and Science, and Career Aspirations of Girls and Boys Ages 9–15."
Washington, DC: American Association of University Women, 1994.

Sidorowicz, Laura S., and G. Sparks Lunney. "Baby X Revisited." *Sex Roles* 6,
no. 1 (February 1980): 67–73. https://doi.org/10.1007/BF00288362.

Silverman, Hollie. "2 More States Will Offer a 3rd Gender Option on Driver's
Licenses." CNN, August 1, 2019. https://www.cnn.com/2019/08/01/health
/washington-pennsylvania-gender-x-id/index.html.

Singh, Anita. "New Staging of Enid Blyton's Malory Towers Story Suggests
'Tomboy' Bill Is Really Transgender." *Telegraph,* June 25, 2019. https://

www.telegraph.co.uk/news/2019/06/25/malory-towers-enid-blytons
-tomboy-bill-actually-transgender/.

Sioux City Journal. May 13, 1917.

Stevens, Heidi. "Boys Are Wearing U.S. Women's National Team Jerseys
and That Feels Like Progress." *Chicago Tribune*. Accessed July 13, 2019.
https://www.chicagotribune.com/columns/heidi-stevens/ct-heidi
-stevens-thursday-boys-wearing-womens-soccer-jerseys-0620-20190620
-7qgm7t2j2rgonkosjfjwm4digq-story.html.

Strangio, Chase. "An Open Letter to Those Praising the *New York Times*
'Tomboy' Piece." Medium.com, April 20, 2017. https://medium.com/the
-establishment/an-open-letter-to-those-praising-the-new-york-times
-tomboy-piece-755e655ce31c.

Stryker, Susan. *Transgender History*. Cambridge, MA: Da Capo Press, 2009.
https://www.google.com/books/edition/Transgender_History/kEfZ1kn
AguMC?hl=en&gbpv=1&bsq=(trans-).

Sweet, Elizabeth. "Guys and Dolls No More?" *New York Times*, December 21,
2012. https://www.nytimes.com/2012/12/23/opinion/sunday/gender-based
-toy-marketing-returns.html.

———. "Toys Are More Divided by Gender Now Than They Were 50 Years
Ago." *Atlantic*, December 9, 2014. https://www.theatlantic.com/business
/archive/2014/12/toys-are-more-divided-by-gender-now-than-they-were
-50-years-ago/383556/.

Thomson Reuters Foundation. "The World's Five Most Dangerous Countries
for Women 2018." poll2018.trust.org. Accessed October 27, 2019. http://
poll2018.trust.org/stories/item/?id=${mainContent.identifier}.

Thorne, Barrie. *Gender Play: Girls and Boys in School*. New Brunswick, NJ:
Rutgers University Press, 1993.

Thorpe, JR. "Why We Need to Stop Calling Girls 'Tomboys.'" Bustle.com,
August 24, 2016. https://www.bustle.com/articles/180131-why-we-need-to
-stop-calling-girls-tomboys.

Tolley, Kimberley. *The Science Education of American Girls: A Historical Perspective*. Abingdon, UK: Psychology Press, 2003.

The Toy Association. "The Toy Association | Insipiring Generations of Play."
Accessed October 10, 2019. https://www.toyassociation.org.

Treaster, Joseph B. "Little League Baseball Yields to 'Social Climate' and
Accepts Girls." *New York Times*. June 13, 1974.

Trebay, Guy. "For Capitalism, Every Social Leap Forward Is a Marketing
Opportunity." *New York Times*, September 18, 2018, sec. Style. https://www
.nytimes.com/2018/09/18/style/gender-nonbinary-brand-marketing.html.

Ulrichs, Karl Heinrich. *The Riddle of "Man-Manly Love": The Pioneering Work on Male Homosexuality*. University of Michigan: Prometheus Books. Accessed October 26, 2019. https://books.google.com/books/about/The _Riddle_of_man_manly_Love.html?id=iOrtAAAAMAAJ.

"U.S. Transgender Survey." National Center for Transgender Equality, 2016. https://transequality.org/issues/us-trans-survey.

Van Droogenbroeck, Filip, Bram Spruyt, and Gil Keppens. "Gender Differences in Mental Health Problems Among Adolescents and the Role of Social Support: Results from the Belgian Health Interview Surveys 2008 and 2013." *BMC Psychiatry* 18 (January 10, 2018). https://doi .org/10.1186/s12888-018-1591-4.

Vasey, Paul L., and Nancy H. Bartlett. "What Can the Samoan 'Fa'afafine' Teach Us About the Western Concept of Gender Identity Disorder in Childhood?" *Perspectives in Biology and Medicine* 50, no. 4 (2007): 481–90. https://doi.org/10.1353/pbm.2007.0056.

Vincent, Alice. "Here's the Story from A to Z: How the Spice Girls Made Wannabe." *Telegraph*, July 8, 2016. https://www.telegraph.co.uk/music /artists/heres-the-story-from-a-to-z-how-the-spice-girls-made-wannabe/.

"Virginia Woolf and Her Sister, Vanessa Bell." Accessed October 30, 2019. https://www.smith.edu/woolf/vanessawithtranscript.php.

Walker, Peter. "Popularity of Tomboys Is Encouraging Girls to Swap Gender, Says NHS Psychologist." *Telegraph*, May 8, 2017. https://www.telegraph .co.uk/science/2017/05/08/popularity-tomboys-encouraging-girls-swap -gender-says-nhs-psychologist/.

Weeks, Linton. "Baseball in Skirts, 19th-Century Style." NPR History Dept., NPR.org, July 12, 2015. https://www.npr.org/sections/npr-history-dept/2015 /07/12/421818565/women-s-baseball-in-the-1800s.

Werber, Cassie. "In the United States Gender Equality Is 208 Years Away from Being Recognised." World Economic Forum, August 21, 2019. https:// www.weforum.org/agenda/2019/08/women-walk-bar-208-years-later -paid-same-men/.

West, Candace, and Don H. Zimmerman. "Doing Gender." *Gender and Society* 1, no. 2 (1987): 125–51.

"Where We Are on TV." Accessed October 30, 2019. https://glaad.org/files /WWAT/WWAT_GLAAD_2017-2018.pdf.

Wilder, Laura Ingalls. *Pioneer Girl: The Annotated Autobiography*. Pamela Smith Hill, ed. Pierre, SD: South Dakota Historical Society Press, 2014. https:// www.amazon.com/Pioneer-Girl-Laura-Ingalls-Wilder/dp/0984504176.

Bibliography

Williams, Katherine, Marilyn Goodman, and Richard Green. "Parent-Child Factors in Gender Role Socialization in Girls." *Journal of the American Academy of Child Psychiatry* 24, no. 6 (November 1985): 720–31. https://doi.org/10.1016/S0002-7138(10)60115-X.

"Women and Hollywood, 2018 Statistics." Accessed October 10, 2019. https://womenandhollywood.com/resources/statistics/2018-statistics/.

Women You Should Know. "Little Girl from 1981 Gender Neutral Lego Ad Tells the Story in Her Own Words." Bustle.com, February 12, 2014. https://www.bustle.com/articles/15378-little-girl-from-1981-gender-neutral-lego-ad-tells-the-story-in-her-own-words.

Woods, Rebecca. "The Life and Loves of Anne Lister." BBC.com, May 3, 2019. https://www.bbc.co.uk/news/resources/idt-sh/the_life_and_loves_of_anne_lister.Smith.edu.

Woolf, Virginia. *The Selected Works of Virginia Woolf.* Wordsworth Editions, 2007.

Worldbank.org. "Women, Business and the Law - Gender Equality, Women Economic Empowerment - World Bank Group." Accessed October 10, 2019. https://wbl.worldbank.org/.

WPATH World Professional Association for Transgender Health. "Standards of Care." Accessed August 9, 2019. https://www.wpath.org/publications/soc.

Zajonc, Robert B. "Attitudinal Effects of Mere Exposure." *Journal of Personality and Social Psychology* 9, no. 2, Part.2 (1968): 1–27. https://doi.org/10.1037/h0025848.

Zucker, Kenneth J. "The DSM Diagnostic Criteria for Gender Identity Disorder in Children." *Archives of Sexual Behavior* 39, no. 2 (April 2010): 477–98. https://doi.org/10.1007/s10508-009-9540-4.

Zucker, Kenneth J., and Robert L. Spitzer. "Was the Gender Identity Disorder of Childhood Diagnosis Introduced into DSM-III as a Backdoor Maneuver to Replace Homosexuality? A Historical Note." *Journal of Sex & Marital Therapy* 31, no. 1 (February 2005): 31–42. https://doi.org/10.1080/00926230590475251.

ENDNOTES

Introduction: A Tomboy Emerges

1. Janet S. Hyde, B. G. Rosenberg, and Jo Ann Behrman, "Tomboyism," *Psychology of Women Quarterly* 2, no. 1 (September 1, 1977): 73–75, https://doi.org/10.1111/j.1471-6402.1977.tb00574.x.
2. Betsy Levonian Morgan, "A Three Generational Study of Tomboy Behavior," *Sex Roles* 39, no. 9 (November 1, 1998): 787–800, https://doi.org/10.1023/A:1018816319376.
3. "Do You Know How to Say Tomboy in Different Languages?," accessed December 5, 2019, https://www.indifferentlanguages.com/words/tomboy.
4. BBC News, "Kim Jong-Un's Sister: 'Sweet but with a Tomboy Streak,'" BBC.com, February 7, 2018, https://www.bbc.com/news/world-asia-36210695.
5. "Virginia Woolf and Her Sister, Vanessa Bell," Smith.edu, accessed October 30, 2019, https://www.smith.edu/woolf/vanessawithtranscript.php.
6. "How Common Is Intersex? | Intersex Society of North America," INSA, accessed October 31, 2019, https://isna.org/faq/frequency/.
7. Sheana Ahlqvist et al., "The Potential Benefits and Risks of Identifying as a Tomboy: A Social Identity Perspective," *Self and Identity* 12, no. 5 (September 1, 2013): 563–81, https://doi.org/10.1080/15298868.2012.717709.

Chapter 1: What the Heck Is a Tomboy, Anyway?

1. Josephine Pollard, *Freaks and Frolics of Little Girls & Boys* (New York: McLoughlin Bros, 1887), https://ufdc.ufl.edu/UF00055359/00001/6j.
2. "Newspapers.com Search," Newspapers.com, accessed October 30, 2019, http://www.newspapers.com/search/.
3. "Our Daughters—Tom-Boys," *Lancaster Examiner*, March 16, 1859.
4. Renée M. Sentilles, *American Tomboys, 1850–1915* (Amherst and Boston: University of Massachusetts Press, 2018), https://muse.jhu.edu/chapter/2242189.
5. Laura Ingalls Wilder, *Pioneer Girl: The Annotated Autobiography*, Pamela Smith Hill, ed. (Pierre, SD: South Dakota Historical Society Press, 2014), 103.

6. E. Lynn (Elizabeth Lynn) Linton, Sallie Bingham Center for Women's History and Culture, NcD, and Leona Bowman Carpenter Collection of English and American Literature, NcD, *The Girl of the Period: And Other Social Essays* (London: Richard Bentley & Son, 1883), 138.

7. "Pocahontas | Biography, History, & Cultural Legacy," Britannica.com, accessed October 21, 2019, https://www.britannica.com/biography/Pocahontas-Powhatan-princess; Florence Cornelia Fox, *The Indian Primer* (American Book Company, 1906), 97.

8. Eliza Bisbee Duffey, *What Women Should Know: A Woman's Book About Women, Containing Practical Information for Wives and Mothers* (J. M. Stoddart & Company, 1873), 35.

9. Michelle Ann Abate, *Tomboys: A Literary and Cultural History* (Philadelphia: Temple University Press, 2008), 6, https://www.jstor.org/stable/j.ctt14bt346.

10. Sentilles, *American Tomboys, 1850–1915*, 11.

11. *Evening Star*, August 27, 1898, 17, accessed October 9, 2019, http://www.newspapers.com/image/46348407/.

12. *Sioux City Journal*, May 13, 1917.

13. Miriam Forman-Brunell and Leslie Paris, *The Girls' History and Culture Reader: The Nineteenth Century* (University of Illinois Press, 2011), 226.

14. Miriam Forman-Brunell and Leslie Paris, *The Girls' History and Culture Reader: The Nineteenth Century* (University of Illinois Press, 2011), 234.

15. Linton Weeks, "Baseball in Skirts, 19th-Century Style," NPR History Dept., NPR.org, July 12, 2015, https://www.npr.org/sections/npr-history-dept/2015/07/12/421818565/women-s-baseball-in-the-1800s.

16. Joseph B. Treaster, "Little League Baseball Yields to 'Social Climate' and Accepts Girls," *New York Times*, June 13, 1974.

17. Maddie Koss, "Madison Girls Soccer Team Bristles at Critics Who Say Players Are Boys," *Milwaukee Journal Sentinel*, accessed October 25, 2019, https://www.jsonline.com/story/news/2017/08/05/madison-girls-soccer-team-bristles-critics-who-say-players-boys/459741001/.

18. Chuck Schilken, "Girl with Short Hair Kicked Out of Soccer Tournament: 'They Only Did It Because I Look Like a Boy,'" *Los Angeles Times*, June 6, 2017, https://www.latimes.com/sports/sportsnow/la-sp-girl-disqualified-soccer-20170606-story.html.

19. Sheana Ahlqvist et al., "The Potential Benefits and Risks of Identifying as a Tomboy: A Social Identity Perspective," *Self and Identity* 12, no. 5 (September 1, 2013): 563–81, https://doi.org/10.1080/15298868.2012.717709.

20. Abate, *Tomboys*, xxii.

Chapter 2: Tomboys? Okay! Sissies? No Way!

1. "When Did Girls Start Wearing Pink?," Smithsonian, accessed November 25, 2019, https://www.smithsonianmag.com/arts-culture/when-did-girls-start-wearing-pink-1370097/.
2. "Our Daughters—Tom-Boys."
3. Jack Drescher, "Out of DSM: Depathologizing Homosexuality," *Behavioral Sciences* 5, no. 4 (December 4, 2015): 565–75, https://doi.org/10.3390/bs5040565.
4. Elizabeth Sweet, "Toys Are More Divided by Gender Now Than They Were 50 Years Ago," *Atlantic*, December 9, 2014, https://www.theatlantic.com/business/archive/2014/12/toys-are-more-divided-by-gender-now-than-they-were-50-years-ago/383556/.
5. Anna de Koven, "Athletic Activity of Women Is Nation-Wide," *Good Housekeeping*, August, 1912.
6. Regina Lee Blaszczyk and Uwe Spiekermann, *Bright Modernity—Color, Commerce, and Consumer Culture* (London: Palgrave Macmillan, 2017), 5.
7. "Homogenizing Fashion," *Time*, November 14, 1927, accessed October 17, 2019, http://users.rowan.edu/~mcinneshin/5120/wk13/fashion5.htm.
8. Richard Johnson, "Iowa's Pink Visiting Locker Room: 6 Things to Know," SBNation.com, September 23, 2017, https://www.sbnation.com/college-football/2017/9/23/16320460/iowa-hawkeyes-pink-locker-rooms.
9. Dorothy Barclay, "'TOMBOY' PHASE CALLED NATURAL; Pamphlet Says That 'Rowdy' Period for Girls 7 to 10 Is Common Occurrence," *New York Times*, September 20, 1950, sec. Archives, https://www.nytimes.com/1950/09/20/archives/tomboy-phase-called-natural-pamphlet-says-that-rowdy-period-for.html.
10. Blaszczyk and Spiekermann, *Bright Modernity*.

Katharine

1. Charlotte Chandler, *I Know Where I'm Going: Katharine Hepburn, A Personal Biography* (Simon and Schuster, 2010), 29.
2. "Arresting Dress: A Timeline of Anti-Cross-Dressing Laws in the United States," *PBS NewsHour*, May 31, 2015, https://www.pbs.org/newshour/nation/arresting-dress-timeline-anti-cross-dressing-laws-u-s.
3. Charles Higham, *Kate: The Life of Katharine Hepburn* (W. W. Norton & Company, 2004), 71.
4. Mary McNamara, "It Was Her Defining Role: Life," *Los Angeles Times*, July 1, 2003, sec. A.

5. Katharine Hepburn, 1981 Barbara Walters Interviews of a Lifetime, accessed November 25, 2019, https://www.youtube.com/watch?v=Bdr9FMhJRaA.

Chapter 3: Sporty Spice Dropkicks the Tomboy

1. Alice Vincent, "Here's the Story from A to Z: How the Spice Girls Made Wannabe," *Telegraph*, July 8, 2016, https://www.telegraph.co.uk/music/artists/heres-the-story-from-a-to-z-how-the-spice-girls-made-wannabe/.
2. Abate, *Tomboys*, 222.
3. Peggy Orenstein, "What's Wrong with Cinderella?," *New York Times*, December 24, 2006, https://www.nytimes.com/2006/12/24/magazine/24princess.t.html.
4. Nancy Lee, "Focusing on Diversity," Google, June 30, 2016, https://blog.google/topics/diversity/focusing-on-diversity30/.
5. Elizabeth Sweet, "Guys and Dolls No More?," *New York Times*, December 21, 2012, https://www.nytimes.com/2012/12/23/opinion/sunday/gender-based-toy-marketing-returns.html.
6. LEGO Systems Inc, "LEGO Systems Built Tenth Consecutive Year of Growth in U.S. Toy Market," accessed December 4, 2019, https://www.prnewswire.com/news-releases/lego-systems-built-tenth-consecutive-year-of-growth-in-us-toy-market-300035004.html.
7. Judith E. Owen Blakemore and Renee E. Centers, "Characteristics of Boys' and Girls' Toys," *Sex Roles* 53, no. 9 (November 1, 2005): 619–33, https://doi.org/10.1007/s11199-005-7729-0.
8. Women You Should Know, "Little Girl from 1981 Gender Neutral Lego Ad Tells the Story in Her Own Words," Bustle.com, February 12, 2014, https://www.bustle.com/articles/15378-little-girl-from-1981-gender-neutral-lego-ad-tells-the-story-in-her-own-words.
9. Jason Bainbridge, "Beyond Pink and Blue: The Quiet Rise of Gender-Neutral Toys," *The Conversation*, June 5, 2018, http://theconversation.com/beyond-pink-and-blue-the-quiet-rise-of-gender-neutral-toys-95147.
10. Elizabeth A. Harris, "Family of Boy Who Wears Dresses Sues Education Department," *New York Times*, August 29, 2017, sec. New York, https://www.nytimes.com/2017/08/29/nyregion/family-of-boy-who-wears-dresses-sues-education-department.html.
11. Lauren Spinner, Lindsey Cameron, and Rachel Calogero, "Peer Toy Play as a Gateway to Children's Gender Flexibility: The Effect of (Counter)Stereotypic Portrayals of Peers in Children's Magazines," *Sex Roles* 79, no. 5 (September 1, 2018): 314–28, https://doi.org/10.1007/s11199-017-0883-3.

Chapter 4: Ode to Jo

1. *The Facts of Life*, "A Death in the Family" (TV Episode 1984), IMDb, accessed November 22, 2019, http://www.imdb.com/title/tt0575285/characters/nm0 924075.

2. *Shortchanging Girls, Shortchanging America: Executive Summary: A Nationwide Poll That Assesses Self-Esteem, Educational Experiences, Interest in Math and Science, and Career Aspirations of Girls and Boys Ages 9–15* (Washington, DC: American Association of University Women, 1994).

3. AAPF, "Black Girls Matter: Pushed Out, Overpoliced and Underprotected," December 30, 2014, http://aapf.org/recent/2014/12/coming-soon -blackgirlsmatter-pushed-out-overpoliced-and-underprotected.

4. George Gerbner and L. Gross, "Living With Television: The Violence Profile," *Journal of Communication* 26 (June 1, 1976): 182, https://doi .org/10.1111/j.1460-2466.1976.tb01397.x.

5. "Where We Are on TV," accessed October 30, 2019, https://glaad.org/files /WWAT/WWAT_GLAAD_2017-2018.pdf.

6. Gallup Inc, "In U.S., Estimate of LGBT Population Rises to 4.5%," Gallup .com, May 22, 2018, https://news.gallup.com/poll/234863/estimate-lgbt -population-rises.aspx.

7. Enid Blyton, *Third Year* (New York: Hachette Children's, 2016); Anita Singh, "New Staging of Enid Blyton's *Malory Towers* Story Suggests 'Tomboy' Bill Is Really Transgender," *Telegraph*, June 25, 2019, https://www .telegraph.co.uk/news/2019/06/25/malory-towers-enid-blytons-tomboy -bill-actually-transgender/.

8. "Hello, Arya! 'Game of Thrones' Baby Names Are for Girls," *New York Times*, accessed December 4, 2019, https://www.nytimes.com/2019/04/29 /style/game-of-thrones-baby-names.html.

9. Dr. Dafna Lemish and Dr. Colleen Russo Johnson, *The Landscape of Children's Television in the US & Canada* (The Center for Scholars & Storytellers, April 2019), https://static1.squarespace.com/static/5c0da585da02bc56793a 0b31/t/5cb8ce1b15fcc0e19f3e16b9/1555615269351/The+Landscape+of +Children%27s+TV.pdf.

10. May Ling Halim, Diane N. Ruble, and Catherine S. Tamis-LeMonda, "Four-Year-Olds' Beliefs About How Others Regard Males and Females," *British Journal of Developmental Psychology* 31, no. 1 (March 2013): 128 –35, https://doi.org/10.1111/j.2044-835X.2012.02084.x.

11. Bureau of Labor Statistics, "Employment Characteristics of Families— 2018," April 18, 2019, https://www.bls.gov/news.release/pdf/famee.pdf.

Chapter 5: The Best of Both Worlds

1. Candace West and Don H. Zimmerman, "Doing Gender," *Gender and Society* 1, no. 2 (1987): 125–51.
2. Carol Lynn Martin and Lisa M. Dinella, "Congruence Between Gender Stereotypes and Activity Preference in Self-Identified Tomboys and Non-Tomboys," *Archives of Sexual Behavior* 41, no. 3 (June 2012): 599, https://doi.org/10.1007/s10508-011-9786-5.
3. Ahlqvist et al., "The Potential Benefits and Risks of Identifying as a Tomboy," 564.
4. Katherine Williams, Marilyn Goodman, and Richard Green, "Parent-Child Factors in Gender Role Socialization in Girls," *Journal of the American Academy of Child Psychiatry* 24, no. 6 (November 1985): 723, https://doi.org/10.1016/S0002-7138(10)60115-X.
5. Kristina R. Olson and Elizabeth A. Enright, "Do Transgender Children (Gender) Stereotype Less Than Their Peers and Siblings?," *Developmental Science* 21, no. 4 (July 2018): e12606, https://doi.org/10.1111/desc.12606.
6. Ahlqvist et al., "The Potential Benefits and Risks of Identifying as a Tomboy," 564.
7. C. Lynn Carr, "Tomboy Resistance and Conformity: Agency in Social Psychological Gender Theory," *Gender and Society* 12, no. 5 (1998): 528–53.
8. Esther Newton, *My Butch Career* (Durham: Duke University Press, 2018), 57, accessed May 6, 2019, https://www.dukeupress.edu/my-butch-career.
9. Sandra L. Bem, "Beyond Androgyny: Some Presumptuous Prescriptions for a Liberated Sexual Identity," in *The Psychology of Women: Future Directions in Research* (New York: Psychological Dimensions, 1978), 1–23.
10. Newton, *My Butch Career*, 57.
11. A. Kathleen O'Neil. "Childhood Tomboyism and Adult Androgyny." *Sex Roles* 34, no. 5 (n.d.): 419–28.
12. Kathryn D. Hilgenkamp and Mary Margaret Livingston, "Tomboys, Masculine Characteristics, and Self-Ratings of Confidence in Career Success," *Psychological Reports* 90, no. 3, Part 1 (June 2002): 743–49, https://doi.org/10.2466/pr0.2002.90.3.743.
13. E. Paul Torrance, *Guiding Creative Talent* (Pickle Partners Publishing, 2018), 94.
14. Virginia Woolf, *The Selected Works of Virginia Woolf* (Wordsworth Editions, 2007), 627.

Chapter 6: Are Tomboys Born or Made?

1. Jane Houlihan, Sonya Lunder, and Anila Jacob, "Timeline: BPA from Invention to Phase-Out," EWG, April 22, 2008, https://www.ewg.org /research/timeline-bpa-invention-phase-out.

2. Melissa Hines et al., "Testosterone During Pregnancy and Gender Role Behavior of Preschool Children: A Longitudinal, Population Study," *Child Development* 73, no. 6 (December 2002): 1678–87, https://doi .org/10.1111/1467-8624.00498.

3. Until quite recently most girls with CAH were given "normalizing" genital surgeries, though that is starting to be illegal, and at the least discouraged, in some states, due to intersex activism and because girls with CAH have a higher potential of non-female gender identity than the general population.

4. John Money and Anke A. Ehrhardt, *Man and Woman, Boy and Girl: Differentiation and Dimorphism of Gender Identity from Conception to Maturity* (Oxford, England: Johns Hopkins U. Press, 1972).

5. This study as well as the studies on intersex people resulting in the term "gender role" were conducted in part by Johns Hopkins psychologist and sexologist John Money. While he did a lot of groundbreaking and important work, he is a controversial, often reviled, figure. Because he was so convinced that gender was socially constructed, he infamously convinced the parents of a boy with a botched circumcision, David Reimer, to raise him as a girl, which didn't work; Reimer later killed himself (though some have pointed out to me that his family had a history of depression).

6. Sheri A. Berenbaum and J. Michael Bailey, "Effects on Gender Identity of Prenatal Androgens and Genital Appearance: Evidence from Girls with Congenital Adrenal Hyperplasia," *Journal of Clinical Endocrinology & Metabolism* 88, no. 3 (March 1, 2003): 1102–6, https://doi.org/10.1210/jc .2002-020782.

7. Sheri A. Berenbaum, Kristina L. Korman Bryk, and Adriene M. Beltz, "Early Androgen Effects on Spatial and Mechanical Abilities: Evidence from Congenital Adrenal Hyperplasia," *Behavioral Neuroscience, Hormones and Cognition: Perspectives, Controversies, and Challenges for Future Research* 126, no. 1 (February 2012): 86–96, https://doi.org/10.1037/a0026652.

8. Andrew R. Flores et al., "How Many Adults Identify as Transgender in the United States?" (The Williams Institute, June 2016), https:// williamsinstitute.law.ucla.edu/wp-content/uploads/How-Many-Adults -Identify-as-Transgender-in-the-United-States.pdf.

9. "Prevalence of Homosexuality Study," accessed October 25, 2019, https://kinseyinstitute.org/research/publications/kinsey-scale.php.

10. People with an intersex condition called androgen-insensitivity syndrome, or AIS, generally have XY chromosomes and produce testosterone and other androgens, but their bodies don't respond, or are insensitive, to them. So they are genetically male but don't develop male-typical genitals and are usually raised as female until their condition is discovered at puberty, when they don't menstruate. Sometimes their genitals are not easily classifiable as either male or female at birth. They generally have female gender identities. See: https://ghr.nlm.nih.gov/condition/androgen-insensitivity-syndrome.

11. Simon Baron-Cohen, "The Essential Difference: The Truth About the Male and Female Brain" (2003), https://www.researchgate.net/publication/232430614_The_Essential_Difference_The_Truth_About_The_Male_And_Female_Brain.

12. Hironao Okahana and Enyu Zhou, "Graduate Enrollment and Degrees: 2006 to 2016," September 28, 2017, https://cgsnet.org/ckfinder/userfiles/files/CGS_GED16_Report_Final.pdf.

13. "Google's Ideological Echo Chamber," accessed October 30, 2019, https://web.archive.org/web/20170809220001if_/https://diversitymemo-static.s3-us-west-2.amazonaws.com/Googles-Ideological-Echo-Chamber.pdf.

14. Karissa Sanbonmatsu:, *The Biology of Gender, from DNA to the Brain*, TED Talk, accessed October 25, 2019, https://www.ted.com/talks/karissa_sanbonmatsu_the_biology_of_gender_from_dna_to_the_brain/transcript?language=en.

15. Sarah Ditum, "What Is Gender, Anyway?," *New Statesman*, May 16, 2016, https://www.newstatesman.com/politics/feminism/2016/05/what-gender-anyway.

16. Bob Ostertag, *Sex Science Self: A Social History of Estrogen, Testosterone, and Identity* (Amherst: University of Massachusetts Press, 2017), https://www.amazon.com/Sex-Science-Self-Estrogen-Testosterone-ebook/dp/B07CHB9B7Y.

17. "Usual Weekly Earnings of Wage and Salary Workers Third Quarter 2019," n.d., 10.

18. "NAACP | Criminal Justice Fact Sheet," NAACP, accessed December 5, 2019, https://www.naacp.org/criminal-justice-fact-sheet/.

19. Mary Beth Flanders-Stepans, "Alarming Racial Differences in Maternal Mortality," *Journal of Perinatal Education* 9, no. 2 (2000): 50–51, https://doi.org/10.1624/105812400X87653.

20. Irma T. Elo and Samuel H. Preston, Racial and Ethnic Differences in Mortality at Older Ages (National Academies Press (US), 1997), https://www.ncbi.nlm.nih.gov/books/NBK109843/.

21. "How Gender Affects Health," Rush University Medical Center, accessed October 10, 2019, https://www.rush.edu/health-wellness/discover-health/how-gender-affects-health.

22. Kimberley Tolley, *The Science Education of American Girls: A Historical Perspective* (Abingdon, UK: Psychology Press, 2003).

23. Jessica J. Good, Julie A. Woodzicka, and Lylan C. Wingfield, "The Effects of Gender Stereotypic and Counter-Stereotypic Textbook Images on Science Performance," *Journal of Social Psychology* 150, no. 2 (April 2010): 132–47, https://doi.org/10.1080/00224540903366552.

24. Leonard Sax, *Why Gender Matters, Second Edition: What Parents and Teachers Need to Know About the Emerging Science of Sex Differences* (New York: Doubleday, 2005), 150.

25. Jane E. Prather, "When the Girls Move in: A Sociological Analysis of the Feminization of the Bank Teller's Job," *Journal of Marriage and Family* 33, no. 4 (1971): 777–82, https://doi.org/10.2307/349451.

26. Penelope Eckert and Sally McConnell-Ginet, *Language and Gender* (Cambridge University Press, 2013), 27.

27. Berenbaum, Bryk, and Beltz, "Early Androgen Effects on Spatial and Mechanical Abilities."

28. Melissa Hines et al., "Prenatal Androgen Exposure Alters Girls' Responses to Information Indicating Gender-Appropriate Behaviour," *Philosophical Transactions of the Royal Society B: Biological Sciences* 371, no. 1688 (February 19, 2016), https://doi.org/10.1098/rstb.2015.0125.

Becky

1. Penn Bullock Byand and Brandon K. Thorp, "Reporters Find Tragic Story amid Embarrassing Scandal," CNN.com, June 10, 2011, http://webcache.googleusercontent.com/search?q=cache:JPo3F35KLLYJ:www.cnn.com/2011/US/06/08/rekers.sissy.boy.experiment/index.html+&cd=1&hl=en&ct=clnk&gl=us.

2. George Rekers, "Treatment of Gender Identity Confusion in Children: Research Findings and Theoretical Implications for Preventing Sexual Identity Confusion and Unwanted Homosexual Attractions in Teenagers and Adults," *University of South Carolina School of Medicine*, 2009, https://www.genesisce.org/docs/IdentityConfusion.pdf.

Chapter 7: Beware the End of the Princess Phase

1. Rajini Vaidyanathan, "Before Clinton, There Was Chisholm," BBC News, January 26, 2016, sec. Magazine, https://www.bbc.com/news/magazine -35057641.
2. Diane N. Ruble, Leah E. Lurye, and Kristina M. Zosuls, "Pink Frilly Dresses (PFD) and Early Gender Identity," *Princeton Report on Knowledge* (P-ROK), 2011, 5.
3. May Ling Halim, Diane N. Ruble, and David M. Amodio, "From Pink Frilly Dresses to 'One of the Boys': A Social-Cognitive Analysis of Gender Identity Development and Gender Bias: Changes in Gender Identity and Gender Bias," *Social and Personality Psychology Compass* 5, no. 11 (November 2011): 933–49, https://doi.org/10.1111/j.1751-9004.2011.00399.x.
4. Gerianne M. Alexander, "An Evolutionary Perspective of Sex-Typed Toy Preferences: Pink, Blue, and the Brain," *Archives of Sexual Behavior* 32, no. 1 (February 2003): 7–14.
5. This may also happen with boys at the same age, that they insist that they are girls, either because they are trans and/or because they have developed a love of PFD without being trans. Kristina Olson's TransYouth Project has documented trans kids going through very similar gender trajectories as cisgender kids.
6. Halim, Ruble, and Amodio, "From Pink Frilly Dresses to 'One of the Boys,'" 937.
7. "Women's Wages: Equal Pay for Women and the Wage Gap," NWLC (blog), accessed December 5, 2019, https://nwlc.org/issue/equal-pay-and -the-wage-gap/.
8. Simone de Beauvoir, *The Second Sex* (New York: Vintage Books, 1952), 335.
9. Robert B. Zajonc, "Attitudinal Effects of Mere Exposure," *Journal of Personality and Social Psychology* 9, no. 2, Part 2 (1968): 1–27, https://doi .org/10.1037/h0025848.

Coco

1. Linda Simon, *Coco Chanel* (London: Reaktion Books, 2011), https://www .bookdepository.com/Coco-Chanel-Linda-Simon/9781861898593.

Chapter 8: Why Do Tomboys Wear Boys' Clothes?

1. Jenny Nordberg, *The Underground Girls of Kabul* (New York: Crown Publishers, 2014), 14.

2. Thomson Reuters Foundation, "The World's Five Most Dangerous Countries for Women 2018," accessed October 27, 2019, http://poll2018.trust.org.
3. "The American Tomboy: She Often Becomes a Woman That Men Admire and Worship," *San Francisco Call*, August 2, 1891.
4. Williams, Goodman, and Green, "Parent-Child Factors in Gender Role Socialization in Girls."
5. Mitra Abrahams, "Gender Stereotypes in Kids Clothing—a Data Blog," July 5, 2019, http://mitraabrahams.co.uk/gender-stereotypes.
6. Sara Clemence, "The Gender Divide in Preschoolers' Closets," *New York Times*, August 28, 2018, https://www.nytimes.com/2018/08/28/well/family /the-gender-divide-in-preschoolers-closets.html.
7. Larry O'Dell, "Christian School Pressured 'Tomboy' Not to Come Back | The Spokesman-Review," Spokesman.com, March 30, 2014, https://www .spokesman.com/stories/2014/mar/30/christian-school-pressured -tomboy-not-to-come-back/.
8. American Civil Liberties Union, "R.G. & G.R. Harris Funeral Homes v EEOC & Aimee Stephens," accessed October 25, 2019, https://www.aclu .org/cases/rg-gr-harris-funeral-homes-v-eeoc-aimee-stephens.
9. Lacey Henry, "Change Cumberland Polytechnic High School Graduation Dress Code c/o 2019 and After," Change.org, 2019, https://www.change .org/p/daniel-krumanocker-change-cumberland-polytechnic-high -school-graduation-dress-code-c-o-2019-and-after.

Chapter 9: Parenting Between the Pink and Blue

1. Ahlqvist et al., "The Potential Benefits and Risks of Identifying as a Tomboy."
2. Letitia E. Kotila, Sarah J. Schoppe-Sullivan, and Claire M. Kamp Dush, "Boy or Girl? Maternal Psychological Correlates of Knowing Fetal Sex," *Personality and Individual Differences* 68 (October 1, 2014): 195–98, https:// doi.org/10.1016/j.paid.2014.04.009.
3. Carr, "Tomboy Resistance and Conformity."
4. Williams, Goodman, and Green, "Parent-Child Factors in Gender Role Socialization in Girls."
5. Katie M. Lawson, Ann C. Crouter, and Susan M. McHale, "Links Between Family Gender Socialization Experiences in Childhood and Gendered Occupational Attainment in Young Adulthood," *Journal of Vocational Behavior* 90 (October 1, 2015): 26–35, https://doi.org/10.1016/j.jvb.2015.07.003.

6. Lawson, Crouter, and McHale, "Links Between Family Gender Socialization Experiences in Childhood and Gendered Occupational Attainment in Young Adulthood."

7. Carol A. Seavey, Phyllis A. Katz, and Sue Rosenberg Zalk, "Baby X: The Effect of Gender Labels on Adult Responses to Infants," *Sex Roles* 1, no. 2 (n.d.): 103–9.

8. Laura S. Sidorowicz and G. Sparks Lunney, "Baby X Revisited | SpringerLink," *Sex Roles* 6, no. 1 (February 1980): 67–73, https://doi.org/10.1007 /BF00288362.

9. Elaine Mondschein, Karen E. Adolph, and Catherine S. Tamis-LeMonda, "Gender Bias in Mothers' Expectations About Infant Crawling," *Journal of Experimental Child Psychology* 77, no. 4 (2000): 304–16, https://doi.org /10.1006/jecp.2000.2597.

10. David Reby et al., "Sex Stereotypes Influence Adults' Perception of Babies' Cries," *BMC Psychology* 4 (April 14, 2016), https://doi.org/10.1186 /s40359-016-0123-6.

11. Eckert and McConnell-Ginet, *Language and Gender*, 11. A recent meta-analysis concluded that studies from the 1970s and '80s and those from after the '90s show different kinds of sex-typed parenting. J. J. Endendijk, M. G. Groeneveld, M. J. Bakermans-Kranenburg, and J. Mesman, in "Gender-Differentiated Parenting Revisited: Meta-Analysis Reveals Very Few Differences in Parental Control of Boys and Girls" (*PLOS ONE* 11, no. 7: e0159193, https://doi.org/10.1371/journal.pone.0159193), suggested that "studies published in the 1970s and 1980s reported more autonomy-supportive strategies with boys than toward girls, but from 1990 onwards parents showed somewhat more autonomy-supportive strategies with girls than toward boys." They concluded: "in general the differences between parenting of boys versus girls are minimal." I have not found that to be the case.

12. "Women and Hollywood, 2018 Statistics," https://womenandhollywood.com, accessed October 10, 2019, https://womenandhollywood.com/resources /statistics/2018-statistics/; "Women, Business and the Law—Gender Equal ity, Women Economic Empowerment - World Bank Group," Worldbank.org, accessed October 10, 2019, https://wbl.worldbank.org/.

13. Erica Reitman, "10 Gender-Neutral Nursery Decorating Ideas," *HGTV's Decorating & Design Blog*, HGTV.com, accessed October 25, 2019, https://www .hgtv.com/design-blog/design/10-gender-neutral-nursery-decorating-ideas.

14. Mona Chalabi, "How Many Parents-to-Be Want to Know the Baby's Sex?," *FiveThirtyEight*, July 22, 2015, https://fivethirtyeight.com/features/how -many-parents-to-be-want-to-know-the-babys-sex/.

15. Robert W. Blum, MD, MPH, PhD, "Achieving Gender Equality by 2030: Putting Adolescents at the Center of the Agenda—Global Early Adolescent Study," June 2019, https://static1.squarespace.com/static/54431bbee4b0ba652295db6e /t/5c87bd9ea4222fba7f4f2444/1552399776334/Bellagio_Report_030419.pdf; Robert W. Blum, Kristin Mmari, and Caroline Moreau, "It Begins at 10: How Gender Expectations Shape Early Adolescence Around the World," *Journal of Adolescent Health* 61, no. 4 (October 1, 2017): S3–4, https://doi.org/10.1016/j .jadohealth.2017.07.009.
16. "Ban on Harmful Gender Stereotypes in Ads Comes into Force," ASA | CAP, accessed December 5, 2019, https://www.asa.org.uk/news/ban-on -harmful-gender-stereotypes-in-ads-comes-into-force.html.

Chapter 10: What Happens to Tomboys When Puberty Hits? (A Brief Introduction to a Giant Question)

1. Morgan, "A Three Generational Study of Tomboy Behavior."
2. "What Is Gender Dysphoria?," accessed August 6, 2019, https://www.psych iatry.org/patients-families/gender-dysphoria/what-is-gender-dysphoria.
3. Joseph Lee, *The Playground* (Executive Committee of the Playground Association of America, 1919), 229.

Chapter 11: I Used to Be a Tomboy. Now I'm a Full-Grown Lesbian.

1. Guerrilla Girls (group of artists), *Bitches, Bimbos, and Ballbreakers: The Guerrilla Girls' Illustrated Guide to Female Stereotypes* (New York: Penguin Books, 2003), 14.
2. That the same words mean very different things to different people is a constant challenge in this book. Many people object to my use of the words "boys" and "girls" as referring to physically distinct people: that is, people assigned male at birth and people assigned female. "Boy" and "girl," "man" and "woman," to many people refer only to a gender identity, regardless of any physical characteristics. And, of course, to even more people, they are interchangeable with "male" and "female." How to balance the beliefs of different groups eludes me, but I've made an attempt to acknowledge different definitions, while hewing, generally, to the definitions used in the academic and scientific research I've relied on. "Butch" is yet another word that can have many definitions. In this chapter, butch mostly means "mannish" lesbian.
3. Kathryn Hughes, "Gender Roles in the 19th Century," The British Library, May 15, 2014, https://www.bl.uk/romantics-and-victorians/articles/gender -roles-in-the-19th-century.

Endnotes

4. Sharon Marcus, *Between Women: Friendship, Desire, and Marriage in Victorian England* (Princeton University Press, 2007), https://www.jstor.org /stable/j.ctt7rkz8.

5. Louisa May Alcott, *Little Women* (Penguin, 1989), xiii.

6. Peter Boag, *Re-Dressing America's Frontier Past* (Berkeley: University of California Press, 2012), 52.

7. Sigmund Freud, "The Psychogenesis of a Case of Homosexuality in a Woman," (1920), accessed October 26, 2019, https://psycnet.apa.org/record /1999-04164-001.

8. Karl Heinrich Ulrichs, *The Riddle of "Man-Manly Love": The Pioneering Work on Male Homosexuality* (University of Michigan: Prometheus Books), accessed October 26, 2019, https://books.google.com/books/about /The_Riddle_of_man_manly_Love.html?id=iOrtAAAAMAAJ.

9. Allison Miller, *Boyhood for Girls: American Tomboys and the Transformation of Eroticism, 1900–1940* (New Brunswick, NJ: Rutgers University, 2012), 7.

10. Abate notes that, due to the Comstock Act and the Hays Code in media and film, lesbianism could not be portrayed as normal and healthy and happy. These tomboys-turned-butch-women didn't just have to be tamed, but portrayed as deviant. She notes the use of words like "odd" or "warped" in these novels, as well as the fact that they were designed as much to stoke the interest of straight men as lesbian women.

11. Jack Drescher, "Out of DSM: Depathologizing Homosexuality," *Behavioral Sciences* 5, no. 4 (December 4, 2015): 565–75, https://doi.org/10.3390 /bs5040565.

12. Abate, *Tomboys*, xxi.

13. Randi Ettner et al., "Tomboys Revisited: A Retrospective Comparison of Childhood Behavioral Patterns in Lesbians and Transmen," *Journal of Child and Adolescent Psychiatry* 1, no. 1 (May 30, 2018): 1, https://doi.org/10.14302 /issn.2643-6655.jcap-18-2086.

14. Carolyn (Caz) Rowland, "What Is the Netflix Special Everyone Is Talking About?," CAZINC, accessed October 27, 2019, https://www.cazinc.com.au /home/2018/7/20/what-is-the-netflix-special-everyone-is-talking-about.

15. Rebecca Woods, "The Life and Loves of Anne Lister," BBC.com, May 3, 2019, https://www.bbc.co.uk/news/resources/idt-sh/the_life_and_loves_of _anne_lister.

16. Katherine Hiestand and Heidi Levitt, "Butch Identity Development: The Formation of an Authentic Gender," *Feminism & Psychology* 15 (February 1, 2005): 64, https://doi.org/10.1177/0959353505049709.

17. C. Lynn Carr, "Where Have All the Tomboys Gone? Women's Accounts of Gender in Adolescence," *Sex Roles* 56 (April 5, 2007): 439–48, https://doi .org/10.1007/s11199-007-9183-7.

18. Jack Halberstam, "Toward a Trans* Feminism," *Boston Review*, January 18, 2018, http://bostonreview.net/gender-sexuality/jack-halberstam-towards -trans-feminism.

Chapter 12: War of the Words: Tomboy or Trans Boy?

1. Ernest Hemingway, *The Garden of Eden* (New York: Scribner's, 1986), https://www.bookdepository.com/Garden-Eden-Ernest-Hemingway /9780684804521.

2. After the *New York Times* piece was published and people began referring to the title (but not the content) of the *Parenting* piece as proof that I had a trans kid, I asked, through a friend who once worked at *Parenting* and knew editors at *Parents* (which had purchased *Parenting*), that the title be changed. They chose to change it to "My Daughter Is a Tomboy!"

3. Chase Strangio, "An Open Letter to Those Praising the *New York Times* 'Tomboy' Piece," Medium.com, April 20, 2017, https://medium.com/the -establishment/an-open-letter-to-those-praising-the-new-york-times -tomboy-piece-755e655ce31c.

4. WPATH World Professional Association for Transgender Health, "Standards of Care," 97, accessed August 9, 2019, https://www.wpath.org/publi cations/soc.

5. Susan Stryker, *Transgender History* (Cambridge, MA: Da Capo Press, 2009), 1, https://www.google.com/books/edition/Transgender_History/kE fZ1knAguMC?hl=en&gbpv=1&bsq=(trans-).

6. Halberstam, "Toward a Trans* Feminism."

7. "What Is Gender Dysphoria?"

8. Drescher, "Out of DSM."

9. Kenneth J. Zucker, "The DSM Diagnostic Criteria for Gender Identity Disorder in Children," *Archives of Sexual Behavior* 39, no. 2 (April 2010): 477– 98, https://doi.org/10.1007/s10508-009-9540-4.

10. Carr, "Where Have All the Tomboys Gone?"

11. Kenneth J. Zucker and Robert L. Spitzer, "Was the Gender Identity Disorder of Childhood Diagnosis Introduced into DSM-III as a Backdoor Maneuver to Replace Homosexuality? A Historical Note," *Journal of Sex & Marital Therapy* 31, no. 1 (February 2005): 31–42, https://doi .org/10.1080/00926230590475251.

12. Jeff Muskus, "George Rekers, Anti-Gay Activist, Caught with Male Escort 'Rentboy' [UPDATE: Escort Says Rekers Is Gay]," *HuffPost*, July 5, 2010, https://www.huffpost.com/entry/george-rekers-anti-gay-ac_n_565142.

13. Sarah Anne Hughes, "Family of Kirk Murphy Says 'Sissy Boy' Experiment Led to His Suicide - The Washington Post," *Washington Post*, June 10, 2011, https://www.washingtonpost.com/blogs/blogpost/post/family-of-kirk -murphy-says-sissy-boy-experiment-led-to-his-suicide/2011/06/10/AGYf gvOH_blog.html.

14. "What Is Gender Dysphoria?"

15. Ibid.

16. Peter Walker, "Popularity of Tomboys Is Encouraging Girls to Swap Gender, Says NHS Psychologist," *Telegraph*, May 8, 2017, https://www .telegraph.co.uk/science/2017/05/08/popularity-tomboys-encouraging -girls-swap-gender-says-nhs-psychologist/.

17. Ibid.

Chapter 13: Breaking the Binary

1. Abrams, "Mere·Their."

2. Hollie Silverman, "2 More States Will Offer a 3rd Gender Option on Driver's Licenses," CNN, August 1, 2019, https://www.cnn.com/2019/08/01/health /washington-pennsylvania-gender-x-id/index.html.

3. Merrill Perlman, "Stylebooks Finally Embrace the Single 'They,'" *Columbia Journalism Review*, March 27, 2017, https://www.cjr.org/language _corner/stylebooks-single-they-ap-chicago-gender-neutral.php.

4. Guy Trebay, "For Capitalism, Every Social Leap Forward Is a Marketing Opportunity," *New York Times*, September 18, 2018, sec. Style, https://www .nytimes.com/2018/09/18/style/gender-nonbinary-brand-marketing.html.

5. "Google Trends," Google Trends, accessed October 10, 2019, https://trends .google.com/trends/explore?date=all&geo=US&q=non-binary.

6. David Hicks, *Ritual and Belief: Readings in the Anthropology of Religion* (Lanham, MD: Rowman Altamira, 2010), 319.

7. Nancy H. Bartlett, "A Retrospective Study of Childhood Gender-Atypical Behavior in Samoan Fa'afafine," *Archives of Sexual Behavior* 35, no. 6 (December 2006): 659–66, https://doi.org/10.1007/s10508-006-9055-1.

8. "Samoa | Human Dignity Trust," accessed December 4, 2019, https://www .humandignitytrust.org./country-profile/samoa/.

9. It's important to note that some cultures have a broader view of gender, with third, fourth, or fifth genders but may have a narrower view of sexuality.

That is, some people who would be considered or identify as gay in some Western cultures may identify as another gender in other cultures, where homosexuality is illegal, misunderstood, or culturally frowned upon.

10. "Researching for LGBTQ Health," accessed October 25, 2019, https://lgbtqhealth.ca/community/two-spirit.php.

11. "U.S. Transgender Survey" (National Center for Transgender Equality, 2016), https://transequality.org/issues/us-trans-survey.

Chapter 14: Is It Time to Retire the Word "Tomboy"?

1. *Sioux City Journal*, May 13, 1917.

2. "The Passing of Tomboys," *Wilkes-Barre Times Leader, the Evening News*, July 20, 1926, http://www.newspapers.com/clip/31372987/wilkesbarre_times_leader_the_evening/.

3. Allan Parachini, "Tomboy Label Wears Out," *Berkshire Eagle*, May 1, 1988.

4. Barrie Thorne, *Gender Play: Girls and Boys in School* (New Brunswick, NJ: Rutgers University Press, 1993), 113.

5. JR Thorpe, "Why We Need to Stop Calling Girls 'Tomboys,'" Bustle.com, August 24, 2016, https://www.bustle.com/articles/180131-why-we-need-to-stop-calling-girls-tomboys; Catharine Connors, "I Refuse to Call My Daughter a 'Tomboy,'" *Babble*, accessed October 20, 2019, https://www.babble.com/parenting/i-refuse-to-call-my-daughter-a-tomboy/; Meredith Hale, "Don't Call My Daughter a Tomboy," *HuffPost*, January 11, 2016, https://www.huffpost.com/entry/dont-call-my-daughter-a-tomboy_b_8950530.

6. Lizzy Acker, "Lady Things: The Plight of the Modern Tomboy," *Willamette Week*, January 26, 2016, https://www.wweek.com/arts/2016/01/26/lady-things-the-plight-of-the-modern-tomboy/.

Conclusion: The Pink Ponytail

1. Shannon Hale, "What Are We Teaching Boys When We Discourage Them from Reading Books About Girls?," *Washington Post*, October 10, 2018, https://www.washingtonpost.com/entertainment/books/parents-and-teachers-please-stop-discouraging-boys-from-reading-books-about-girls/2018/10/09/f3eaaca6-c820-11e8-b1ed-1d2d65b86d0c_story.html.

2. Simon Ragoonanan, "Star Wars: Where Is Princess Leia?," Let Toys Be Toys, May 4, 2015, http://lettoysbetoys.org.uk/star-wars-leia-toy-marketing/.

3. "Statistics & Research on Eating Disorders," National Eating Disorders Association, February 19, 2018, https://www.nationaleatingdisorders.org/statistics-research-eating-disorders.

4. "Do You Know the Factors Influencing Girls' Participation in Sports?," Women's Sports Foundation, accessed November 26, 2019, https://www.womenssportsfoundation.org/do-you-know-the-factors-influencing-girls-participation-in-sports/.

5. Connors, "I Refuse to Call My Daughter a 'Tomboy'."

6. Sule Alan, Seda Ertac, and Ipek Mumcu, "Gender Stereotypes in the Classroom and Effects on Achievement," *Review of Economics and Statistics* 100, no. 5 (July 16, 2018): 876–90, https://doi.org/10.1162/rest_a_00756.

7. Sarah J. McKenney and Rebecca S. Bigler, "Internalized Sexualization and Its Relation to Sexualized Appearance, Body Surveillance, and Body Shame Among Early Adolescent Girls," *Journal of Early Adolescence* 36, no. 2 (November 3, 2014): 171–97, https://doi.org/10.1177/0272431614556889.

8. Dana Kanze et al., "Male and Female Entrepreneurs Get Asked Different Questions by VCs—and It Affects How Much Funding They Get," *Harvard Business Review*, June 27, 2017, https://hbr.org/2017/06/male-and-female-entrepreneurs-get-asked-different-questions-by-vcs-and-it-affects-how-much-funding-they-get.

9. Cassie Werber, "In the United States Gender Equality Is 208 Years Away from Being Recognised," World Economic Forum, August 21, 2019, https://www.weforum.org/agenda/2019/08/women-walk-bar-208-years-later-paid-same-men/.

10. "Watching Gender: How Stereotypes in Movies and on TV Impact Kids' Development," Common Sense Media, accessed November 22, 2019, https://www.commonsensemedia.org/research/watching-gender.

11. Heidi Stevens, "Boys Are Wearing U.S. Women's National Team Jerseys and That Feels Like Progress," *Chicago Tribune*, accessed July 13, 2019, https://www.chicagotribune.com/columns/heidi-stevens/ct-heidi-stevens-thursday-boys-wearing-womens-soccer-jerseys-0620-20190620-7qgm7t2j2rgonkosjfjwm4digq-story.html.

12. "The Toy Association | Inspiring Generations of Play," The Toy Association, accessed October 10, 2019, https://www.toyassociation.org.

13. McKenna Pope, "Petition · Hasbro: Feature Boys in the Packaging of the Easy-Bake Oven," Change.org, 2012, https://www.change.org/p/hasbro-feature-boys-in-the-packaging-of-the-easy-bake-oven.

14. Tanya Edwards, "Store Removes Boys and Girls Labels from Kids Clothes," September 3, 2017, https://www.yahoo.com/lifestyle/uk-retailer-john-lewis-removes-boys-girls-labels-kids-clothes-155813055.html.

15. "Team-Style Graphic Flutter-Sleeve Tee for Girls," Old Navy, accessed November 22, 2019, https://oldnavy.gap.com/browse/product.do?pid=449844.

16. Siri Hedreen, "The Dangers of Gendered Jobs," *Business News Daily*, August 14, 2019, https://www.businessnewsdaily.com/10085-male-female -dominated-jobs.html.

17. Kim Parker, Nikki Graf, and Ruth Igielnik, "Generation Z Looks a Lot Like Millennials on Key Social and Political Issues," Pew Research Center's Social & Demographic Trends Project (blog), January 17, 2019, https:// www.pewsocialtrends.org/2019/01/17/generation-z-looks-a-lot-like -millennials-on-key-social-and-political-issues/.

18. "Half of Young People Believe Gender Isn't Limited to Male and Female," accessed November 26, 2019, https://splinternews.com/half-of -young-people-believe-gender-isnt-limited-to-mal-1793844971.

19. Filip Van Droogenbroeck, Bram Spruyt, and Gil Keppens, "Gender Differences in Mental Health Problems Among Adolescents and the Role of Social Support: Results from the Belgian Health Interview Surveys 2008 and 2013," *BMC Psychiatry* 18 (January 10, 2018), https://doi .org/10.1186/s12888-018-1591-4.

20. Paul L. Vasey and Nancy H. Bartlett, "What Can the Samoan 'Fa'afafine' Teach Us About the Western Concept of Gender Identity Disorder in Childhood?," *Perspectives in Biology and Medicine* 50, no. 4 (2007): 481–90, https://doi.org/10.1353/pbm.2007.0056.

21. Shepherd Laughlin, "Gen Z Goes Beyond Gender Binaries in New Innovation Group Data," JWT Intelligence, March 11, 2016, https:// www.jwtintelligence.com/2016/03/gen-z-goes-beyond-gender-binaries -in-new-innovation-group-data/.

INDEX

Index

Index

Index